T0320164

International Perspectives on Industrial Ecology

STUDIES ON THE SOCIAL DIMENSIONS OF INDUSTRIAL ECOLOGY

Series Editor: Frank Boons, *Sustainable Consumption Institute, University of Manchester, UK*

The Studies on the Social Dimensions of Industrial Ecology series aims to publish contributions to the field of industrial ecology which shed light on the way in which material and energy flows are shaped by, and shape, production and consumption practices in industrialized societies. Material and energy flows emerge from and affect the actions of consumers, firms, governments and NGOs in various social systems (regional industrial clusters, supply and product chains, and cities). This series aims to promote innovative research in which disciplinary boundaries are transcended, and thus theoretical, empirical, and normative work from social scientists, engineers, and natural scientists is welcomed. The series endeavours to provide insight into empirical and theoretical developments in various regions of the world, and strives to keep abreast of emerging topics such as social LCA, governance of sustainable urban systems and industrial ecosystems, social practice theory and sustainable consumption, and the political economy of Industrial Ecology (trade networks and material flows).

International Perspectives on Industrial Ecology

Edited by

Pauline Deutz

Senior Lecturer, University of Hull, UK

Donald I. Lyons

Professor, University College Cork, Republic of Ireland

Jun Bi

Professor, Nanjing University, China

STUDIES ON THE SOCIAL DIMENSIONS OF INDUSTRIAL ECOLOGY

Cheltenham, UK • Northampton, MA, USA

Published by
Edward Elgar Publishing Limited
The Lypiatts
15 Lansdown Road
Cheltenham
Glos GL50 2JA
UK

Edward Elgar Publishing, Inc.
William Pratt House
9 Dewey Court
Northampton
Massachusetts 01060
USA

A catalogue record for this book
is available from the British Library

Library of Congress Control Number: 2015941468

This book is available electronically in the **Elgar**online
Social and Political Science subject collection
DOI 10.4337/9781781003572

ISBN 978 1 78100 356 5 (cased)
ISBN 978 1 78100 357 2 (eBook)

Typeset by Servis Filmsetting Ltd, Stockport, Cheshire
Printed and bound in Great Britain by TJ International Ltd, Padstow

Contents

Figures

Tables

Contributors

Weslynne Ashton is an assistant professor of environmental management and sustainability at the Illinois Institute of Technology, US. Her research focuses on industrial ecology, industrial symbiosis and collaborative approaches to sustainability, and sustainable economic development in emerging economies. Originally from Trinidad and Tobago, she holds an SB degree in Environmental Engineering from MIT and a PhD from Yale University.

Leo Baas, PhD, is an expert in cleaner production and industrial ecology concepts. He is Emeritus Professor Industrial Ecology at Linköping University, Sweden, and staff member of the International Off-Campus PhD Programme in Cleaner Production, Cleaner Products, Industrial Ecology and Sustainability at Erasmus University Rotterdam, the Netherlands.

Henrikke Baumann is an associate professor of Environmental Systems Analysis, Chalmers University of Technology, Sweden, who teaches methods of life cycle assessment and environmental management. Her research centres on methodology development in the field of industrial ecology – she explores socio-material combinations of quantitative environmental flow studies with qualitative organizational studies in the context of product chains and urban environmental flows.

Jun Bi is a professor in the School of Environment at Nanjing University, China. With a background in environmental policy, planning and management, he has research, study and teaching experience at several universities in Asia and North America.

Frank Boons was appointed Professor of Innovation and Sustainability at the Sustainable Consumption Institute, University of Manchester, UK, January 2015, following several years as Associate Professor of Public Administration at Erasmus University Rotterdam.

Robin Branson has been arranging bilateral industrial symbiosis in Australia since 1989. He has a PhD on the topic from Sydney University (2011), an MBA from the University of New South Wales and a BSc (Hons) Civil Engineering from Imperial College, London. Drawing on his highly varied career, Robin's interests focus on applied industrial symbiosis and on industrial ecology education.

Sabrina Brullot is a teacher-researcher and works on industrial ecology in a multidisciplinary way. Her research interests relate to the following themes: social and human aspects of industrial ecology, governance, cooperation and coordination of actors, the decision-making process, and sustainable regional development.

Inês Costa is an environmental consultant for 3Drivers, focusing on sustainable resource use and waste management. She holds a PhD degree on Industrial Ecology and specializes in resource recovery and industrial symbiosis networks. She continues to collaborate on university research on IS, especially in bridging the gap between public policy and industrial implementation of this type of networks.

Chris Davis is currently a postdoctoral researcher at the Faculty of Technology, Policy and Management at the Delft University of Technology, the Netherlands, where he also received his PhD degree. His research focuses on how data analytics, open data, machine learning and agent-based modelling can aid the study of industrial ecology and industrial symbiosis.

Pauline Deutz is a senior lecturer in the Department of Geography Environment and Earth Sciences at the University of Hull, UK. With degrees in Geography from Oxford and Ohio State Universities and in Geology from the University of California Riverside, Pauline's research takes an interdisciplinary social science approach to the coordination of environmental issues with other priorities. She is the Vice President of the International Sustainable Development Research Society.

Mats Eklund is Professor in Environmental Technology and Management at Linköping University, Sweden, where he is scientific leader of the Centre of Excellence Biogas Research Centre, and carries out research into industrial symbiosis, addressing collaborative approaches to green and groundbreaking innovation.

David Gibbs is Professor of Human Geography at the University of Hull, UK. His research focuses on local and regional economic development, and he has been an expert advisor to the European Commission's DG REGIO on climate change and cohesion policy, to the OECD on green jobs, and to the Local Government Association on sustainable economic development.

Lan Hu is an independent scholar, originally from China. She completed an MSc degree at the University of North Texas, US, in 2013, and is about to enrol on an MSc Software Engineering programme at the University of Texas at Arlington, Texas. She has research interests in geographic information systems, sustainable development and industrial ecology.

Ralf Isenmann is a professor for sustainable future management at the Munich University of Applied Sciences, Germany. His research areas are in the interface between the management of innovation and technologies on the one hand and sustainable management, industrial ecology and corporate social responsibility on the other.

Gijsbert Korevaar is an assistant professor of industrial symbiosis at the Delft University of Technology, the Netherlands. His research and teaching is about industrial ecology, sustainable chemical process engineering, circular economy business models, and eco-industrial park development. He has an MSc and PhD degree in Chemical Engineering, both from Delft University of Technology.

Yue Lei has a master's degree from the Environmental School of Nanjing University, China, majoring in environmental planning and management. Yue's research focused on local low carbon development (especially industrial parks), and also on POE (post-occupancy evaluation) of China's green building and building energy consumption. Yue now works for Dow Chemical (Zhangjiagang) as a plant engineer.

Lingxuan Liu is a social scientist who focuses on environmental policy, public participation, and political science. He received his PhD in Environmental Governance of Climate Change Issues from Nanjing University, China. He is now a lead researcher and project manager of the China team at The Sustainability Consortium at Arizona State University, US.

Peter Lowitt, FAICP, is the Director of the Devens Enterprise Commission and administers the Devens Eco-Industrial Park as part of the sustainable redevelopment of the former Fort Devens in Massachusetts, US. He is Chair of the Eco-Industrial Development/Industrial Symbiosis Section of the International Society of Industrial Ecology and Chair of the Eco-Industrial Development Council of North America.

Donald I. Lyons is Professor of Geography at University College Cork, Republic of Ireland, where has worked since 2012. Previously, he spent 20 years as Assistant and Associate Professor of Geography at the University of North Texas, Denton, Texas. His research centres on urban and economic geography, and the spatial implications of sustainable development as it relates to the concept of industrial ecology. His research has appeared in numerous leading journals.

Guillaume Massard is Founding Partner at Sofies SA (Geneva, Switzerland) and researcher at the Université de Lausanne in Switzerland. He is currently working on field projects and research on industrial ecology, and industrial and urban development in Western Europe, Asia and North Africa. Guillaume has a PhD in Environmental Science from the University of Lausanne (Switzerland) and a master's degree in Environmental Engineering from the Swiss Federal Institute of Technology (EPFL).

Phil McManus has an educational background in urban planning (Curtin, Australia), environmental studies (York, Canada) and geography (Bristol, UK). He is Professor of Urban and Environmental Geography and Head of the School of Geosciences at the University of Sydney, Australia. His research interests include environmental management and urban sustainability.

Olawale Emmanuel Olayide is a research fellow in the Centre for Sustainable Development, University of Ibadan, Nigeria. He holds a PhD in Agricultural Economics from the University of Ibadan, Nigeria. His research interests include agricultural production and food security, industrial ecology, governance and gender. Olawale is a board member of the International Sustainable Development Society and is a member of the editorial team of the *African Journal of Sustainable Development*.

Jerry Patchell is associate professor of social science at the Hong Kong University of Science and Technology. His research examines the mechanisms and structures of cooperation among firms and institutions to explain production and regional economic systems. He has explored these systems in the robotics, electric vehicle, housing, wine, fisheries and ski industries, usually with regard to sustainability. His current research focuses on oligopoly as a global climate governance platform.

Murray Rice is Associate Professor of Geography at the University of North Texas, US. His research focuses on metropolitan corporate development and entrepreneurship, including interests in infrastructure and material flows. His research also addresses the intersection of businesses and regional change, focusing on the impact of retail development on urban communities. He holds a BE in Engineering Physics and an MA and PhD in Geography from the University of Saskatchewan in Saskatoon.

Elena Romero Arozamena is an industrial engineer and holds her PhD from the University of Cantabria, Spain. Since 2011 she has been an assistant professor of the Department of Transport and Projects Technology and Processes at the University of Cantabria. Her area of work is complex systems modelling and industrial symbiosis. Her current research is focused on agent-based modelling of eco-industrial systems.

Carmen Ruiz Puente is an associate professor of engineering and industrial ecology at the University of Cantabria, Spain. She has a degree and a PhD in Industrial Engineering. Her research interests include industrial symbiosis and the modelling of industrial ecosystems with a focus on the socio-technically systemic thinking and complexity. She has been a visiting researcher at the Universities of Cambridge (UK, 2013) and Cincinnati (USA, 1998) and at the Instituto de Catálisis y Petroquímica (Argentina, 1995).

Megha Shenoy is an independent consultant in India working on sustainability research, scientific editing and infographics. The recommendations of the research she led at the Resource Optimization Initiative, India, have been implemented to optimize resource flows in a range of industrial contexts. She completed a postdoctoral fellowship at the Center for Industrial Ecology, at Yale University, USA, following an Integrated PhD programme at the Indian Institute of Science, Bangalore.

Wouter Spekkink is a postdoctoral researcher at Delft University of Technology, the Netherlands, working on an EU-funded project on the role of bottom-up sustainability initiatives in the diffusion of green lifestyles. Before starting in this position, Wouter did his PhD research at Erasmus University in Rotterdam. He wrote his PhD thesis on the process through which communities of governments, firms, knowledge institutes and other relevant actors build up the capacity to collaborate on industrial symbiosis.

Bart van Hoof is a Dutch industrial ecologist with strong roots in Latin America. He is an associate professor at the Universidad de Los Andes School of Management, Colombia. His academic work studies management for change in supply networks and regional industrial systems networks in emerging markets, mainly Colombia and Mexico. Bart has a PhD from Erasmus University, Rotterdam.

Veerle Verguts works as a coordinator of scientific research at the Manure Policy Unit of the Division for Rural Development and Manure Policy of the Flemish Land Agency. At the time of writing this chapter, Veerle worked as a scientific researcher at the Social Sciences Unit of the Institute for Agricultural and Fisheries Research (ILVO).

Haikun Wang is an associate professor in the School of Environment at Nanjing University, China. He received his PhD at Tsinghua University in 2010. His research focuses on energy consumption and related impacts on greenhouse gas emissions, air pollution and public health, with a particular emphasis on China's urban areas. He is also interested in the field of regional climate change mitigation and adaptation.

Qiaozhi Wang is a lecturer of human geography in the School of Resource and Environmental Engineering at the Wuhan University of Science and Technology, China. She has a PhD from the University of Hull, UK. Her research interest is eco-industrial development and knowledge transfer in collaborations.

Bing Zhang is a professor in the School of Environment and School of Government at Nanjing University, China and Director of the Centre for Environmental Management and Policy Analysis (supported by Nanjing University and Jiangsu Environmental Protection Department). He holds a doctorate in Environmental Planning and Management from Nanjing and Rutgers University. His research examines the social, political and legal contexts shaping environmental governance in China.

Foreword

The notion that waste has value is as old as the hills. For centuries human beings have reused and recycled stone blocks to replace old structures with new ones. Rag-and-bone men, a common sight in nineteenth-century Paris and London, scavenged unwanted rags, bones, metal and other waste from households and sold them to traders; rags were often used for making paper, bones were used as knife handles, toys and ornaments. In 1954, when I worked as an apprentice machinist at a factory near Birmingham, UK, the swarf produced by the lathe I was operating was picked up every afternoon to be baled eventually and sold to a scrap merchant. In 1970, as a member of a World Bank Group delegation meeting with leaders of the Japanese textile industry, a senior official of a cotton spinning mill in Osaka informed me that the person handling the sale of waste cotton ranked on a par with his colleagues handling operations, marketing and finance. The company President explained that the so-called waste from carding and combing operations was, in fact, quite valuable; it was good cotton fibre but of a staple length shorter than what was required for his operation. However, it would be good material for mills spinning coarser count yarns. At the end of the cotton fibre chain, the remaining fibre would be used for the production of blankets, which, in turn, at the end of their life would probably end up as rags for papermaking. Similar examples of intuitive recycling and reuse can be found in many other sectors of production worldwide.

Over the past 25 years, industrial ecology, a multidisciplinary pursuit of knowledge, began looking at non-human ecosystems as models for industrial activity. Many biological ecosystems are especially effective at recycling resources and thus are held out as exemplars for the efficient cycling of materials and energy in industry and society. The multi-industry park in Kalundborg, Denmark, where facilities share resources – materials as well as energy – and also exchange by-products, led to a body of research on 'industrial symbiosis' providing an example for the biological analogy.

In recent years, academics in the field of industrial ecology have focused on input-output analysis, studies of resource criticality (using tools of material flow analysis), the integration of social science and operations research, agent-based complexity modelling, and urban metabolism, among other subjects. Long-term socio-ecological research has become central to the field.

Progress on the academic front of industrial ecology in recent years has, unfortunately, come at a cost. There is a growing divide between the academics and the practitioners; and, at the same time, there is a risk that the field of industrial ecology could splinter into geographical sub-groups and perhaps also into clusters of sub-specialties. The growing divide between academia and the industrial world can only be detrimental to the greater use of industrial ecological principles and their implementation in practice. Industrial ecology has been defined as the study of resource flows in industrial and consumer activities with the ultimate objective of minimizing their use. Based on my observation, most economies, particularly the emerging ones, could benefit greatly by examining their resource flows using industrial ecology tools.

It is precisely for this reason that I welcome the publication of *International Perspectives on Industrial Ecology*, jointly edited by Dr Pauline Deutz of the University of Hull, England, Professor Jun Bi of Nanjing University, China, and Professor Donald I. Lyons of University College Cork, Ireland.

The volume benefits greatly from the international perspective of the three editors who have individually studied and taught at reputable universities around the world. In addition, each of the editors, having had an opportunity to interact first hand with academics and practitioners in various regions of the world, is able to identify the problems and potential of transferring experience from one location to others.

The editors have assembled a qualified and experienced group of international and interdisciplinary contributors to share their views of the state of industrial ecology in their regions. The reader is thus enabled to draw comparisons between different national situations. The contributions, although presented in an academic paper format, are clearly and simply written to be accessible equally to the practitioner in industry or in a policy-making institution and to graduate students seeking new avenues for further research. The focus in the contributions is primarily on industrial symbiosis and the development of eco-industrial parks. These are precisely the areas that present the greatest scope for further research and also rapid implementation on the ground.

Chevy Chase, Maryland USA
March 2015

M.V. Dehejia
President, Alliance for Sustainable Industry and Energy, LLC
Chevy Chase, MD, USA
Formerly
Vice President – Engineering and Technical Assistance,
International Finance Corporation,
World Bank Group,
Washington DC, USA

Acknowledgements

Many thanks to everyone who has contributed to this volume. As editors, we are very grateful to all the authors for their work and patience as we constructed this compilation. Thanks to anonymous reviewers for their constructive contribution. On behalf of the authors, we also wish to thank everyone who contributed either by participation in the research or by providing support behind the scenes. We thank Frank Boons for inviting us to develop our ISDRS conference sessions into this book, and indeed we thank all the people who have contributed to those sessions over the past decade, thereby contributing to our international understanding. Erin McVicar and Alan Sturmer at Edward Elgar are thanked for their support in putting the volume together.

A special thank you is due to our families for their patience and support, especially over the last few challenging months of what has been a lengthy project. We are indebted to Pauline's daughter, Hazel Deutz, for her meticulous proofreading of the entire book; she reports that she now knows all she needs to know about industrial ecology. The contribution of the University of Hull to this work was part-funded by the UK Natural Environment Research Council (with the Economic and Social Research Council and DEFRA: NE/I019468/1).

To Dr Jalal Etriki, who is fondly remembered by everyone who knew him in Hull. We can only imagine how much more he is missed by his family in Tripoli.

1. Introducing an international perspective on industrial ecology

Pauline Deutz and Donald I. Lyons

The aim of this book is to promote a debate about the relationship between industrial ecology (IE), as a business, community and academic endeavour, and the places in the world where examples of industrial ecology can be found. We present analyses of IE demonstrating its context and variability on a global scale. After 25 years of activity, industrial ecology studies and practices can be found across the globe. The commonalities, associated constraints and opportunities are widely discussed in the burgeoning literature. An additional commonality, seldom explored, is that these examples are all happening *somewhere*. The significance of location for the IE activity attempted, the outcome of that attempt, and the transferability of lessons to other locations are rarely considered. Furthermore, studies are conducted *from* somewhere, not necessarily the same place where the IE activities are rooted.

Originally inspired by a session on IE and geography at the International Sustainable Development Research Society conference in Hong Kong in 2010, we have expanded the range of contributions to the book to provide a genuinely global reach in terms of both case studies and authorship. This book provides contextualised overviews of the current state of IE in specific countries or continents, it explores case studies of different types of IE, in a variety of settings (including developed and developing countries), and provides comparisons between different national contexts. Authors draw on several methodological and theoretical frameworks, offering approaches to comparative work, and contributing to the theoretical understanding of the field.

INDUSTRIAL ECOLOGY TODAY

IE is both an academic field of research and a practice that rests on the assumption that the impact of society on the environment can be reduced by drawing on lessons from natural ecosystems. It concerns the flows of materials and energy that comprise the industrial ecosystem and the scientific, technical, economic, political, social and cultural issues related to those flows (White, 1994). A quintessentially multidisciplinary discipline, IE incorporates a wide range of methodological approaches. These take a system-scale approach based ultimately on biological ecosystems, in some cases adapted by engineering or business approaches. IE work is often normative, though an emerging theme is investigating systems theory or other social science perspectives (see Deutz and Ioppolo, 2015 for an overview of the field).

A substantial component of IE research concerns analysis of the potential for, and/or empirical examples of, industrial symbiosis (Yu et al., 2014). Part of a series on social science perspectives on IE, this book is also primarily, but not exclusively, concerned with industrial symbiosis (IS). IS refers to the flow of residue material/energy between entities, which can occur in a range of socio-spatial contexts (Lombardi et al., 2012; Deutz, 2014). These may include local to regional networks of interconnected companies, such as those that comprise the industrial ecosystem at Kalundborg, Denmark, or the Styrian recycling network in Austria (Ehrenfeld and Gertler, 1997; Schwarz and Steininger, 1997). IS may also be a component of activities associated with an eco-industrial park (EIP), i.e., a site-specific cluster of companies with a collaborative approach to environmental management (Côté and Cohen-Rosenthal, 1998). Recent studies have applied a range of social science approaches to IS in different forms, building on earlier work (e.g., Boons and Howard-Grenville, 2009) for example, applying social network theory to regional IS networks (e.g., Ashton and Bain, 2012; Schiller et al., 2014), or investigating institutional capacity building with respect to EIPs (Boons and Spekkink, 2012).

Significantly, IE is not just an academic field of enquiry but also an area of business activity and policy application that pre-dates academic interest (see Erkman, 1997). Currently, IE-related ideas, such as the Circular Economy and industrial symbiosis, are receiving high-level policy attention, e.g., from China, the European Union (EU) and the United Nations (UNEP/SETAC, 2009; Tian et al., 2014; European Commission, n.d.), and are enjoying support from both NGOs and industry (e.g., Ellen MacArthur Foundation [n.d.] and partners in the UK); public and private sector-led IS projects have been attempted at locations across the world (Lombardi et al., 2012).

Recent years have seen an increase in academic IE contributions, with case studies and collaboration from beyond the initial developed country focus held in common with other fields of academic enquiry (e.g., Rigg, 2007). The initial geographic expansion of interest in IE from North America to Europe and other industrialised countries brought a disciplinary expansion to encompass social science perspectives (Vermeulen, 2006) to what had been a predominantly engineering approach to sustainability (e.g., Frosch and Gallopoulos, 1989; Allenby and Richards, 1994).

Over the past decade, IE research has extended to Newly Industrialised Countries (e.g., South Korea, Park et al., 2008) and emerging economies such as China (Yuan et al., 2006;), India (Ashton and Bain, 2012), South Africa (Brent et al., 2008) and developing countries (e.g., Bangladesh, Gregson et al., 2012; Thailand, Manomaivibool and Vassanadumrongdee, 2011; and Liberia, Alfaro and Miller, 2013). This further geographic expansion has been conducted by researchers from those countries and by previously established IE researchers. There is thus a global-scale knowledge transfer network, both within academia and between academics and practitioners. This empirical expansion has not been accompanied by a significant shift in disciplinary focus. IE now needs not just to encompass an awareness of economic development and developed country sustainability issues, but also to appreciate the nuances of developing country contexts.

The need for an appreciation of geographic context in IE is underscored by recent developments in both practice and theory. Within academic IE, there is increasing concern for usability of IE tools by industry, rather than primarily as academic research (Despeisse et al., 2012; Arzoumanidis et al., 2014). Such considerations are likely to be of increasing interest to academics at a time when their work is judged in part on its impact beyond academia (Deutz and Ioppolo, 2015). Attention to implementation has not always been a strong feature of academic work on environmental initiatives, even when ostensibly producing tools for industry (Baumann et al., 2002). Improving the usability of IE tools is partly a case of better understanding practice (in industry and policy circles), but also of recognising geographic variability not just of practice but of the circumstance to which it may be applied.

It is surely appropriate for researchers to develop their theories from the empirical contexts on which their research has been based. Consequently, though, theorisations of IE (largely IS) have thus far been rooted in the developed world context (e.g., Boons et al., 2011; Doménech and Davies, 2011; Chertow and Ehrenfeld, 2012). Greater attention needs to be paid to the cultural and institutional context of the developing world. However, caution is advised on the transferability of practices from developed to developing countries given that seemingly basic terms such as 'waste' may have geographic specificities arising from the intersect of policy and practice (Deutz, 2014).

The extension of IE from developed economies to emerging and developing economies is to be welcomed in as much as those places are in need of resource efficiencies associated with sustainable development (Olayide,

Chapter 3, this volume). However, the particular circumstances in the Global South may impact on the forms that IE takes. Even within the developed country context, limited attention has been paid to geographic context, including potential policy transfers from one country's context to another's (Jiao and Boons, 2014). The remainder of this chapter briefly outlines the contribution of each chapter of the book in the context of current debates.

THE CASE FOR PLACE IN INDUSTRIAL ECOLOGY

IE activities are happening, or are desired to happen, in places. Although IS networks may be related to a place most obviously (be it a town, or region, or nation), even process-oriented IE systems are measuring, modelling or planning flows that start, pass through and stop at places. Place is a deceptively simple term which encompasses more than defining coordinates on the Earth's surface (e.g., Hubbard, 2005). As alluded to above, socially and economically, as well as culturally, places are highly variable. Despite the potentials of modern communications and an increasingly interconnected world (in terms of trade and finance flows), there are still locations that are significantly more attractive to investment than others (e.g., Cumbers and MacKinnon, 2004); IE projects are not immune to the economic realities of their locations (Deutz and Gibbs, 2008).

Perhaps unsurprisingly spatial variability has been under-analysed within the IE literature. The field is after all based on a metaphor with nature, which although geographically variable in outcome has underlying principles which are invariable. IE activity relates to materials, processes and techniques that are in principle the same anywhere. For example, engineers and ecological economists draw on the principles of thermodynamics (Daly, 1977; Layton et al., 2012). If a substance can be used, or reused, in a certain way in one location, then physically it could in another. Nonetheless, economically viable, culturally acceptable and socially/politically achievable options are likely to be just as geographically variable as biological ecosystems. A good example of a contextual requirement is supplied by Wang H. et al.'s chapter (Chapter 13, this volume), which develops a model for calculating greenhouse gas (GHG) emissions from Chinese EIPs. In contrast to the relatively small-scale EIPs of co-located firms in the USA, Chinese EIPs are of a larger scale and incorporate residential neighbourhoods. Modelling therefore must incorporate elements of urban as well as industrial settings. The case study used is Suzhou Industrial Park, which has a developed area of 80 km^2 and a population of

0.7 million (Wang H. et al., Chapter 13, this volume), and which resembles a medium-sized city rather than an EIP in European or US usage.

The twofold classification of countries into the Global North and Global South (Brandt, 1981) as a summary of development level remains depressingly valid (Arrighi, 2001/2002), albeit that there are overlapping sub-groups of newly industrialising countries, emerging and transition economies. Large and widening gaps of wealth exist between developed and developing countries (e.g., Oxfam, 2014; Dutta, 2015), not to mention within countries (e.g., the north–south divide in the UK, McSmith, 2015). For industrial ecologists, the challenge is both to be aware of the circumstances of a particular place as well as to understand its connections to a global and globalising capitalist economy (e.g., Dicken, 2011). In a highly interconnected world linked by commodity and residue flows on a global scale (e.g., Lyons, 2007), residue flows are as globalised as resource flows and the patterns in the North are firmly linked to those in the South (Massey, 1991; Gregson et al., 2012). The interconnections comprising globalisation can have positive effects for development, but not without creating stresses (both environmental and social) (Martens and Raza, 2010).

Development-related issues for IE are well illustrated by Ashton and Shenoy's chapter (Chapter 2, this volume) and Olayide's chapter (Chapter 3, this volume) on India and Africa respectively. These chapters consider the current status of IE across places where the states of development and future trajectories are very heterogeneous. Extractive industry and agriculture (both traditional and large scale) remain economically prominent in Africa, providing opportunities as well as constraints for IE (Olayide, Chapter 3, this volume). Ashton and Shenoy describe how similar conditions are faced by smaller traditional industries and the agricultural sector in India. Much of the developed world-style practice of IE in India is carried out either by branches of multinational companies or by India's indigenous conglomerates.

Issues surrounding IE in those locations can be contrasted with those explored by Lowitt (Chapter 4, this volume) and Boons et al. (Chapter 5, this volume) with respect to the industrialised and post-industrial landscapes of the USA and Europe respectively. Lowitt explores current EIP and regional IS projects in the USA in a policy context where the drive for economic development is more strongly supported than that for resource efficiency. State-level resource/waste policies in the USA contrast with the supranational scale of environmental regulation overlying national policies in the EU.

Whereas the chapters in this book provide relevant material for comparisons of IE in different contexts, most are not themselves undertaking a comparison. Boons et al.'s chapter (Chapter 5, this volume) is an exception, comprising a large-scale comparison of IS achieved by a collaboration of 16 researchers in nine different European countries. Explicitly exploring the form and development of IE examples between different locations is entering the realms of comparative research, which brings methodological challenges of its own alongside potential insights (e.g., Kennett, 2013). Three major forms of IS emerge, with significant variation within as well as between countries.

Some of the policy applications of IE, most notably of industrial symbiosis, have been consciously learning from/adopting examples from elsewhere (Geng et al., 2012; Tian et al., 2014). Both the politics and geography literatures have explored the complexities of transferring policies (even within, let alone between, countries), and the manner in which policies influence and are influenced by the places in which they are employed (e.g., Peck, 2011; Stone, 2012). In the case study explored by Wang Q. et al.'s chapter (Chapter 6, this volume) there is a deliberate effort to transfer an approach to IS facilitation between very distinct geographic contexts (the UK and a Chinese EIP). The chapter explores the impact of the differing multi-scalar policy regimes in the two contexts and the implications for the effectiveness of the particular approach for facilitating IS connections.

A weakness in the underpinning of IS research has been the reliance on a small number of successful case studies. Lyons et al.'s chapter (Chapter 7, this volume) and Branson and McManus' chapter (Chapter 8, this volume) expand the empirical foundation of IS with contrasting studies of non-hazardous industrial waste flows from Pennsylvania, USA, and non-park based symbioses in Australia respectively. Thereby, they contribute invaluable insight to debates on the importance of proximity and industrial diversity to IS (Chertow, 2000; Van Beers et al., 2007; Jensen et al., 2011). Contrasting the densely industrialised regions of Pennsylvania with relatively sparsely populated Australia firmly indicates the importance of context to outcome.

Institutions are emerging as an important contextual factor for IS and provide the framework for several chapters in this book. Institutions are the formal and informal rules and structures governing behaviour in society (North, 1990). Spekkink (Chapter 9, this volume) discusses how institutional forms in different locations will impact on the form of IS development. Significantly, the form and function of institutions can have distinctive impacts in the context of developing countries (Braveboy-Wagner, 2008) with issues like corruption, which are not unique to the Global South, nonetheless representing a particular challenge (e.g., Bissessar and Owoye, 2014).

Liu et al. (Chapter 10, this volume) consider the particular institutional context of EIP development that has arisen in conjunction with, and in response to, the rapid industrialisation of China. National-scale regulations stress resource conservation requirements, with implementation at the local to regional scale via a network of industrial parks undergoing transformation to EIPs. This can be compared with the situation in Japan, which is analysed in Patchell's chapter (Chapter 11, this volume). Japan has taken a distinctive approach to IE, favouring eco-towns over EIPs (Ohnishi et al., 2012). Patchell extends this analysis by examining the interplay of eco-towns designed to eliminate domestic waste and extended producer responsibility regulations giving companies liability for post-consumer electronics.

An important characteristic of institutions with respect to the implementation of IE is their ability to learn and develop, i.e., institutional capacity (Healey, 1998; Boons and Spekkink, 2012). Spekkink's chapter addresses this theoretically, using an Event Sequence Analysis (Boons et al., 2014) to explore the development of the institutional context over time. Van Hoof's chapter (Chapter 12, this volume) extends the application of institutional capacity in IE beyond IS to examine a government programme aiming to foster cleaner production in industry. His study of Caldas, Colombia, also extends the application to an emerging economy context.

In the concluding chapter we briefly explore the themes emerging from the book and propose an agenda for further work.

REFERENCES

Alfaro, J. and S. Miller (2013), 'Applying industrial symbiosis to smallholder farms', *Journal of Industrial Ecology*, **18**, 145–154. Doi: 10.1111/jiec.12077.

Allenby, B.R. and D.J. Richards (1994), *The Greening of Industrial Ecosystems*, Washington, DC: National Academy Press.

Arrighi, G. (2001/2002), 'Global capitalism and the persistence of the north–south divide', *Science & Society*, **65** (4), 469–475.

Arzoumanidis, I., A. Raggi and L. Petti (2014), 'Considerations when applying simplified LCA approaches in the wine sector', *Sustainability*, **6**, 5018–5028.

Ashton, W.S. and A.C. Bain (2012), 'Assessing the "short mental distance" in eco-industrial networks', *Journal of Industrial Ecology*, **16**, 70–82.

Ashton W. and M. Shenoy (2015), 'Industrial ecology in India: converging traditional practice and modern environmental protection', in P. Deutz, D. Lyons and J. Bi (eds), *International Perspectives on Industrial Ecology*, Cheltenham, UK and Northampton, MA, USA: Edward Elgar, pp. 12–29.

Baumann, H., F. Boons and A. Bragd (2002), 'Mapping the green product development field: engineering, policy and business perspectives', *Journal of Cleaner Production*, **10**, 409–425.

Bissessar, N. and O. Owoye (2014), 'Corruption in African countries: a symptom of leadership and institutional failure', *Challenges to Democratic Governance in Developing Countries*, **11**, 227–245.

Boons, F.A.A. and J. Howard-Grenville (eds) (2009), *The Social Embeddedness of Industrial Ecology*, Cheltenham, UK and Northampton, MA, USA: Edward Elgar.

Boons, F.A.A. and W.A.H. Spekkink (2012), 'Levels of institutional capacity and actor expectations about industrial symbiosis', *Journal of Industrial Ecology*, **16**, 61–69.

Boons, F.A.A., W.A.H. Spekkink and Y. Mouzakitis (2011), 'The dynamics of industrial symbiosis: a proposal for a conceptual framework based upon a comprehensive literature review', *Journal of Cleaner Production*, **19** (9–10), 905–911.

Boons, F.A.A., W.A.H. Spekkink and W. Jiao (2014), 'A process perspective on industrial symbiosis', *Journal of Industrial Ecology*, **18** (3), 341–355.

Boons, F., W. Spekkink, R. Isenmann, L. Baas, M. Eklund, S. Brullot, P. Deutz, D. Gibbs, G. Massard, E. Romero, M.C. Ruiz, V. Verguts, C. Davis, G. Korevaar, I. Costa, H. Baumann (2015), 'Comparing industrial symbiosis in Europe: towards a conceptual framework and research methodology', in P. Deutz, D. Lyons and J. Bi (eds), *International Perspectives on Industrial Ecology*, Cheltenham, UK and Northampton, MA, USA: Edward Elgar, pp. 69–88.

Brandt, W. (1981), *North–South: A Programme for Survival: Report of the Independent Commission on International Development Issues*, London: Pan.

Branson R. and P. McManus (2015), 'Bilateral symbiosis in Australia and the issue of geographic proximity', in P. Deutz, D. Lyons and J. Bi (eds), *International Perspectives on Industrial Ecology*, Cheltenham, UK and Northampton, MA, USA: Edward Elgar, pp. 126–141.

Braveboy-Wagner, J.A. (2008), *Institutions of the Global South*, London and New York: Routledge.

Brent, A.C., S. Oelofse and L. Godfrey (2008), 'Advancing the concepts of industrial ecology in South African institutions', *South African Journal of Science*, **104**, 9–12.

Chertow, M.R. (2000), 'Industrial symbiosis: literature and taxonomy', *Annual Review of Energy and Environment*, **25**, 313–337.

Chertow, M.R. and J. Ehrenfeld (2012), 'Organizing self-organizing systems: toward a theory of industrial symbiosis', *Journal of Industrial Ecology*, **16**, 13–27.

Côté, R. and E. Cohen-Rosenthal (1998), 'Designing eco-industrial parks: a synthesis of some experiences', *Journal of Cleaner Production*, **6**, 181–188.

Cumbers, A. and D. McKinnon (2004), 'Introduction: clusters in urban and regional development', *Urban Studies*, **41**, 959–969.

Daly, H.E. (1977), *Steady-state Economics: The Economics of Biophysical Equilibrium and Moral Growth*, San Francisco, CA: W.H. Freeman.

Despeisse, M., P.D. Ball, S. Evans and A. Levers (2012), 'Industrial ecology at factory level – a conceptual model', *Journal of Cleaner Production*, **31**, 30–39.

Deutz, P. (2014), 'Food for thought: seeking the essence of industrial symbiosis', in R. Salomone and G. Saija (eds), *Pathways to Environmental Sustainability: Methodologies and Experiences*, Switzerland: Springer International Publishing, pp. 3–11.

Deutz, P. and D. Gibbs (2008), 'Industrial ecology and regional development: eco-industrial development as cluster policy', *Regional Studies*, **42** (10), 1313–1328.

Deutz, P. and G. Ioppolo (2015), 'From theory to practice: enhancing the potential policy impact of industrial ecology', *Sustainability*, **7**, 2259–2273. Doi: 10.3390/su7022259.

Dicken, P. (2011), *Global Shift*, sixth edition, London: Sage.

Doménech, T. and M. Davies (2011), 'The role of embeddedness in industrial symbiosis networks: phases in the evolution of industrial; symbiosis networks', *Business Strategy and the Environment*, **20**, 281–296.

Dutta, K. (2015), 'Wealthiest 1% set to be richer than other 99% combined', *The Independent*, **8823**, 19 January 2015, 4–5.

Ehrenfeld, J. and N. Gertler (1997), 'Industrial ecology in practice: the evolution of interdependence at Kalundborg', *Journal of Industrial Ecology*, **1**, 67–79.

Ellen MacArthur Foundation (n.d.) http://www.ellenmacarthurfoundation.org/.

Erkman, S. (1997), 'Industrial ecology: an historical view', *Journal of Cleaner Production*, **5**, 1–10.

European Commission (n.d.), accessed 17 March 2015 at http://ec.europa.eu/environment/circular-economy/.

Frosch, R.A. and N.E. Gallopoulos (1989), 'Strategies for manufacturing', *Scientific American*, **261**, 94–102.

Geng, Y., J. Fu, J. Sarkis and B. Xue (2012), 'Towards a national circular economy indicator system in China: an evaluation and critical analysis', *Journal of Cleaner Production*, **23**, 216–224.

Gregson, N., M. Crang, F.U. Ahamed, N. Akter, R. Ferdous, S. Foisal and R. Hudson (2012), 'Territorial agglomeration and industrial symbiosis: Sitakunda-Bhatiary, Bangladesh, as a secondary processing complex', *Economic Geography*, **88**, 37–58.

Healey, P. (1998), 'Building institutional capacity through collaborative approaches to urban planning', *Environment and Planning A*, **30** (9), 1531–1546.

Hubbard, P. (2005), 'Space/place', in D. Atkinson, P. Jackson, D. Sibley and N. Washburne (eds), *Cultural Geography: A Critical Dictionary of Key Concepts*, London and New York: I.B. Tauris & Co. Ltd.

Jensen P.D., L. Basson, E.E. Hellawell, M.R. Bailey and M. Leach (2011), 'Quantifying "geographic proximity": experiences from the United Kingdom's National Industrial Symbiosis Programme', *Resources, Conservation and Recycling*, **55**, 703–712.

Jiao, W. and F.A.A. Boons (2014), 'Toward a research agenda for policy intervention and facilitation to enhance industrial symbiosis based on a comprehensive literature review', *Journal of Cleaner Production*, **67**, 14–25.

Kennett, P. (ed.) (2013), *A Handbook of Comparative Social Policy*, Cheltenham, UK and Northampton, MA, USA: Edward Elgar.

Layton, A., J. Reap, B. Bras and M. Weissburg (2012), 'Correlation between thermodynamic efficiency and ecological cyclicity for thermodynamic power cycles', *PLOS One*. Doi: 10.1371/journal.pone.0051841.

Liu, L., B. Zhang and J. Bi (2015), 'Institutional context of eco-industrial parks development in China: environmental governance in industrial parks and zones', in P. Deutz, D. Lyons and J. Bi (eds), *International Perspectives on Industrial Ecology*, Cheltenham, UK and Northampton, MA, USA: Edward Elgar, pp. 154–174.

Lombardi, R.D., D. Lyons, H. Shi and A. Agarwal (2012), 'Industrial symbiosis: testing the boundaries and advancing knowledge', *Journal of Industrial Ecology*, **16**, 2–7.

Lowitt, P. (2015), 'Eco-industrial development in the United States: analysing progress from 2010–2015', in P. Deutz, D. Lyons and J. Bi (eds), *International*

Perspectives on Industrial Ecology, Cheltenham, UK and Northampton, MA, USA: Edward Elgar, pp. 46–68.

Lyons, D.I. (2007), 'A spatial analysis of loop closing among recycling, remanufacturing and waste treatment firms in Texas', *Journal of Industrial Ecology*, **11**, 43–54.

Lyons D., M. Rice and L. Hu (2015), 'Industrial waste management improvement: a case study of Pennsylvania', in P. Deutz, D. Lyons and J. Bi (eds), *International Perspectives on Industrial Ecology*, Cheltenham, UK and Northampton, MA, USA: Edward Elgar, pp. 108–125.

Manomaivibool, P. and S. Vassanadumrongdee (2011), 'Extended producer responsibility in Thailand: prospects for policies on waste electrical and electronic equipment', *Journal of Industrial Ecology*, **15**, 185–205.

Martens, P. and M. Raza (2010), 'Is globalisation sustainable?', *Sustainability*, **2** (1), 280–293.

Massey, D. (1991), 'A global sense of place', *Marxism Today*, **June**, 24–29.

McSmith, A. (2015), 'Divided UK: for every 12 jobs created in the South, one is lost in the North', *The Independent*, **8823**, 19 January 2015, 1 and 4.

North, D.C. (1990), *Institutions, Institutional Change and Economic Performance*, Cambridge, UK: Cambridge University Press.

Ohnishi, S., T. Fujita, X.D. Chen and M. Fujii, (2012), 'Econometric analysis of the performance of recycling projects in Japanese Eco-Towns', *Journal of Cleaner Production*, **33**, 217–225.

Olayide, O.A. (2015), 'Industrial ecology, industrial symbiosis and eco-industrial parks in Africa: issues for sustainable development', in P. Deutz, D. Lyons and J. Bi (eds), *International Perspectives on Industrial Ecology*, Cheltenham, UK and Northampton, MA, USA: Edward Elgar, pp. 30–45.

Oxfam (2014), accessed 10 March 2015 at http://www.oxfam.org/en/research/working-few.

Park, H.S., E.R. Rene, S.M. Choi and A.S.F. Chiu (2008), 'Strategies for sustainable development of industrial park in Ulsan, South Korea – from spontaneous evolution to systematic expansion of industrial symbiosis', *Journal of Environmental Management*, **87**, 1–13.

Patchell, J. (2015), 'Intersection of industrial symbiosis and product-based industrial ecologies: considerations from the Japanese home appliance industry', in P. Deutz, D. Lyons and J. Bi (eds), *International Perspectives on Industrial Ecology*, Cheltenham, UK and Northampton, MA, USA: Edward Elgar, pp. 175–190.

Peck, J. (2011), 'Geographies of policy: from transfer-diffusion to mobility-mutation', *Progress in Human Geography*, **35**, 773–797.

Rigg, J. (2007), *An Everyday Geography of the Global South*, London: Routledge.

Schiller, F., A.S. Penn and L. Basson (2014), 'Analyzing networks in industrial ecology: a review of Social-Material Network Analyses', *Journal of Cleaner Production*, **76**, 1–11.

Schwartz, E. and K. Steininger (1997), 'Implementing nature's lesson: the industrial recycling network enhancing regional development', *Journal of Cleaner Production*, **5**, 47–56.

Spekkink, W. (2015), 'Varieties of industrial symbiosis', in P. Deutz, D. Lyons and J. Bi (eds), *International Perspectives on Industrial Ecology*, Cheltenham, UK and Northampton, MA, USA: Edward Elgar, pp. 142–156.

Stone, D. (2012), 'Transfer and translation of policy', *Policy Studies*, **33**, 1–17.

Tian, J., W. Liu, B. Lai, X. Li and L. Chen (2014), 'Study of the performance of eco-industrial park development in China', *Journal of Cleaner Production*, **64**, 486–494.

UNEP/SETAC (2009), *Life Cycle Management: How Business Use It to Decrease Footprint, Create Opportunities and Make Value Chains more Sustainable*, Geneva, Switzerland: UNEP/SETAC.

Van Beers D., G. Corder, A. Bossilkov and R. van Berkel (2007), 'Industrial symbiosis in the Australian minerals industry: the cases of Kwinana and Gladstone', *Journal of Industrial Ecology*, **11**, 55–72.

Van Hoof, B. (2015), 'Institutional capacity for sustainable industrial systems in Caldas, Colombia', in P. Deutz, D. Lyons and J. Bi (eds), *International Perspectives on Industrial Ecology*, Cheltenham, UK and Northampton, MA, USA: Edward Elgar, pp. 191–208.

Vermeulen, W.J.V. (2006), 'The social dimensions of industrial ecology: on the implications of the inherent nature of social phenomena', *Progress in Industrial Ecology*, **3**, 574–598.

Wang, H., Y. Lei and J. Bi (2015), 'Greenhouse gases reduction strategies for eco-industrial parks in China', in P. Deutz, D. Lyons and J. Bi (eds), *International Perspectives on Industrial Ecology*, Cheltenham, UK and Northampton, MA, USA: Edward Elgar, pp. 209–227.

Wang, Q., P. Deutz and D. Gibbs (2015), 'UK-China collaboration for industrial symbiosis: a multi-level approach to policy transfer analysis', in P. Deutz, D. Lyons and J. Bi (eds), *International Perspectives on Industrial Ecology*, Cheltenham, UK and Northampton, MA, USA: Edward Elgar, pp. 89–107.

White, R. (1994), 'Preface', in B. Allenby and D. Richards (eds), *The Greening of Industrial Ecosystems*, Washington, DC: National Academy Press.

Yu, C., C. Davis and G.P.J Dijkema (2014), 'Understanding the evolution of industrial symbiosis research a bibliometric and network analysis (1997–2012)', *Journal of Industrial Ecology*, **18**, 280–293.

Yuan, Z.W., J. Bi and Y. Moriguichi (2006), 'The circular economy: a new development strategy in China', *Journal of Industrial Ecology*, **10**, 4–8.

2. Industrial ecology in India: converging traditional practice and modern environmental protection

Weslynne Ashton and Megha Shenoy

INTRODUCTION

India is a land of contrasts. Poverty exists alongside vast wealth; leaps of technical progress occur alongside traditional industry and agriculture. Resource conservation has been practised in India for millennia, driven primarily by economics and culture, similar to many other societies including Victorian England (Desrochers, 2002). This remains true in communities across the sub-continent and in many industries trying to turn profits on small margins. But, as populations urbanised and industrialised across the Indian sub-continent, the material and energy systems were thrown into a state of flux with a clash between traditional recycling systems and modern materials that have difficulty being recycled through these channels.

Agriculture has traditionally been the dominant economic sector in India, and remains so today, employing about 60% of the working population, and accounting for about one-quarter of economic output (India MoLE, 2012). Modern and traditional manufacturing coexist. The former is characterised by large-scale production in modern factories and the latter by small-scale activities, especially micro-scale 'cottage' industries in rural areas. While manufacturing activities employ approximately 10% of the workforce (India MoLE, 2012), they contribute upwards of one-third of India's formal economic output (Roy, 2002). Both modern and traditional industries are very labour intensive by Western standards, providing employment to large numbers of citizens throughout the country. Both also produce high levels of air and water pollution, and result in significant land degradation and transformation. For the majority of private enterprises, environmental issues have been viewed as costly matters that need to be addressed only when there is public outcry or government attention (Stuligross, 1999).

Despite this, a new trend has emerged – a growing number of companies in India are implementing industrial ecology-type solutions including cleaner production, industrial symbiosis, life cycle management, greening extended producer responsibility (Ashton et al., 2009; Muduli et al., 2013). The motivations and methods are often different across the spectrum from micro-enterprises to multinational corporations. Industrial ecology (IE) research at the regional and national levels is also not often called by that name, but several Indian researchers have conducted studies on materials cycling, waste management and resource conservation. In addition, international IE researchers have shown increasing interest in India.

Drawing on published academic literature, corporate publications and our own research, we illustrate the contemporary implementation of IE solutions. Our own work is based on material and energy flow analyses, combined with an examination of social, economic and policy issues present in a given locale. These follow the Resource Flow Analysis (RFA) methods developed by Erkman and Ramaswamy (2003). We critique the inadequacies of the current systems for waste management and recycling, including the lack of national policies and enforcement, and the low level of trust between industry, government and the public. Finally, we offer opportunities for bridging these gaps through policy development and enforcement, and support for private industry initiatives that go beyond regulatory compliance towards sustainable resource management. These opportunities lay a greater emphasis on environmentally-oriented research, closer and more transparent interaction between the public, private and civil sectors, and policy development to facilitate a shift to 'systems' thinking.

INDUSTRIAL ECOLOGY IN INDIA TODAY

The discussion of current implementation of IE approaches is organised at the firm level, across firms and within regional systems (see Figure 2.1). But, first, an important distinction concerning resource management can be made between traditionally biodegradable and recyclable materials streams and more complex industrial ones. The latter comprise both non-biodegradable materials (such as plastics) and products that are not recyclable by traditional methods (such as electronic equipment). Before 1950, solid waste was either composted or dumped in open sites on the outskirts of settlements (Thompson et al., 2009). As the non-biodegradable waste fraction has increased, composting pits have effectively become un-engineered landfills (Thompson et al., 2009). Through the early 1990s a considerable fraction of recyclable waste (paper, metal, glass and some types of plastics) was either segregated at households and industries and

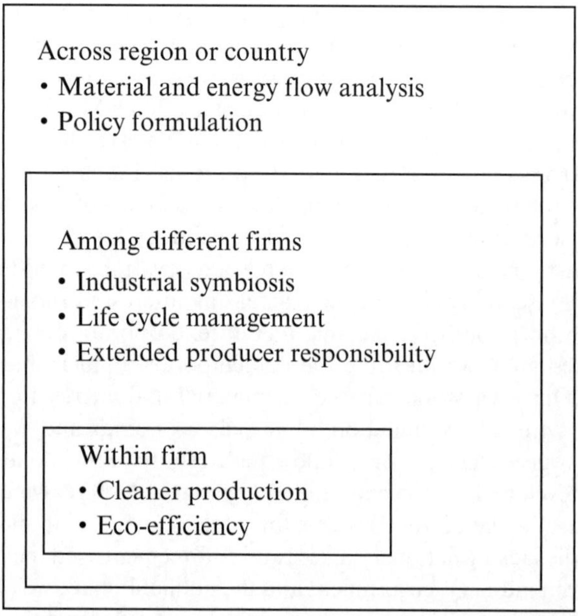

Across region or country
• Material and energy flow analysis
• Policy formulation

Among different firms
• Industrial symbiosis
• Life cycle management
• Extended producer responsibility

Within firm
• Cleaner production
• Eco-efficiency

Figure 2.1   Industrial ecology concepts and methods implemented at three levels: within firm, among different firms, across region or country

sold to scrap dealers, or collected from landfills by rag pickers and sold to larger traders (Van Beukering, 1994; Agarwal et al., 2005; Gidwani and Reddy, 2011). Today, door-to-door collection of scrap from households has decreased due to a combination of factors, from a growing throwaway culture to a rise in apartment complexes and gated communities (Whiteley, 1987; World Bank, 2012). However, scrap dealers continue to collect and effectively manage recyclables from industries.

Within Firm

At the level of an individual firm, IE activities include implementation of cleaner production practices such as minimising and reusing waste, and measures to increase the efficient use of materials and energy, resulting in productivity improvements (Figure 2.1). Large companies, both domestic and foreign owned, are thought-leaders with respect to modern environmental and social sustainability in India (Sharma, 2009). Many have been implementing corporate social responsibility (CSR) and cleaner production projects for decades, albeit not under those names.

Foreign-owned multinationals tend to follow the lead of their corporate mandates in terms of the types and manner of sustainability initiatives such as implementing ISO 14001 or the Global Reporting Initiative (GIZ, 2012). Indigenous companies have developed their own agendas, in response to local needs, such as water pollution; certification programmes, for example Bureau of Energy Efficiency standards (BEE, 2001); and global trends. The Confederation of Indian Industry, the largest trade association on the sub-continent, has two important hubs of activity focused on sustainability awareness and education for business (CII, 2013a). In addition, non-governmental organisations play an important role in India's industrial landscape by closely monitoring and critiquing industrial activities that create significant social and environmental impacts (Pargal and Mani, 2000; Chitra, 2003).

The Tata group of companies, one of India's foremost conglomerates, claims a high prioritisation of sustainability issues, with a special focus on social responsibility and proactively addressing climate-related challenges (Tata Group, 2014). Tata has conducted carbon and water footprint analyses for various facilities in its power, steel, automotive and chemicals manufacturing subsidiaries and has developed strategies for reducing their impacts (IFC et al., 2013). In some cases they have implemented closed loop systems to manage materials within units: for every tonne of steel produced at Tata Steel, approximately 700 kg of various wastes (excluding fly ash) were also generated, of which 83% of these materials were either recycled or reused in its own facilities or sold as raw materials to other industries, with the balance going to landfill (Moraes, 2006). Tata Consultancy Services (TCS), India's largest technology services company, was ranked as the seventh 'greenest' global company in *Newsweek*'s 2011 Green Rankings and eleventh in 2012 (*Newsweek*, 2012; *Hindustan Times*, 2012).

Small-scale enterprises (defined as firms with fixed assets worth less than 10 million Indian Rupees or approximately 100 000 Euros [MSME, 2013]) play a very significant role in the economy, contributing about one-third of exports in 2007 (Bodla and Verma, 2008). Implementing environmental initiatives has been especially challenging in this sector (similar to other parts of the world), as small companies have limited finances and human capital to assess and pursue environmental (and more broadly innovation) opportunities (Van Berkel, 2010; Mathiyazhagan et al., 2013). A recent study by the Resource Optimization Initiative (ROI) in Bangalore highlighted this challenge. ROI researchers identified the material and energy use among cottage-scale silk reelers in Sidlaghatta, Karnataka (Shenoy et al., 2010): producing 1 kg of raw silk required 26 kg of firewood and 112 L of water. However, reelers found it extremely difficult to invest in cleaner technologies that would reduce their operating costs and resource consumption because of the high perceived costs, even with payback periods under two years. Furthermore, as investment in equipment for the cottage-scale sector is currently subsidised by the government of India, owners expect that investment in new greener technology should also be subsidised by the government (Shenoy et al., 2010).

There have been international programmes promoting cleaner production in India, but so far these have had limited effect. In the late 1990s, the World Bank sponsored a technical assistance project focused on 'Environmental Management Capacity Building' that promoted cleaner production, especially in the state of Gujarat (Rathi, 2003). The United Nations Industrial Development Organisation (UNIDO) and United Nations Environment Programme (UNEP) supported the setting up of the National Cleaner Production Centre[1] (NCPC) in New Delhi in 1995, to address environmental problems of Small and Medium Enterprises (SMEs) (Van Berkel, 2010). Four regional cleaner production centres were subsequently planned in Gujarat, Karnataka, Punjab and West Bengal (Rathi, 2003). However, only the Gujarat centre has implemented cleaner production in SMEs in a variety of manufacturing and service sectors (GCPC, 2013). Despite these efforts, some of the most significant barriers to cleaner production and greening activities include lack of internal environmental knowledge, funding and capacity for implementing changes, insufficient external social pressure demanding change, and lax enforcement of regulations (Muduli et al., 2013).

Among Different Firms

The power of IE becomes much more apparent when considered at the level of systems (Figure 2.1). Multiple firms can belong to an industrial ecosystem, whether defined geographically or by the value chain (Boons and Howard-Grenville, 2009).

Industrial symbiosis
Companies in regional networks can engage in industrial symbiosis, i.e., can have utility sharing arrangements (the joint management of utilities and infrastructure such as electricity and steam co-generation and waste treatment plants) and/or by-product synergies (transfer and productive use of one company's 'waste' by another). Utility sharing in the Indian context includes Common Effluent Treatment Plants (CETPs). Under a Ministry of Environment and Forests (MoEF) financial assistance scheme, 88 CETPs having total capacity of 560 million litres per day (MLD) have been set up covering more than 10000 companies (CPCB, 2005). They are especially useful to smaller enterprises by providing an affordable means of

pollution control and wastewater treatment (UNEP, 2001). In some cases these CETPs have also been designed to capture methane, using the gas for generating electricity, providing co-benefits of energy provision and CO_2 emissions reductions (Puppim de Oliveira et al., 2013).

Numerous companies individually investigate ways to optimise their performance through better by-product management and greater coordination with others in their supply chain. The sugar industry is notable as it has explored many innovative uses for its by-products over the years. In some cases, companies have developed vertically integrated operations to maximise profits and manage materials more effectively. The Appropriate Rural Technology Institute (ARTI) has been instrumental in developing innovative technologies and uses for waste materials, such as converting sugar cane bagasse, the fibrous by-product from sugar production, to charcoal for use in domestic cook stoves (Balakrishnan and Batra, 2011). Many sugar mills across the country utilise bagasse as a fuel for electricity and steam production, these are consumed on-site or fed into the electricity grid. Seshasayee Paper and Boards Ltd began operating a sugar mill to secure the supply of the bagasse as the primary raw material for the production of paper (Erkman and Ramaswamy, 2003).

Larger networks with extensive by-product synergies are thought to be commonplace in India, though not yet 'uncovered' as such (Bain et al., 2010). One example is located in the Nanjangud region near Mysore in the state of Karnataka. Many companies in this region utilise agricultural by-products in place of coal for generating energy, thus lowering their CO_2 emissions and operating costs (Figure 2.2). In addition, companies in Nanjangud transfer 13% of their by-products for reuse by others within 20 km of the industrial area. The synergies are driven primarily by the economic savings from replacing more expensive virgin raw materials with locally available by-products. They generate positive environmental benefits such as lowering emissions from transportation because of localised reuse, and reducing the disposal of materials in landfills and the need for energy-intensive processing and supply of raw materials. Despite potential benefits, there are few avenues from which companies can obtain information and coordinate material reuse, beyond standard recyclable materials that are very effectively managed through the informal recycling network of scrap dealers.

There have been several initiatives to promote eco-industrial development (EID) in India, notably in the state of Gujarat at the Naroda Industrial Estate in the 1990s (Singhal and Kapur, 2002). However, little was actually implemented. In the past, public sector efforts to promote environmental activities did not include industries as a primary partner, which limited their willingness to participate in such initiatives. In addition,

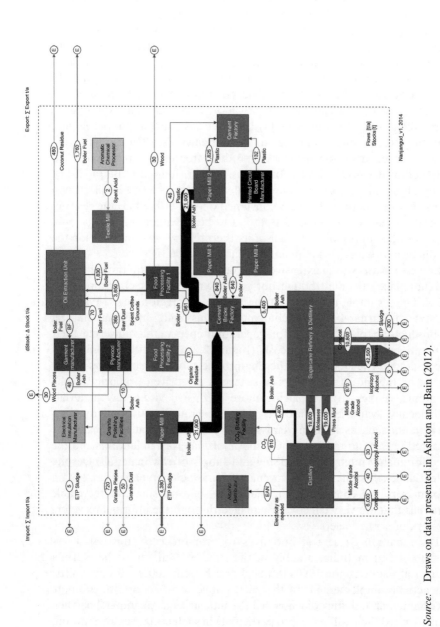

Source: Draws on data presented in Ashton and Bain (2012).

Figure 2.2 *Network depicting inter-firm reuse of industrial by-products generated by facilities in the Nanjangud Industrial Area, Karnataka*

many companies lack faith in the system and corruption is thought to be widespread, further reducing the willingness of companies to participate in government initiatives. More recently GIZ, the German international development agency, began promoting EID in Special Economic Zones (SEZs), especially in the state of Andhra Pradesh, through capacity building workshops with policy makers and industries (Mahadev, 2013). An understanding of local conditions that encourage by-product synergies and cross-country comparison of supporting policies can help to drive top-down and bottom-up strategies for industrial symbiosis.

Life cycle management
Environmental performance in specific industries can be assessed and enhanced when individual companies voluntarily work together to develop standards and codes of best practice. Life cycle assessment (LCA) is used to understand environmental issues at the level of a product, firm or across a value chain.

One of the earliest Indian LCAs, from 1997, focused on the steel industry because of its high forecasted growth to meet the infrastructural needs of the country (Kakkar, 2003). This assessment created a baseline of material and energy use, benchmarked environmental impacts, and devised policies and best practices to inform expansion of the industry. Steel production in India was found to consume much more resources than global averages. For example, it used twice as much coal and about a third more iron to produce a unit of steel. However, it is difficult to determine if any of the recommendations were followed on a large scale. Subsequent LCAs found that the Indian steel industry continues to generate a higher pollution load and higher raw material consumption compared to Western counterparts (Kakkar and Maudgal, 2008; Yellishetty et al., 2011).

Interest in LCAs in India has grown dramatically, with coverage of the sugar industry, building infrastructure and renewable energy taking prominence (Varun et al., 2009; Chauhan et al., 2011; Sharma et al., 2011). Recent interest in biofuels to supply domestic energy needs as well as the export market has spurred numerous LCAs, especially regarding the production of *Jatropha* biofuels (for example, Achten et al., 2010; Gmünder et al., 2010; Pandey et al., 2011). There is an active and growing LCA practitioner community which is supported by the major industry associations and which aims to generate and utilise LCAs in environmental management (Wernet et al., 2011; CII, 2013b; FICCI, 2013).

Extended producer responsibility
Extended producer responsibility (EPR) puts the onus on individual companies to effectively manage the environmental impacts throughout the life

cycles of their products, especially in closing the material and energy loops at the end of the products' useful life (Deutz, 2009). However, such strategies may be challenging within developing country contexts.

Tetra Pak, the global leader in aseptic packaging, has had to develop its own EPR system in India. It adapted collection and recycling methods as formal collection systems were not in place. Partnering with NGOs, such as Saahas in Bangalore, it developed pictorial educational campaigns to create awareness among illiterate collectors that the containers are valuable and explained how they should be collected and stored (Saahas, 2012). Tetra Pak arranges the collection and transportation of these materials to the Daman Ganga paper mill in the state of Maharashtra. The mill separates the constituent materials in the collected cartons and produces recycled paper notebooks and other paper goods, as well as a plastic polymer from the polyethylene and aluminium, which is used for making roofing materials and office furniture (Daman Ganga Industries, 2008; Gokhale and Choudhary, 2009).

The electronic consumer goods sector has played a leading role in EPR initiatives. India imports a growing volume of electronic waste from more developed countries, in addition to generating a large amount of e-waste. Information technology (IT) has become the fastest growing sector in the economy and the population has become more affluent, both of which contribute to the frequent purchase and obsolescence of electronic goods, especially computers and mobile phones. E-waste tends to have high concentrations of toxic substances that are not easily recycled and which pose serious health risks to those who are exposed to them (*Design News*, 2005). In most cases, e-waste is recycled through the informal sector, with very little protection, including gloves or masks, provided to workers who are often the most marginal in societies (Streicher-Porte et al., 2005).

The national *E-waste (management and handling) Rules* came into effect in May 2012 (MoEF, 2011). These regulations made producers liable for reducing and recycling e-waste in the country and provided guidelines for companies to trace the flow of discarded e-waste and ensure legal and responsible recycling in state authorised centres (MoEF and CPCB, 2008; Wath et al., 2010). While there has been an increase in transmission of e-waste from businesses to authorised recyclers, collection systems for consumers have not been enforced (Lalchandani, 2012). Enforcement across sectors will be critical for effective e-waste collection, recycling and proper disposal.

Interestingly, there were some private sector antecedents to the new rules. In August 2010, Samsung India launched the Samsung Takeback and Recycling (STAR) programme – India's first electronics producer-initiated product takeback and recycling programme. Samsung encourages consumers to recycle Samsung branded consumer electronics sold in India, free of cost. The current reach of the programme includes 21 cities across the sub-continent with drop-off centres for smaller electronics and collection for larger goods. Recyclers are directly contracted and continuously monitored by Samsung to ensure that this e-waste is not incinerated, landfilled, exported or otherwise improperly disposed (Samsung India, 2012).

Many companies are voluntarily initiating resource conservation and reuse practices in collaboration with others, including by-product synergies, life cycle management and extended producer responsibility. However, little is known about the effectiveness of these schemes or the likelihood of other companies imitating them. Government efforts often lag or miss opportunities to support industry best practices, thus closer coordination between the private and public sector is necessary in order to reward best practices and promote them across the country.

Across Region or Country

With millions of informal micro-, small- and medium-scale enterprises, IE concepts can also be applied to identify opportunities for reducing total material consumption and disposal across a region (Figure 2.1). Tiripur, in the southern state of Tamil Nadu, is an international hub for textile manufacturing. In the 1980s, manufacturers in the town began using chemical dyes to produce coloured shirts for export, which led to massive pollution of the local river, and the need to have water trucked in from 50 km away (Erkman and Ramaswamy, 2003). While no single textile producer used a lot of resources, in aggregate the more than 4000 individual small-scale units consumed 90 000 kilolitres of water and 1200 tonnes of firewood every day (Erkman and Ramaswamy, 2003). By identifying how raw materials, energy and water were consumed in various stages of the textile processing supply chain, the researchers pinpointed opportunities for improving resource recycling and efficiencies. A local entrepreneur then developed an innovative means to recycle wastewater using waste heat from the dyeing process, thus simultaneously reducing the energy requirements, greenhouse gas emissions and conserving wastewater – a truly systemic solution that was implemented in many dyeing units. Unfortunately, this solution was not implemented in a systemic way, and water supply and pollution problems have persisted. In 2010, more than 100 bleaching and dyeing units were shut down for non-compliance with regulations (Venkatesan and Mayilvaganan, 2010). Serious concerns persist about the future viability of the industry as these units have depleted the existing resource base and overwhelmed the assimilative capacity of the natural environment.

Regional studies can extend beyond the industrial sector to look at the overall metabolism of energy and materials by members of a society – known as social metabolism (Fischer-Kowalski, 1998). Longitudinal studies have been performed on the agrarian society of Trinket in the Nicobar Islands in the Indian Ocean (Singh et al., 2001; Singh and Grünbühel, 2003). These studies captured the changing dynamics of the island's transition from being subsistence based to having increasing trade and interactions with outsiders. More than 90% of the materials needed to satisfy local consumption was sourced locally, with a very small but growing amount of final products, construction materials and fossil fuels being imported and traded for sand and copra (coconut fibre). The 2004 Indian Ocean tsunami had a devastating effect on the island, not only in terms of the loss of lives, crops and livestock during the tsunami, but also due to the dramatic changes in materials consumption from humanitarian aid in the aftermath of the disaster (Singh, 2011). Socio-metabolic studies like this can illustrate changing patterns of material and energy use due to gradual changes and rapid shocks, as well as the sustainability of those patterns.

Industrial Ecology Education

While there are no formal IE degree programmes at the tertiary level, several environmental engineering and science programmes include coverage of IE topics in their coursework (Jain et al., 2013). One of the authors of this chapter (Ashton) taught the first full graduate IE course at TERI University in New Delhi in 2009. Several short courses and seminars related to LCA and IE feature both local and international speakers and are hosted by local institutions. For example, ROI in Bangalore has played a leading role in promoting IE awareness within academia, as well as in the public and private sectors (Resource Optimization Initiative, 2011). ROI's founder, the late Ramesh Ramaswamy, was a passionate advocate for bringing IE to India. He emphasised that IE was much more urgently needed in emerging economies, like India, as their industry and infrastructure was not yet built (Erkman and Ramaswamy, 2003). Many young people interested in working in IE pursue postgraduate studies in more established IE academic institutions in Europe and North America. Conversely, a growing number of young IE researchers from more developed countries travel to India to conduct research and write their theses on challenging issues, many at ROI.

CONCLUSIONS AND RECOMMENDATIONS

Government regulations rarely emphasise resource conservation in India and instead focus on pollution control and treatment. Smaller companies' recovery, reuse and recycling of materials are largely driven by economics; while larger, multinational (both foreign and domestic) companies voluntarily pursue resource conservation strategies to coincide with their global sustainability and/or social responsibility mandates. Furthermore, where regulations exist there is little, if any, oversight and monitoring. Industry associations and advocacy efforts tend to focus on economic rather than environmental issues, and seem to have little influence on environmental regulations. A shift from a 'compliance only' to a 'beyond compliance' mindset in the public and private sectors is needed to foster more innovative practices around resource circulation within the economy. In addition, closer coordination between these sectors can result in the creation of policies that align with the interests and capabilities of the private sector to act upon them.

IE research in India so far has focused on conducting baseline assessments of material flows, product life cycles and opportunities for loop closing and symbiosis, and in the future should examine:

1. Why numerous government-led initiatives (e.g., eco-industrial development) have failed to bring lasting changes in industry, and how better to engage the private sector in the design and establishment of such programmes.
2. The impact of IE seminars and outreach events on attendees.
3. City- and regional-level metabolism of resources, including waste generation and disposition, and the impact of various indigenous policy or cultural interventions.
4. How corporate practices and sustainability programmes impact environmental and human health across the supply chains, product life cycles and diverse communities in which they operate.
5. How better to integrate and account for manual labour in LCAs, which can be an important and unique contribution from India to the global LCA community.
6. How to include the needs of different social groups (e.g., rural and urban dwellers) in resource management policies, with special regard to negotiations between parties of unequal power (such as between farmers and industry), and the potential for corruption and inefficiencies in monitoring and expansion.

The systems approach associated with IE commands attention to all the possible resource problems a company might face, not just to a single issue within its walls. Indeed, in expanding boundaries to nearby companies as in Nanjangud or across the product life cycle as in the steel sector, IE expands the solution set for Indian companies to tackle challenges from local pollution, waste disposal and the sourcing of raw materials to global climate change.

National and state governments can develop policies which support business in effective environmental and waste management while giving them the flexibility to innovate and devise profitable solutions for resource management problems. While much relevant government activity in India is at the state level through the Pollution Control Boards, there is also scope for activity at the national level. Germany and Japan were pioneers in devising legislation to encourage 'recycling-oriented' or 'sound material-cycle' societies, and China has recently followed suit (Mathews and Tan, 2011). A similar framework for India could help to develop a cohesive framework for the reduction, reuse and recycling of resources through their life cycles. IE certainly has much scope for implementation in India due to the large infrastructure and production planning required to meet future needs. For India, more resource-cognisant policies will be able to better situate industrial activities on the sub-continent so that they do not irrevocably harm natural resources and people.

NOTE

1. See http://wmc.nic.in/chapter2-environmentalmanagement.asp#3.3.3.2, accessed 18 February 2015.

ORGANISATIONS REFERENCED

Appropriate Rural Technology Institute, last accessed May 2015 at www.arti-india. org.
Centre for Science and Environment, last accessed May 2015 at www.cseindia.org.
CII-Sohrabji Godrej Green Business Centre, last accessed May 2015 at www.green-businesscentre.com.
CII-ITC Centre of Excellence for Sustainable Development, last accessed May 2015 at www.sustainabledevelopment.in.
Greenpeace India (Bangalore), last accessed May 2015 at www.greenpeace.org/india/en/.
GIZ Pathway to Eco-industrial Development in India, last accessed May 2015 at http://www.igep.in/live/hrdpmp/hrdpmaster/igep/content/e48745/e50194/e50195/121004_Pathway_EID_ISOX3uncoated-1.pdf.
Resource Optimization Initiative, last accessed January 2014 at www.roionline.org.
Saahas, last accessed January 2014 at www.saahas.org.

Toxics Link, last accessed January 2014 at www.toxicslink.org.
UNEP-UNIDO joint RECP Programme (Formerly the National Cleaner Production Centres Programme), last accessed May 2015 at http://www.unep.org/resourceeffi ciency/Business/CleanerSaferProduction/ResourceEfficientCleanerProduction/ UNEP-UNIDOjointRECPProgramme/tabid/78757/Default.aspx.

REFERENCES

Achten, W.M.J., J. Almeida, V. Fobelets, E. Bolle, E. Mathijs, V.P. Singh, D.N. Tewari, L.V. Verchot and B. Muys (2010), 'Life cycle assessment of Jatropha biodiesel as transportation fuel in rural India', *Applied Energy*, **87**, 3652–3660.

Agarwal, A., A. Singhmar, M. Kulshrestha and A.K. Mittal (2005), 'Municipal solid waste recycling and associated markets in Delhi, India', *Resources, Conservation and Recycling*, **44**, 73–90.

Ashton, W.S. and A. Bain (2012), 'Assessing the "short mental distance" in eco-industrial networks', *Journal of Industrial Ecology*, **16**, 70–82.

Ashton, W., M. Chertow and M. Shenoy (2009), 'Industrial ecology – developing systemic solutions to climate change and other environmental challenges in Indian industry', *Sustainability Tomorrow*, New Delhi, India: Confederation of Indian Industry.

Bain, A., M. Shenoy, W. Ashton and M. Chertow (2010), 'Industrial symbiosis and waste recovery in an Indian industrial area', *Resources, Conservation and Recycling*, **54**, 1278–1287.

Balakrishnan, M. and V.S. Batra (2011), 'Valorization of solid waste in sugar factories with possible applications in India: a review', *Journal of Environmental Management*, **92**, 2886–2891.

BEE (2001), *BEE Initiatives: Standards & Labeling Programme*, accessed November 2013 at http://bee-dsm.in/PoliciesRegulations_1_4.aspx#L2.

Bodla, B.S. and S.R. Verma (2008), 'An analysis of the performance of SSIs in the era of globalization', *ICFAI Journal of Managerial Economics*, **6**, 40–53.

Boons, F.A. and J. Howard-Grenville (eds) (2009), *The Social Eembeddedness of Industrial Ecology*, Cheltenham, UK and Northampton, MA, USA: Edward Elgar.

Chauhan, M.K., C.S. Varun, S. Kumar and S. Samar (2011), 'Life cycle assessment of sugar industry: a review', *Renewable & Sustainable Energy Reviews*, **15**, 3445–3453.

Chitra, A. (2003), 'Role of NGOs in protecting environment and health', in M.J. Bunch, V.M. Suresh and T.V. Kumaran (eds), *Proceedings of the Third International Conference on Environment and Health*, Chennai, India, Department of Geography, University of Madras and Faculty of Environmental Studies, 15–17 December 2003, York University, 105–112.

CII (2013a), *Confederation of Indian Industry – Centres of Excellence*, accessed 2013 at http://www.cii.in/Centres_of_Excellence.aspx.

CII (2013b), *LCI India Network*, Confederation of Indian Industry – Sohrabji Godrej Green Business Centre, accessed February 2013 at http://www.greenbusi nesscentre.com/lcanetwork.

CPCB (2005), *Performance Status of Common Effluent Treatment Plants in India New Delhi*, Central Pollution Control Board, Government of India.

Daman Ganga Industries (2008), TetraPak Recycling, accessed May 2015 at http://www.damanganga.com/index.html.

Design News (2005), 'Toxic e-waste in China and India dumps', *Design News*, **60**, 34, accessed May 2015 at http://www.designnews.com/author.asp?section_id=1386&doc_id=222046).

Desrochers, P. (2002), 'Cities and industrial symbiosis: some historical perspectives and policy implications', *Journal of Industrial Ecology*, **5**, 29–34.

Deutz, P. (2009), 'Producer responsibility in a sustainable development context: ecological modernisation or industrial ecology?', *The Geographical Journal*, **175**, 274–285.

Erkman, S. and R. Ramaswamy (2003), *Applied Industrial Ecology: A New Platform for Planning Sustainable Societies: Focus on Developing Countries with Case Studies from India*, Bangalore, India: Acra Publishers.

FICCI (2013), *India LCA Alliance*, Federation of Indian Chambers of Commerce and Industry, accessed 24 February 2013 at http://indialca.com.

Fischer-Kowalski, M. (1998), 'Society's metabolism: the intellectual history of materials flow analysis, Part I, 1860–1970', *Journal of Industrial Ecology*, **2**, 61–78.

GCPC (2013), *Gujarat Cleaner Production Centre (GCPC) Case studies*, accessed November 2013 at http://www.gcpcgujarat.org.in/layout.php?mid=4.

Gidwani, V. and R.N. Reddy (2011), 'The afterlives of "waste": notes from India for a minor history of capitalist surplus', *Antipode*, **43**, 1625–1658.

GIZ (2012), 'Sustainability reporting: practices and trends in India 2012', New Delhi: Deutsche Gesellschaft für Internationale Zusammenarbeit (GIZ) GmbH.

Gmünder, S.M., R. Zah, S. Bhatacharjee, M. Classen, P. Mukherjee and R. Widmer (2010), 'Life cycle assessment of village electrification based on straight jatropha oil in Chhattisgarh, India', *Biomass & Bioenergy*, **34**, 347–355.

Gokhale, J. and A. Choudhary (2009), 'Re: Tetra Pak India, food for development office' (personal communication with Weslynne Ashton).

Hindustan Times (2012), '13 Indian firms in Newsweek's global green; Wipro no.2', *Hindustan Times*, 27 October 2012.

IFC, TATA and WFN (2013), 'Water footprint assessment for Tata chemicals', Tata Motors, Tata Power and Tata Steel: results and learning, International Finance Coporation, Tata Group, Water Footprint Network.

India MoLE (2012), *Unorganised Sector in India*, Ministry of Labour and Employment, accessed 5 March 2012 at http://labour.nic.in/ss/UNORGANISEDSECTORININDIA-SocialSecurityandWelfareFunds.pdf.

Jain, S., P. Aggarwal, N. Sharma and P. Sharma (2013), 'Fostering sustainability through education, research and practice: a case study of TERI University', *Journal of Cleaner Production*, **61**, 20–24.

Kakkar, M. (2003), 'India', in R. Tan (ed.), *Life Cycle Assessment For Green Productivity: An Asian Perspective*, Singapore: Asian Productivity Organization.

Kakkar, M. and S. Maudgal (2008), *Life Cycle Assessment – An Effective Tool for Cleaner Production in the Steel Sector*, Sustainable Development Solutions for Asia and the Pacific.

Lalchandani, N. (2012), 'No system in place to handle electronic waste', *Times of India*.

Mahadev, R.H. (2013), 'Greening of existing industrial parks – experiences of GIZ in Andhra Pradesh', International Conference on 'Planning of New Industrial Parks and Investment Zones', New Delhi: GIZ.

Mathews, J.A. and H. Tan (2011), 'Progress toward a circular economy in China', *Journal of Industrial Ecology*, **15**, 435–457.

Mathiyazhagan, K., K. Govindan, A. Noorulhaq and Y. Geng (2013), 'An ISM approach for the barrier analysis in implementing green supply chain management', *Journal of Cleaner Production*, **47**, 283–297.

MoEF (2011), *E-waste (management and handling) Rules*, Ministry of Environment and Forests, Government of India.

MoEF and CPCB (2008), *Guidelines for Environmentally Sound Management of E-waste*, New Delhi, India: Government of India: Ministry of Environment and Forests and Central Pollution Control Board.

Moraes, C. (2006), 'Reduce, reuse and recycle', accessed January 2014 at http://www.tata.co.in/article/inside/1tjxIyeO8fs=/TLYVr3YPkMU=.

MSME (2013), *Ministry of Micro, Small and Medium Enterprises – Definitions*, accessed January 2014 at http://dcmsme.gov.in/ssiindia/definition.htm.

Muduli, K., K. Govindan, A. Barve and Y. Geng (2013), 'Barriers to green supply chain management in Indian mining industries: a graph theoretic approach', *Journal of Cleaner Production*, **47**, 335–344.

Newsweek (2012), 'Green rankings 2012 – global companies', accessed 18 February 2015 at http://www.newsweek.com/2012/10/22/newsweek-green-rankings-2012-global-500-list.html.

Pandey, K.K., N. Pragya and P.K. Sahoo (2011), 'Life cycle assessment of small-scale high-input Jatropha biodiesel production in India', *Applied Energy*, **88**, 4831–4839.

Pargal, S. and M. Mani (2000), 'Citizen activism, environmental regulation, and the location of industrial plants: evidence from India', *Economic Development and Cultural Change*, **48**, 829–846.

Puppim de Oliveira, J.A., C.N.H. Doll, T.A. Kurniawan, Y. Geng, M. Kapshe and D. Huisingh (2013), 'Promoting win–win situations in climate change mitigation, local environmental quality and development in Asian cities through co-benefits', *Journal of Cleaner Production*, **58**, 1–6.

Rathi, A.K.A. (2003), 'Promotion of cleaner production for industrial pollution abatement in Gujarat (India)', *Journal of Cleaner Production*, **11**, 583.

Resource Optimization Initiative (2011), *ROI 2010 Annual Report*, Bangalore, India: Resource Optimization Initiative.

Roy, T. (2002), 'Economic history and modern India: redefining the link', *The Journal of Economic Perspectives*, **16**, 109–130.

Saahas (2012), *Tetra Pak Collection and Recycling*, accessed 18 February 2012 at http://saahas.org/index.php?option=com_content&view=article&id=63&Itemid=72.

Samsung India (2012), Samsung Take Back and Recycling (STAR) Programme.

Sharma, A., A. Saxena, M. Sethi, V. Shree and Varun (2011), 'Life cycle assessment of buildings: a review', *Renewable & Sustainable Energy Reviews*, **15**, 871–875.

Sharma, S.G. (2009), 'Corporate social responsibility in India: an overview', *International Lawyer*, **43**, 1515–1533.

Shenoy, M., S. Lokanath, R. Kumari and S.I. Pattanshetti (2010), 'An industrial ecology approach to optimize resources in the silk reeling sector in Sidlaghatta, South India', Bangalore, India: Resource Optimization Initiative, accessed

18 February 2015 at http://www.roionline.org/uploads/ROI_2010_Silk%20 Case%20Study%20Final.pdf.

Singh, S.J. (2011), 'Humanitarian aid and its impact on resource throughput: a case of the Nicobar Islands in the aftermath of the tsunami', *Island Industrial Ecology and Sustainability*, Kona, Hawaii.

Singh, S.J. and C.M. Grünbühel (2003), 'Environmental relations and biophysical transition: the case of Trinket Island', *Geografiska Annaler Series B: Human Geography*, **85**, 191–208.

Singh, S.J., C.M. Grünbühel, H. Schandl and N. Schulz (2001), 'Social metabolism and labour in a local context: changing environmental relations on Trinket Island', *Population and Environment*, **23**, 71–104.

Singhal, S. and A. Kapur (2002), 'Industrial estate planning and management in India – an integrated approach towards industrial ecology', *Journal of Environmental Management*, **66**, 19.

Streicher-Porte, M., R. Widmer, A. Jain, H.-P. Bader, R. Scheidegger and S. Kytzia (2005), 'Key drivers of the e-waste recycling system: assessing and modelling e-waste processing in the informal sector in Delhi', *Environmental Impact Assessment Review*, **25**, 472–491.

Stuligross, D. (1999), 'The political economy of environmental regulation in India', *Pacific Affairs*, **72**, 392–406.

Tata Group (2014), *Our Commitment*, accessed 14 January 2014 at http://tata.com/ ourcommitment/index.aspx?sectid=ei6stgDjpgA=.

Thompson, R.C., S.H. Swan, C.J. Moore and F.S. Vom Saal (2009), 'Our plastic age', *Philosophical Transactions of the Royal Society B: Biological Sciences*, **364**, 1973–1976.

UNEP (2001), *Environmental Management for Industrial Estates: Information and Training Resources*, United Nations Environmental Programme.

Van Berkel, R. (2010), 'Evolution and diversification of National Cleaner Production Centres (NCPCs)', *Journal of Environmental Management*, **91**, 1556–1565.

Van Beukering, P. (1994), 'An economic analysis of different types of formal and informal entrepreneurs, recovering urban solid waste in Bangalore (India)', *Resources, Conservation and Recycling*, **12**, 229–252.

Varun, I.K. Bhat and R. Prakash (2009), 'LCA of renewable energy for electricity generation systems – a review', *Renewable & Sustainable Energy Reviews*, **13**, 1067–1073.

Venkatesan, R. and V. Mayilvaganan (2010), 'Despite green crackdown, Tiripur remains most polluted', *Times of India*, accessed 18 February 2015 at http://articles.timesofindia.indiatimes.com/2010-10-06/chennai/28250860_1_noyyal-river-dyeing-units-water-samples.

Wath, S.B., A.N. Vaidya, P.S. Dutt and T. Chakrabarti (2010), 'A roadmap for development of sustainable e-waste management system in India', *Science of the Total Environment*, **409**, 19–32.

Wernet, G., M. Stucki, M. Shenoy and N. Muthusezhiyan (2011), 'Establishing a data framework for life cycle management in India', LCM 2011, Berlin.

Whiteley, N. (1987), 'Toward a throw-away culture, consumerism, "style obsolescence" and cultural theory in the 1950s and 1960s', *Oxford Art Journal*, **10**, 3–27.

World Bank (2012), 'GNI per capita, Atlas method for India (current US$)', accessed 18 February 2015 at http://data.worldbank.org/indicator/NY.GNP.PCAP.CD.

Yellishetty, M., G.M. Mudd, P.G. Ranjith and A. Tharumarajah (2011), 'Environmental life-cycle comparisons of steel production and recycling: sustainability issues, problems and prospects', *Environmental Science & Policy*, **14**, 650–663.

3. Industrial ecology, industrial symbiosis and eco-industrial parks in Africa: issues for sustainable development

Olawale Emmanuel Olayide

INTRODUCTION

The idea of industry finding uses for non-product outputs (by-products and wastes) is not a new one (Desrochers, 2001). However, local context and incentives change with the global drive towards efficient use of resources (Deutz, 2014) and sustainable development (Posch, 2010). This contrasts with the conventional economic growth trajectories that lead to increased negative ecological impacts (Boons et al., 2011). In Africa, and indeed globally, multiple factors are bringing about a change in attitudes and making the prospects for industrial ecology (IE) more attractive. The growing scarcity of resources together with advances in technology and greater urbanisation are all heightening awareness that the time is ripe for change to more sustainable development (Ellen MacArthur Foundation, 2013).

IE considers non-human 'natural' ecosystems as potential models for industrial activity and places human technological activity (industry) in the larger ecosystems that support it, examining the sources of resources used in society and the sinks that may act to absorb or detoxify wastes. This latter sense of the 'ecological' links IE to the questions of carrying capacity and ecological resilience (Graedel, 1996; Allenby, 2006; Kronenberg, 2006). An eco-industrial park (EIP) is a means of improving resource efficiency within a network of co-located companies (Côte and Cohen-Rosenthal, 1998; Roberts, 2004; Tudor et al., 2007) by employing a range of environmental management strategies. The EIPs aim to implement industrial zones where waste or by-products of one company can be used as resources by another business, that is, industrial symbiosis (IS) (Brent et al., 2008; Lombardi et al., 2012).

There is evidence to show that companies are now utilising various strategies to realise the social, economic, environmental and institutional benefits of increasing the efficiency of their businesses at the organisational level, inter-business level and regional levels (Phillips et al., 2006; Tudor et al., 2007). Examples of IE and applications of the principles of IS transcend the borders and continents of the world (Heeres et al., 2004; Lombardi et al., 2012; Alfaro and Miller, 2013). Successful case studies of EIPs can be found in many continents of the world including Asia and Europe (Chiu and Yong, 2004; Lombardi et al., 2012). However, not much is known of IE in Africa despite the fact that the challenges that IE seeks to solve (e.g., inefficient use of resources and energy, poor transportation, and environmental degradation, etc. [Roberts, 2004]) are more pervasive in Africa than elsewhere.

Efficient management of resources is a key issue for sustainable development of societies at all level. Developed countries have made considerable progress in recent years towards the recovery of value from waste and effective management of disposal facilities through recycling and implementation of EIPs (Deschenes and Chertow 2004; Behera et al., 2012). EIPs have been said to offer the path to sustainable development in the context of developed countries (Ehrenfeld, 2004; Boons et al., 2011). This appears to be an argument for EIPs as a partial solution to sustainable development in Africa. However, due to varying social, political, economic and environmental conditions, the application of the principles of IS and on-the-ground implementation of EIPs in developing countries (e.g., Africa) should be approached with a different emphasis than in developed countries (Brent et al., 2008; Alfaro and Miller, 2013). Hence, this review is a deliberate attempt to bring to the fore the issues and contexts in the implementation of IE ecology through the identifiable mechanisms of IS and EIPs.

Africa is the world's second largest continent both in population and in size. It covers an area of 11.7 million square miles. It is made up of 54 countries with distinct regions of economic development and cooperation (that is, north, west, east and south). Connections between those economic regions are hindered by the distances and physical barriers between them (for example the Sahara Desert region, the Great Rift Valley, the Libyan Desert and the Kalahari Desert). The social and economic infrastructure which circumvents such barriers (whether transport or telecommunications related) is not yet developed to a point where distance ceases to be a significant constraint on business activity. According to the World Development Report of 2009 (World Bank, 2009), there is a need to encourage the transformation of the economies of the developing world such that distance ceases to be a significant constraint on business activity.

Agriculture and mining contribute substantially to the economies of many countries in Africa. Agriculture alone employs about 60% of the continent's workforce and generates more than 32% of its gross domestic product growth on average (World Bank, 2008). Apart from agriculture, income comes from exporting minerals such as gold, diamond and copper. A trend away from economic reliance on commodity exports has been noted in some countries, suggesting the potential expansion of other sectors (*The Economist*, 2015). Variation between countries is considerable, though, as indicated by World Bank data on foreign direct investment (FDI). For example: Ethiopia saw a 70% increase in net inflow of FDI from 2010 to 2013; Cameroon has had fluctuating levels, but in 2013 was only 6% higher than 2010; Nigerian FDI has decreased by a similar amount over the same time period (World Bank, 2015). For the time being, however, as a generalisation, the agricultural and mining sectors appear to offer the most scope (and arguably need) for the development of IE in Africa.

The following sections present and analyse the current experiences of IE and IS in Africa, and then explore how drivers for and barriers to EIPs identified elsewhere relate to the African context. Finally, conclusions are offered for the prospects for IE in Africa.

IE AND EIPS IN AFRICA

This section presents an analysis of the operationalisation of the principles of IE through case studies of EIPs by region and country in Africa as well as a summary of IE in higher education. Table 3.1 provides a summary of some of the cases of EIPs in Africa. The specific region, country, activity, initiative and characteristics of the EIPs are also enumerated. It is a synthesis of the activities, initiatives and characteristics of EIPs in Africa.

Eco-industrial Parks in Southern Africa

South Africa
The cases of IE and EIPs in southern Africa mostly emerge from South Africa. Brent et al. (2008) reported some seven cases of IE and EIPs in South Africa (see Table 3.1). The cases/initiatives involved industrial waste exchanges, EIPs and cleaner production. The Waste Management Department of the Cape Metropolitan Council (CMC) launched an Integrated Waste Exchange (IWE) programme in May 2000 as a pilot project. The primary objectives were to reduce the industrial waste streams going to the Cape Metropolitan Area (CMA) landfill sites and to promote

Table 3.1 Summary of cases of industrial ecology and eco-industrial parks in Africa

Region	Country	Activity	Initiative	Characteristics	Literature
Southern Africa	South Africa	Industrial waste exchange	Sedibeng District Municipality	A model for reducing industrial waste currently disposed of to landfill.	Department of Environmental Affairs and Tourism (2006)
			Cape Metropolitan Council	Virtual eco-industrial parks – industries not in close proximity to each other. Most material listings are for relatively low-value material, i.e. paper and plastic. Producing companies see waste exchange as an opportunity to make money instead of paying for disposal.	Department of Environmental Affairs and Tourism (2005)
		Eco-industrial parks	Krugersdorp and Bronkhorstspruit	Proposed eco-industrial parks with focus on greenhouse farming using bio-organic fertilisers.	*Engineering News* (2000)
			Darling eco-industrial park	A wind farm is being planned in the area. An eco-industrial park is planned to provide local employment in industries that will benefit, not destroy, the environment.	African Development Bank (2004)

Table 3.1 (continued)

Region	Country	Activity	Initiative	Characteristics	Literature
Southern Africa			Pelindaba eco-industrial park	Shared services, including recycling. No by-product exchanges occur.	NECSA (2003)
East Africa	Tanzania	Industrial solid waste management (ISWM)	ISWM and resource recovery practices	Practices pertaining to generation, storage, collection and transportation, processing, and final disposal were investigated. Collection of ISW is done by the source industries (60%) and private contractors (40%).	Mbuligwe and Kaseva, 2006
West Africa	Liberia	Material and energy flows	Material and energy flows in smallholder integrated agriculture	Exchange of energy and materials among agro-industrial processes in an effort to increase value and reduce environmental impact.	Alfaro and Miller, 2013
	Benin Republic	Material and energy flows	Material and energy flows in smallholder integrated agriculture	Exchange of energy and materials among agricultural enterprises in an effort to increase value and reduce enviromental impact.	Songhai (n.d.)

34

the optimal use of the known reserves of valuable materials in the area. The programme was built on a previous industrial symbiosis project, initiated in the 1990s as part of a portfolio of cleaner production demonstration projects in the Cape Town region. The aim was to map and exploit financial, market and supply chain linkages between small- and medium-sized enterprises, and thereby optimise environmental and economic performances. The IWE programme influenced potential material exchanges through a web-based catalogue managed by a contracted broker. By 2002, 85 companies and 166 material listings were entered into the IWE website catalogue (Brent et al., 2008).

The cases of IE and EIPs in South Africa highlight the important role of local government authorities in partnership with local companies through social networking and an effective decision-making process. As Brent et al. (2008) identified, regional efficiency, regional learning and the desire to build a sustainable district are key issues for successful IE and EIPs in South Africa.

Eco-industrial Parks in East Africa

Tanzania

Cleaner product practices relating to resource recovery can be practised more extensively in developing than developed countries. This was revealed by Mbuligwe and Kaseva's (2006) assessment of industrial solid waste management and resource recovery practices in Tanzania. They found that resource recovery had a considerable potential for improving industrial solid waste management there, as most of the industrial solid waste components are reusable or recyclable. The Tanzania case also highlights the importance of foreign assistance in catalysing the process of implementing IE and Cleaner Production Technology (CPT) in Africa. For example, CPT was first introduced in Tanzania in the early 1990s under the auspices of the United Nations Industrial Development Organisation (UNIDO) and was followed by the establishment of the Cleaner Production Technology Centre of Tanzania (CPCT). The CPCT is currently supported by UNIDO and the United Nations Environment Programme (UNEP). Since its inception, the CPCT has been recruiting industries to take part in its cleaner production programmes (Mbuligwe and Kaseva, 2006).

Formal intra-industry IS is not practised nationally in Tanzania. However, some industries practise IE by using only waste materials as their raw materials while also reusing or recycling all their own waste materials (Das, 2005). The pulp and paper industries, which use waste paper and cardboard as raw materials, are a notable example; as are the beverage industries, which reuse beverage bottles at a rate of more than 90% and

provide spent grain and yeast for reuse as animal feed. However, Mbuligwe
and Kaseva (2006) noted that in Tanzania, as well as in most developing
countries, the hazardous component of the industrial solid waste is not
segregated from the rest of the waste. Reuse of industrial solid waste would
therefore carry the risk of exposure to hazardous materials.

Eco-industrial Parks in West Africa

Liberia
Alfaro and Miller (2013) analysed the potential benefits of integrated
material and energy flows in smallholder farming in Liberia. The study
links IS to the growing field of integrated farming research (IFR), which
seeks to create new technologies that increase the production of farms by
viewing the farm as a system. The optimisation model used in the analysis
of the baseline scenario and IFR anticipated high performance of the farm
because of the IS projects. The farm production units were the guest house,
piggery, rabbit farm, fish ponds and rice mill. This case study emphasised
the importance of external stimulus in the facilitation of IE as well as
the potential benefits of smallholder agricultural systems from IS. The IS
projects in Liberia were designed by a missionary group with help from the
University of Michigan in the United States.

Benin Republic
The Songhai farm in Benin Republic, West Africa, is a case in point
(Songhai, n.d.). The Songhai farm is an integrated farm that practices the
principle of zero emissions combining crop farming, aquaculture, livestock production, mushroom production, vegetable and exotic produce
production, farm produce processing and biogas generation.

IE and Education for Sustainable Development in Africa

The universities in Africa are playing a significant role as knowledge
institutes with their involvement in the systematic and consistent development capacity for IE as what Ehrenfeld termed 'science of sustainability'
(2004, p. 1). There are now many universities offering sustainability
science-related courses and promoting sustainable development in sub-
Saharan Africa. Such universities offer a variety of degrees in the sustainability sciences (Togo, 2010). Many are also engaged in community
engagement initiatives and campus operational management practices,
including the establishment of institutes and centres that promote sustainable development (e.g., CESDEV, 2014).

   Also, through the support of the UNEP-initiated Mainstreaming

Environment and Sustainability in African Universities (MESA) Partnership programme, some universities in Africa are now mainstreaming sustainability into their curricula and programmes. Examples of such universities and programmes are: Egerton University, Kenya (Masters degree in Environmental Science); Mekelle University, Egypt (inclusion of a chapter on sustainable development in all courses in the Department of Land Resources); Zanzibar University, Tanzania (introducing a module on sustainable development into the Development Studies curriculum); and the University of Ibadan with its establishment of the Centre for Sustainable Development and graduate-level courses on sustainable development practice (CESDEV, 2014). By 2008, the programme had approximately 77 universities participating from more than 40 countries (UNEP, 2008; GUNi-IAU-AAU, 2011). It is hoped that these examples will engender a critical mass of industry practitioners in IE and sustainable development practice as more graduates are churned out from these institutions. Industrial ecologists possess a unique set of skills that can be deployed to better manage natural resources and emerging industries (Alfaro and Miller, 2013).

ANALYSIS OF THE CASE STUDIES AND FUTURE OUTLOOK ON IE AND EIPS IN AFRICA

Agriculture

Significantly, most of the EIPs (proposed or implemented) are taking place in the agricultural sector thereby reducing industrial waste, promoting greenhouse farming using bio-organic fertilisers, and exchanging energy and materials among agro-industrial processes in an effort to increase value and reduce environmental impact. Unlike industrialised nations, African countries rely heavily on smallholder agriculture, and have few large industrial districts (Alfaro and Miller, 2013). Smallholder agriculture, therefore, presents a unique opportunity for agglomeration and cooperation to implement the principles of industrial symbiosis in a non-industrialised context.

The community development project in Konia, Liberia, is a demonstration of the potential for complementary IS and integrated farming (Alfaro and Miller, 2013). The project is typical of smallholder operations in Africa. The importance of income gains and waste reduction derivable from the IS implementation by such projects could make it attractive to smallholder agricultural economies. However, the time lag between establishing projects and seeing improved results can be a significant barrier, depending on the perspective of stakeholders on sustainability – either as a short time-horizon matter (Hansen, 1996) or as a long time-horizon matter (Olayide et al., 2013).

Interventions towards sustainability are most effective during the early stages of system development, including agricultural and extractive land resources (Nikolic and Dijkema, 2010). Therefore, agricultural resources endowments portend great opportunities for Africa to adopt IS principles as agricultural systems are developed. However, African IE initiatives are subject to similar constraints as those elsewhere, where the potential for success and its delivery have not always gone hand in hand (Lowitt, Chapter 4, this volume; Wang et al., Chapter 6, this volume).

External Stimulus

Notwithstanding the evolution of IS networks in Kalundborg, Denmark (Chertow and Ehrenfeld, 2012), the involvement of external stimuli or third-party agents facilitating IS have been shown to be critical to its implementation (e.g., in the United Kingdom, see Paquin and Howard-Grenville, 2012; and in South Korea, see Behera et al., 2012). This applies also to the emerging cases in Africa. The IS project in Liberia was instrumented and designed by a non-governmental organisation (NGO) called the Christian Revival Church Association (CRCA). In some of the African cases however, there was additional support from international bodies. The University of Michigan in the United States helped the CRCA in Konia. In Tanzania, UNIDO played a significant role in what has led to the intra- and inter-industrial reuse and recycling waste materials through the formal CPTs. A similar situation is found in South Africa where the characteristics of foreign EIPs manifest in the planning of South African Industrial Development Zones (Mbuligwe and Kaseva, 2006; Brent et al., 2008; Alfaro and Miller, 2013).

ISSUES FOR SUSTAINABLE DEVELOPMENT OF IE AND EIPS IN AFRICA

Arising from the various cases on the implementation of EIPs in Africa are the drivers and limitations of EIPs. Table 3.2 highlights the issues identified in the literature as factors enhancing the successful implementation of IE. The issues are classified under related sustainability dimensions. That is, social/governance, economic and environmental dimensions. For instance, out of the 16 issues identified in the literature as factors affecting the implementation of IE, more than half (nine) of them are related to social/governance issues. Therefore, if IE is not working properly in Africa,

Table 3.2   Summary of literature on issues around the implementation of industrial ecology and eco-industrial parks

Factors identified for IE and EIP projects	Sustainability dimension	References
1. Cooperation (between firms and between firms and local government) with a view to improving environmental and business performance.	Social/ governance	Kolpron Consultants, 1998; Van der Veeken, 1998; Pellenbarg, 2002; Chiu and Yong, 2004; Heeres et al., 2004; Vermeulen, 2006; Aston, 2008; Behera et al., 2012; Faquin and Howard-Grenville, 2012
2. The initiative involve firms and government.		
3. Active participation from a range of stakeholders and organizations including labour, community and environmental organizations and industry, as well as experts in various fields such as architecture, engineering, economics, ecology and environmental management.		
4. A level of trust should exist between participants which may be promoted by proximity.		
5. A widespread support system should be created, fostering networking and ongoing collaboration.		
6. Good public relations are essential.		
7. Clear understanding of what constitutes an eco-industrial development by all stakeholders.		
8. Ability to measure accurately the development and functioning of the EIPs.		
9. Clear roles for various public bodies during its development and operation.	Economic	Pellenbarg, 2002; Heeres et al., 2004; Chertow, 2007; Tudor et al., 2007; Aston, 2008; Posch, 2010; Boons et al., 2011; Behera et al., 2012
10. The presence of a large firm which acts as a 'magnet' for other enterprises.		
11. The organisations should not be in direct competition with each other.		
12. A diverse range of firms with complementary materials and needs should be involved.		
13. The existing management systems should be utilised as much as possible.		
14. Information gathering on a number of issues (e.g., basic company information, resource streams, employees, future plans, markets) is required.		
15. Access to finance.	Environmental	Van der Veeken, 1998; Kolpron Consultants, 1998
16. Strategies should ensure full integration of environmental, ecological and spatial concepts.		

it would be important to consider the underlying factors, especially social/ governance issues. The economic issues are also germane and compelling. With only 2% of the African countries ranked as high-income groups, according to the World Bank (2013), it might be a Herculean task to muster the high financial outlay to investigate opportunities for IS, for example, or to put collective management procedures in place. The environmental issues are also mutually reinforcing the mirage of barriers (including social and economic issues) to implementing successful EIPs in Africa.

Generally, the analysis shows that much effort would be needed to ensure the effective implementation and sustainability ideals of IE in Africa. In addition, flexible and facilitated planning systems are needed in order to provide a strategic opportunity to create the most effective combinations of industries, technologies, skills, resources and legal frameworks, as well as incentives to encourage integration (Roberts, 2004; Lombardi et al., 2012) for effective implementation of IE with its attendant sustainability dimensions in Africa.

The sustainability dimensions of the equation also indicate the need for promoting sustainable economic opportunities in Africa. African countries generally have low economic rankings as a reflection of the dimension of pervasive economic poverty in the continent. For example, the majority of countries in Africa are in the World Bank's lower and lower-middle income groups (51% and 28% respectively). There has been a complete disappearance of the middle income group, with 19% in the upper-middle and only 2% (i.e., one country, Equatorial Guinea) in the high income group (World Bank, 2013; Ibrahim Index of African Governance, 2014). Although low national income levels tend to be associated with low rates of waste production per capita (Scheinberg et al., 2010), they are also associated with an inadequate level of waste collection and disposal services (Wilson et al., 2012). Lack of financial resources can be compounded by a deficit of institutional capacity comprising, for example, unclear governmental responsibilities, regulations lacking in specific requirements or guidance, and a lack of power or resources to punish offenders (Etriki, 2013). Institutional capacity has been identified as an important factor underlying IE development (Boons and Spekkink, 2012; van Hoof, Chapter 12, this volume), which has also been indicated in the African context (Brent et al., 2008).

Thus, the general economic weakness of the African nations may hamper the process of effective implementation of IE due to the initial high financial outlay – notwithstanding the potentially short payback period identified in other contexts (e.g., South Korea, Behera et al., 2012). Overall, the social, economic and environmental scenarios in Africa vis-à-vis the implementation of IE will require a broader transformation to sustainability in order to achieve the potential resource efficiencies associated with IE. For instance, social and governance issues need to involve the various stakeholders from community level to regional level. Environmental issues will also require awareness creation and support for stakeholders' participation. Economic issues on the other hand will require some financial support and empowerment for bringing about the agglomeration of industries and for ensuring standards of operation for IE in Africa.

CONCLUSION

Africa has a diverse resource base that potentially favours the implementation of IE and IS. However, presently, unsustainable exploration and/or exploitation of these resources poses grave dangers to sustainable economic development. The issues of IE in Africa as presented in this chapter underscore the need for the implementation of sustainable principles and practices. The sustainability dimension and the general situation in Africa vis-à-vis the implementation of IE for sustainable development have been enumerated. The agricultural sector was identified as the potential sector for implementing principles and practices of IE in Africa. It was suggested that the agricultural sector could present a unique opportunity for agglomeration and cooperation to implement the principles of IS in a non-industrialised or agricultural context in Africa.

Given that the time lag between establishing IE projects and seeing the improved results can be significant, planning for the implementation of IE in Africa will require the balancing of short-term survival with long-term sustainability (Hansen, 1996; Olayide et al., 2013). Hansen (1996) explains that, in developing countries, sustainability is considered a short-time horizon matter, with farmers thinking about how to survive now. IS and IE, on the other hand, are focused on a long-time horizon of sustainability (Alfaro and Miller, 2013); although short payback has also been recorded (Behera et al., 2012). Lack of institutional and regulatory supports can serve as limitations to the application and implementation of IE principles in Africa. Del Rio et al. (2010) explain that with a lack of institutional support, innovations can remain stagnant because of cost and due to a lack of implementation, creating a vicious cycle. Even as the lack of appropriate institutional, legal and policy support systems could be barriers to the application of IE in Africa (Brent et al., 2008).

Notably, though, the implementation of IE has been challenging in all contexts. It appears to require a complex institutional, legal and policy support system, which may be more scarce in developing countries than in developed countries (Chertow, 2007; Boons et al., 2011). Given the potential benefits of resource efficiencies to lower-income countries, perhaps the key is to find a style of implementation that works, rather than to dismiss IE as a developed country tool. Although there are limited cases of EIPs in Africa, there are numerous potential institutions for the take-off of IS networks (Brent et al., 2008; Behera et al., 2012). However, the relative lack of IE examples from Africa may also reflect differing research priorities to date among African colleagues and a relative scarcity of international IE researchers compared to other regions of the world. The work of Ashton and Shenoy in India (Chapter 2, this volume) suggests that developing countries may have their own forms of IE ripe for discovery, as also suggested by the experience in Tanzania (Mbuligwe and Kaseva, 2006).

Overall, the need for a systematic and consistent development of human capacity for IE in Africa is gradually emerging. African higher education institutions are now integrating sustainable development and sustainability issues in their institutions. In this regard, Africa needs to muster its abundant resources with the adoption of appropriate technologies in order to progressively accommodate the transition to sustainable development.

REFERENCES

African Development Bank (2004), *The Darling Wind Farm – A Kick Start for Wind Power in South Africa?*, Finesse Africa Newsletter, accessed 20 February 2015 at http://kbb2.com/en/darlipp.htm.

Alfaro, J. and S. Miller (2013), 'Applying industrial symbiosis to smallholder farms: modeling a case study in Liberia, West Africa', *Journal of Industrial Ecology*, **18**, 145–154.

Allenby, B. (2006), 'The ontologies of industrial ecology?', *Progress in Industrial Ecology*, **3** (1/2), 28–38.

Ashton, W. (2008), 'Understanding the organization of industrial ecosystems: a social network approach', *Journal of Industrial Ecology*, **12**, 34–51.

Ashton W. and M. Shenoy (2015), 'Industrial ecology in India: converging traditional practice and modern environmental protection', in P. Deutz, D. Lyons and J. Bi (eds), *International Perspectives on Industrial Ecology*, Cheltenham, UK and Northampton, MA, USA: Edward Elgar, pp. 12–29.

Behera, S.K., J.H. Kim, S.Y. Lee, S. Suh and H.S. Park (2012), 'Evolution of "designed" industrial symbiosis networks in the Ulsan Eco-industrial Park: "research and development into business" as the enabling framework', *Journal of Cleaner Production*, **29–30**, 103–112.

Boons, F. and W. Spekkink (2012), 'Levels of institutional capacity and actor expectations about industrial symbiosis', *Journal of Industrial Ecology*, **16** (1), 61–69.

Boons, F., W. Spekkink and Y. Mouzakitis (2011), 'The dynamics of industrial symbiosis: a proposal for a conceptual framework based upon a comprehensive literature review', *Journal of Cleaner Production*, **19**, 905–911.

Brent, A.C., S. Oelofse and L. Godfrey (2008), 'Advancing the concepts of industrial ecology in South African institutions', *South African Journal of Science*, **104**, 9–12.

CESDEV (2014), Centre for Sustainable Development, accessed 22 December 2014 at http://cesdev.ui.edu.ng/.

Chertow, M.R. (2007), '"Uncovering" industrial symbiosis', *Journal of Industrial Ecology*, **11** (1), 11–30.

Chertow, M.R. and J.R. Ehrenfeld (2012), 'Organizing self-organizing systems: toward a theory of industrial symbiosis', *Journal of Industrial Ecology*, **16**, 13–27.

Chiu, A.S.F. and G. Yong (2004), 'On the industrial ecology potential in Asian developing countries', *Journal of Cleaner Production*, **12**, 1037–1045.

Côte, R.P. and E. Cohen-Rosenthal (1998), 'Designing eco-industrial parks: a synthesis of some experiences', *Journal of Cleaner Production*, **6**, 181–188.

Das, T.K. (2005), *Towards Zero Discharge: Innovative Methodology and Technologies for Process Pollution Prevention*, New Jersey: John Wiley & Sons.

Del Rio, P., J. Carrillo-Hermosilla and T. Konnola (2010), 'Policy strategies to promote eco-innovation', *Journal of Industrial Ecology*, **14** (4), 541–557.

Department of Environmental Affairs and Tourism (2005), *National Waste Management Strategy Implementation – Recycling – Review of Industrial Waste Exchange*, accessed 20 February 2015 at http://sawic.environment.gov.za/documents/235.pdf.

Department of Environmental Affairs and Tourism (2006), *National Waste Management Strategy: Industrial Waste Exchange Baseline Study Report*, Sedibeng District Municipality, accessed 20 February 2015 at http://www.docstoc.com/docs/18652606/Department-of-Environmental-Affairs.

Deschenes P.J. and M. Chertow (2004), 'An island approach to industrial ecology: towards sustainability in the island context', *Journal of Environmental Planning and Management*, **47** (2), 201–217.

Desrochers, P. (2001), 'Cities and industrial symbiosis: some historical perspectives and policy implications', *Journal of Industrial Ecology*, **5** (4), 29–34.

Deutz, P. (2014), 'Food for thought: seeking the essence of industrial symbiosis', in R. Salomone and G. Saija (eds), *Pathways to Environmental Sustainability: Methodologies and Experiences*, Switzerland: Springer International Publishing, pp. 3–11.

Ehrenfeld, J.R. (2004), 'Editorial: Can industrial ecology be the "science of sustainability"?', *Journal of Industrial Ecology*, **8** (1–2), 1–3.

Ellen MacArthur Foundation (2013), *Towards the Circular Economy: Opportunities for the Consumer Goods Sector*, Ellen MacArthur Foundation, accessed 20 February 2015 at http://www.ellenmacarthurfoundation.org/business/reports/ce2013.

Engineering News (2000), 'New era in solid-waste disposal', accessed May 2015 at http://www.engineeringnews.co.za/article/new-era-in-solidwaste-disposal-2000-03-10.

Etriki, J. (2013), 'Municipal solid waste management and institutions in Tripoli, Libya: applying the Environmentally Sound Technologies (ESTs) concept', PhD Thesis, Department of Geography, Environment and Earth Sciences, University of Hull, accessed 19 December 2014 at https://hydra.hull.ac.uk/assets/hull:8239a/content.

Graedel, T.E. (1996), 'On the concept of industrial ecology', *Annual Review of Energy and the Environment*, **21** (1), 69–98.

GUNi-IAU-AAU (2011), *Promotion of Sustainable Development by Higher*

Education Institutions in Sub-Saharan Africa, Association of African Universities (AAU) Global University Network for Innovation (GUNi) and the International Association of Universities (IAU). Project funded in part by the Spanish Agency for International Development and Cooperation (AECID).

Hansen, J.W. (1996), 'Is agricultural sustainability a useful concept?', *Agricultural Systems*, **50** (2), 117–143.

Heeres, R.R., W.J.V. Vermeulen and F.B. de Walle (2004), 'Eco-industrial park initiatives in the USA and the Netherlands: first lessons', *Journal of Cleaner Production*, **12**, 985–995.

Ibrahim Index of African Governance (2014), accessed 20 November 2014 at http://www.moibrahimfoundation.org/interact/.

Kolpron Consultants (1998), *Werken aan Vernieuwing: duurzame Bedrijventerreinen*, Project number 98142/juli, Rotterdam: Kolpron.

Kronenberg, J. (2006), 'Industrial ecology and ecological economics', *Progress in Industrial Ecology*, **3** (1/2), 95–113.

Lombardi, D.R., D. Lyons, H. Shi and A. Agarwal (2012), 'Editorial: Industrial symbiosis: testing the boundaries and advancing knowledge', *Journal of Industrial Ecology*, **16** (1), 2–7.

Lowitt, P. (2015), 'Eco-industrial development in the United States: analyzing progress from 2010–2015', in P. Deutz, D. Lyons and J. Bi (eds), *International Perspectives on Industrial Ecology*, Cheltenham, UK and Northampton, MA, USA: Edward Elgar, pp. 46–68.

Mbuligwe, S.E. and M.E. Kaseva (2006), 'Assessment of industrial solid waste management and resource recovery practices in Tanzania', *Resources, Conservation and Recycling*, **47**, 260–276.

NECSA (2003), 'NESCA eco-industrial park – approach map', accessed 20 November 2014 at http://www.primeproductmanufacturing.com/downloads/Download%20NECSA%20Approach%20Map.pdf.

Nikolic, I. and G.P.J. Dijkema (2010), 'On the development of agent-based models for infrastructure evolution', *International Journal of Critical Infrastructure*, **6** (2), 148–167.

Olayide, O.E. and A.E. Ikpi (2013), *Agricultural Production and Rural Welfare in Nigeria: Assessing Agricultural Production and Rural Welfare*, Saarbrücken, Germany: Scholars' Press, AV Akademikerverlag GmbH & Co. KG.

Olayide, O.E., L. Popoola, O. Olaniyan, F. Dapilah and R.Y.A. Issahaku (2013), 'Assessing the transition from survival to sustainability: case of Wechiau Community Hippo Sanctuary in Upper West Region of Ghana, West Africa', *Journal of Sustainable Development*, **6** (10), 47–56.

Paquin, R.L. and J. Howard-Grenville (2012), 'The evolution of facilitated industrial symbiosis', *Journal of Industrial Ecology*, **16** (1), 83–93.

Pellenbarg, P.H. (2002), 'Sustainable business sites in the Netherlands: a survey of policies and experiences', *Journal of Environmental Planning and Management*, **45** (1), 59–84.

Phillips, P.S., R. Barnes, M.P. Bates and T. Coskeran (2006), 'A critical appraisal of an UK county waste minimisation programme: the requirements for regional facilitated development of industrial symbiosis/ecology', *Resources, Conservation and Recycling*, **46** (3), 242–264.

Posch, A. (2010), 'Industrial recycling networks as starting points for broader sustainability-oriented cooperation?', *Journal of Industrial Ecology*, **14** (2), 242–257.

Roberts, B.H. (2004), 'The application of industrial ecology principles and planning guidelines for the development of eco-industrial parks: an Australian case study', *Journal of Cleaner Production*, **12**, 997–1010.

Scheinberg, A., D. Wilson and L. Rodic (2010), *Solid Waste Management in the World's Cities*, 3rd edition, UN-Habitat's State of Water and Sanitation in the World's Cities Series, London and Washington, DC: Earthscan for UN-Habitat.

Songhai (n.d.) (online), accessed 8 March 2015 at https://www.songhai.org/index.php?lang=en.

The Economist (2015), 'Why Africa is becoming less dependent on commodities', accessed 18 March 2015 at http://www.economist.com/blogs/economist-explains/2015/01/economist-explains-5.

Togo, M. (2010), *Environmental Science and Water Masters Degrees. Dialogue*, Rhodes University, pp. 48–49.

Tudor, T., E. Adam and M. Bates (2007), 'Drivers and limitations for the successful development and functioning of EIPs (eco-industrial parks): a literature review', *Ecological Economics*, **61**, 199–207.

UNEP (2008), *Mainstreaming Environment and Sustainability in African Universities Partnership: Supporting Universities to Respond to Environment, Sustainable Development and Climate Change Challenges, 2004–2008*, Report, Nairobi: UNEP.

Van der Veeken, T. (1998), 'Overheid wil ontwikkeling duurzame bedrijventerreinen gaan stimuleren', *ROM Magazine*, **11**, 5–7.

Van Hoof, B. (2015), 'Institutional capacity for sustainable industrial systems in Caldas, Colombia', in P. Deutz, D. Lyons and J. Bi (eds), *International Perspectives on Industrial Ecology*, Cheltenham, UK and Northampton, MA, USA: Edward Elgar, pp. 191–208.

Vermeulen, W.J.V. (2006), 'The social dimension of industrial ecology: on the implications of the inherent nature of social phenomena', *Progress in Industrial Ecology*, **3**, (6), 574–598.

Wang, Q., P. Deutz and D. Gibbs (2015), 'UK-China collaboration for industrial symbiosis: a multi-level approach to policy transfer analysis', in P. Deutz, D. Lyons and J. Bi (eds), *International Perspectives on Industrial Ecology*, Cheltenham, UK and Northampton, MA, USA: Edward Elgar, pp. 89–107.

Wilson, D.C., L. Rodic, A. Scheinberg, C.A. Velis and G. Alabaster (2012), 'Comparative analysis of solid waste management in 20 cities', *Waste Management and Research*, **30** (3), 237–254.

World Bank (2008), World Development Report (WDR) 2008, *Agriculture for Development*, Washington, DC: The World Bank.

World Bank (2009), World Development Report, *Reshaping Economic Geography*, Washington, DC: The World Bank.

World Bank (2013), *The 2012/2013 Little Data Book on Africa*, Washington, DC: The World Bank.

World Bank (2015), 'Data (net inflows of foreign direct investment)', accessed 11 March 2015 at http://data.worldbank.org/indicator/BX.KLT.DINV.CD.WD/countries?display=default.

4. Eco-industrial development in the United States: analysing progress from 2010–2015

Peter Lowitt

INTRODUCTION

Eco-industrial development (EID) involves co-operation between firms with a goal of improving their combined environmental and economic performance. There are many different types of EID activities (e.g., energy and material efficiencies, exchange of unwanted materials/energy, co-operating over transport, utility sharing and developing markets for new materials) (Cohen-Rosenthal, 2003). A wave of optimism for EID in the US in the late 1990s produced some 30 projects (Chertow, 2007; Gibbs and Deutz, 2007). Whilst there were a similar number of active eco-industrial projects in 2010 as there were then, almost all of the original projects had disappeared.

Notwithstanding the widely observed challenges faced by the first wave of EIDs in the US (Chertow, 2007; Gibbs and Deutz, 2007), in the last few years there has been an upsurge in interest. Over 33 new, self-identified, EIDs were announced by 2010. This chapter reviews the new wave of EIDs in the US from the vantage point of 2015. It aims to provide a characterisation of present activity, analyse its drivers and assess the future prospects for EID in the US. The following sections briefly outline the major characteristics of the first wave of developments (1995 to 2002), and then present an analysis of the new wave. Subsequent sections consider the drivers, funding and policy support for the new parks, before offering some thoughts for the future.

ECO-INDUSTRIAL DEVELOPMENTS IN THE US

First Wave Developments

A significant landmark in EID in the US was the roundtable meeting at Cape Charles Virginia in 1996. The resulting definition of an eco-industrial park has become a standard definition: '. . . community of businesses that cooperate with each other and with the local community to efficiently share resources (information, materials, water, energy, infrastructure and natural habitat) . . . leading to economic gains, gains in environmental quality and equitable enhancement of human resources for the business and local community' (Cohen-Rosenthal, 2003: 19). Major drivers for the roundtable were the recognition of EID given by the President's Council for Sustainable Development (PCSD) alongside the enthusiastic support of Ed Cohen-Rosenthal from the Cornell Work and Environmental Initiative (CWEI; Cohen-Rosenthal, 2000). Representatives of 12 EIPs attended the meeting, including the four PCSD demonstration projects (Cape Charles, VA; Chattanooga, TN; Fairfield (Baltimore), MD; and Brownsville, TX). Several additional developments joined the network co-ordinated from Cornell by 2000.

These first wave projects were predominantly driven by economic development considerations (Gibbs and Deutz, 2007). Several were developed by local economic development bodies (e.g., Londonderry, NH; Front Royal, VA; Cape Charles, VA); others were a combination of state and local economic development projects such as Mesa del Sol and the Red River Ecoplex; others were non-profit initiatives (e.g., the Green Institute, Minneapolis, MN). Some had additional incentives such as the reuse of military facilities at Devens, MA, or the remediation of contaminated industrial facilities (e.g., Front Royal). PCSD projects benefited from access to federal grant funding and technical assistance from networking with colleagues under the auspices of the CWEI, itself funded by the PCSD. The US Business Council for Sustainable Development launched their by-product exchange programme for the Kansas City metro area in this time frame as well. These initial US projects have, with notable exceptions such as Devens (Veleva et al., 2015), fallen by the wayside of history and their fates recorded by Gibbs and Deutz (2007) and Chertow (2007). Only four of these first wave projects were still operational in 2010 (Table 4.1), but the Green Institute closed in 2011, leaving two park-based and one regional EID (Table 4.1).

Notwithstanding the disappointing outcome of most of the first wave of EID projects, a new series of eco-industrial projects have emerged. This chapter seeks to analyse these new projects and their economic sustainability based on progress between 2010 and 2015, thereby providing a current register of eco-industrial projects in the US.

Table 4.1 First wave eco-industrial parks and eco-industrial projects operating in the year 2000 and still active in 2010

Project	Type	Status 2015	Brown-field	Theme	Leadership	
Devens, MA	EIP	Operational	x	Sustainability	Economic development	Sustainable Devens (n.d.) accessed 14 March 2015 at http://www.devensec.com/sustain.html
Green Institute, MN	EIP	Closed in 2011 for financial reasons, though some components may survive	x	Recycling, re-use; community project	Economic development	*Star Tribune* Business 5 August 2011 accessed 14 March 2015 at http://www.startribune.com/business/126863523.html
Cabazon Resource Recovery Park, Mecca, CA	EIP	Operational		CHP	Economic development	Cabazon Resource Recovery Park (n.d.) accessed 14 March 2015 at http://wei-mecca.com/cabazon.php
Kansas City, MO	Regional	Operational		BPS	B2B USBCSD	Green Business Network KC (2015) accessed 14 March 2015 at https://www.bridgingthegap.org/green-business-network-events/

METHODS

This longitudinal review of self-identified eco-industrial projects in the US (including Puerto Rico) was conducted initially by reviewing all Google Search references to EID and industrial symbiosis for the year 2010. The identification of projects with 'eco-industrial development' and/or related terms (eco-industrial network and districts, by-product synergy, industrial symbiosis) is significant because it indicates a level of awareness of environmental principles in the design and operation of industrial parks, networks and systems. Internet searches were supplemented by an interview with Andy Mangan, of the US Business Council for Sustainable Development, by personal conversations with Professor Marian Chertow of Yale, and by involvement with the eco-industrial community, e.g., via networking events held at Devens, where the author plays a leading role in EID network co-ordination. The second phase of the study comprised an internet search in March 2015 to update the status of the second wave and surviving first wave projects from 2010.

Given the challenging experience of the first wave projects, this study provides critical perspective on whether the second wave sites have been more embedded as an economic-environmental institution than the first wave. A limitation of this research method is the difficulty of knowing whether actions outlined on the internet have come to fruition in practice. The longitudinal aspect of the study, in conjunction with the author's personal experience, is important for triangulation. Projects for which there is no internet presence more recent than the announcement of the intention to engage with EID are listed as 'currently inactive', which in many cases may be euphemistic. For only three projects (one first wave and two second wave) were local government or press announcements found confirming a change in direction or outright closure.

One current strand of EID in the US continues to pursue the approach of the first wave developments, focusing on incorporating eco-industrial networking into the development of industrial parks and land development projects, including eco-industrial parks (EIPs). The second strand of EID continues to be the US Business Council for Sustainable Development (USBCSD) and their by-product synergy programmes, which attempt to develop physical exchanges of waste and by-products between existing firms (also known as industrial symbiosis) in their present locations (Cimren et al., 2011). A third strand comprises by-product exchanges that have been negotiated independently by the companies involved. Uncovering this type of activity can be a fruitful starting point for building a larger symbiosis network (Chertow, 2007). However, these activities rarely identify themselves as industrial symbiosis specifically or EIDs and are therefore excluded from this study.

NEW WAVE PROJECTS

Thirty new EID projects were identified in the US in 2010 (Table 4.2). Twenty of these were projects attempting to develop EIPs along the lines proposed by many of the first wave EID projects. This implies collaborative environmental management features to be (or actually) established within the confines of an industrial park. Of these, six were already operational in 2010, and, promisingly, all six remain operational in 2015 (Keystone Industrial Port Complex, PA; Piedmont Biofuels, NC; Silver Bay Eco-Industrial Business Park, MN; Eco Sustainable Systems, Charleston, SC; Camden EIP, NC; and ReVenture Park, NC) (Table 4.2). In addition, two municipalities Boston (Newmarket District) and King County, WA, zoned districts to promote collaborations (such as by-product exchange) between firms.

However, of the 14 EIPs planned in 2010 only one (New Belgium, Golden, CO) is operational and one other (Itasaca) appears to have reached the point of recruiting tenants. Ten of them have no current web presence, and in several cases no remaining indication of the former intentions. Two others had some activity in 2011, but nothing since. The abandonment of the Gaylord development (on the site of a former particleboard mill) was announced in the press in 2013 (Woodworking Network, 2013). This rather poor rate of transitioning of projects from the drawing board to reality is in line with the experience of the first wave parks, several of which never got beyond the 'drawing board' stages (Chertow, 2007).

Seven of the new wave projects were regional non-park EIDs resulting from USBCSD's projects (Table 4.2). The USBCSD approach to facilitating industrial symbiosis between firms in their existing location influenced the approach taken by the UK National Industrial Symbiosis Programme (NISP; Wang, 2013). Unlike NISP, however, the USBCSD has not enjoyed public funding. Relying on the willingness of participants to pay, USBCSD has not approached the same level of success as NISP, which by 2012 had over 12 000 companies in its database (Wang, 2013). Nonetheless, USBCSD has programmes in various stages of deployment throughout the US in addition to those identified in 2010 and in Kansas City, Missouri, from the first wave. Andy Mangan, of the USBCSD, also has a number of new tools in development to further facilitate exchanges, including a GIS mapping tool showing linkages established in a geographic area:

Table 4.2 New wave eco-industrial developments in the US active in 2010

Project	Type	Status 2010	Theme	Leadership	Status 2015	Web address (date of last access 15 March 2015)
Keystone Industrial Port Complex, Bucks Co., PA	EIP, H, B	Operational	Port, Renewable Energy, Biomass	Private sector	Operational	http://www.naikipc.com/
Piedmont Biofuels Pittsboro, NC	EIP	Operational	Agriculture Renewable Energy, Biomass	Private sector	Operational	http://www.biofuels.coop/
Camden EIP, Camden, NC	EIP	Operational	Encourages renewable energy projects and other R&D	EDA	Operational	http://www.camdencountync. gov/departments/economic- development/ development-sites/ camden-eco-industrial-park
ReVenture, Charlotte, NC	EIP, H, B	Operational	Waste to Energy, Renewable Energy, Biomass	Private sector	Operational	http://www.reventurepark.com/
Silver Bay Eco-Industrial Business Park, MN	EIP, H	Operational	Renewable energy produced on site for tenant use, water capture, local food production	EDA	Operational	www.pca.state.mn.us/ index.php/view-document. html?gid=18195

Table 4.2 (continued)

Project	Type	Status 2010	Theme	Leadership	Status 2015	Web address (date of last access 15 March 2015)
Eco Sustainable Systems, Charleston, SC	EIP	Operational	Incubator for environmental technology industries	Private sector	Operational	http://ecosustainable systems.com/ technology_development
New Belgium, Golden, CO	EIP H	Planned	Agriculture	Private sector	Operational	http://www.newbelgium.com/ events.aspx
Itasca, MN	EIP H, B	Planned	Timber related products and biofuels using former paper mill site	EDA	Recruiting	http://www.itascadv.org/ IEDC%202013%20 Annual%20Report.html
Canastota, NY	EIP H	Planned	Renewable Energy, Agriculture	Private sector	In progress	http://www.syracuse.com/news/ index.ssf/2011/03/plan_to_ turn_canastota_farmlan.html
Fairfield Renewable Energy and Resource Recovery Plant Fairfield, MD, 2nd iteration	EIP H	Planned	Waste to Energy, CHP, Port, Materials Recovery	EDA	Construction delayed	http://www.energyanswers.com/ development/current_ projects/fairfield_renewable_ energy_project http://www.wbaltv.com/news/ state-halts-construction-on- fairfield-renewable-energy- plant/26681382

52

Name	Type	Status	Description	Sector	Notes	Source
Eco-industrial Business Park Anderson, IN	EIP H	Planned	Detailed plan for environmentally-friendly site aiming at inter-firm co-operation	EDA	Recruiting	http://www.mccog.net/Eco%20Industrial%20Park%20Template.pdf
Port Townsend, WA	EIP H	Planned	Eco-friendly products/ services, mode of operation and site design	EDA	Feasibility study completed by 2011	http://portofpt.com/wp-content/uploads/JCIA-Feasibility-Aug2011-electronic21.pdf
Puerto Rico Wanan, PR	EIP H	Planned	Waste to Energy, Biomass	Private sector	Still listed as planned concept, but no location	http://wananinternational.com/wanan-pr
Gaylord, MI	EIP H, B	Planned	Biomass-based EIP on site of former particleboard mill	EDA	Plans abandoned in 2013	http://grandrapidseda.com/property-for-sale-grand-rapids-mn/industrial-property-for-sale/2-eo-road-63-itasca-eco-industrial-park.html
South Portland, ME	EIP H	Planned	Renewable Energy, CHP	EDA	Currently inactive	
Infinitus, Destiny, FL 5	EIP H	Planned	Renewable Energy, Biomass, Solar, Aquaculture	Private sector	Re-located to Montgomery, AL	http://www.bizjournals.com/tampabay/stories/2010/02/22/story1.html?page=all http://infinitus-energy.com/

Table 4.2 (continued)

Project	Type	Status 2010	Theme	Leadership	Status 2015	Web address (date of last access 15 March 2015)
Tiverton, RI	EIP H	Planned	Renewable Energy Generation	EDA	Currently inactive	http://sustainablesakonnet.blogspot.co.uk/2010/02/eco-industrial-park-presents-its-case.html
South Bronx	EIP H, B	Planned		Non-profit	Currently inactive	http://community-wealth.org/content/oak-point-eco-industrial-park-sustainable-economic-development-proposal-south-bronx
Reno, NV	EIP H, B	Planned	Waste to Energy		Currently inactive	
Forsyth Co GA	EIP H	Planned	Renewable Energy	EDA	Currently inactive	
Greater Chicago Waste to Profit Network, Chicago, IL	Regional	Operational	BPS	Private sector UCBCSD	Operational	http://wtpnetwork.org/
Great Houston By-product Synergy Network, TX	Regional	Operational	BPS	Private sector UCBCSD	Operational	http://houstonbps.org/about/

Name	Scale	Status	Type	Funding/Partners	Current status	URL
Ohio By-product Synergy Network	Regional	Operational	BPS	EDA and private sector USBCSD	Operational	http://www.sustainable-ohio.org/
By-product Synergies Northwest Puget Sound, WA	Regional	Operational	Materials exchange; part of more general eco-efficiency project for business	Private and public partners USBCSD	Operational, assuming current evidence refers to the same project	http://www.materialsinnovationexchange.com/ http://www.pprc.org/synergy/brochure.pdf
Detroit/Lansing	Regional			Private and public sector USBCSD	Operational	http://usbcsd.org/category/by-product-synergy/
Mobile, AL	Regional	Active	BPS	Private sector USBCSD	Operational	http://usbcsd.org/documents/USBCSD%202011%20EPA%20Proposed%20DSW%20Comments%20Final%20%281%29.pdf
King County Eco-Industrial District, WA 9	District	Planned		EDA	Dropped environmental credentials in 2012 (King County Industrial District)	http://www.psrc.org/about/boards/edd

Table 4.2 (continued)

Project	Type	Status 2010	Theme	Leadership	Status 2015	Web address (date of last access 15 March 2015)
Portland, OR	Regional	Planned		Private sector and EDA Initiative	Operational	
Newmarket Eco-Industrial Zone, Boston, MA 10	District	Planned	Environmental efficiency savings	EDA	Operational	http://newmarket.wikidot.com/
New Bedford, MA	Regional	Planned	BPS	EDA	City is promoting green economy (e.g., renewables jobs), not BPS	Chelsea Center (2002) http://www.chelseacenter.org/pdfs/RBED_NewBedford.pdf

Notes:
Abbreviations: H: holistic (see text for explanation); B: brownfield development; CHP: includes combined heat and power plant; BPS: by-product synergies; EIP: eco-industrial park; EDA: economic development agency.
District or Regional refers to the scale on which projects seek collaboration between firms in their existing locations.
Renewable energy may indicate either the onsite generation of renewable energy or the manufacturing of renewable energy technologies.

In 2010, the US BCSD by-product synergy process brought financial gains, along with social and environmental benefits to participating companies and organizations in the Ohio By-Product Synergy Network and the Greater Houston By-Product Synergy Project. Leveraging our collaborative methodology, life cycle assessment tools, and our new Cirrus national database, we've set a strong foundation to take the success of these projects to a national level. (Mangan, 2010: 7)

Significantly, now that NISP is charging membership fees (NISP, 2014), there may be further lessons to be learnt from the US model.

DRIVERS FOR THE NEW WAVE EIDS

Examining the new EID projects, a number of features emerge which are considered in turn in this section: economic development and employment creation; concern for the environment; academic interest, energy; clean-up of contaminated land; policy; and funding.

Economic Development, Green Jobs and Green Marketing

Almost by definition, EIDs have economic and environmental benefits (Dunn and Steinman, 1998). An optimism in that twin benefit was a feature of the first wave of EIDs (Deutz and Gibbs, 2008), and remains prominent now. Local economic development initiatives continue to play an important role in the creation of this round of EID projects, with 20 projects identifying themselves in this category. Several of the new park-/district-based projects stress the economic motivation: the key purpose of the development being to attract investment in industries which are seen as providing desirable jobs. In some cases this is, or was, to help revitalise a declining industrial base (e.g., King County, WA); in others it is to regenerate disused brownfield sites (Ithasca, MN; South Bronx, NY). The ReVenture site in Charlotte, North Carolina, had expectations of attracting 1100 so-called green collar jobs (ReVenture, 2011).

From the planning perspective, a number of concepts have converged in projects embracing the ideal of an EIP. These concepts include the romance of all things green epitomised by the smart growth movement; the various US Green Building Council (USGBC) Leadership in Energy and Environmental Design (LEED) programmes; the Congress of New Urbanism (CNU); and an increased emphasis on urban sustainability. Most of these movements recognise the importance of jobs, yet focus on green building design issues and creating energy efficient housing. In many cases the jobs envisioned in these plans are hard to find, e.g., confined to coffeehouses tucked into the new housing neighbourhoods. EIPs have an appeal to those promoting the green jobs agenda as they provide an answer to the question of 'Where are the jobs?' Making economic development and environmental protection compatible in the form of an EIP has an appeal on its own and has motivated many people to become involved in this field. Action towards solving the compatibility of the economy and environment provides hope for the future and a pathway for others to follow.

Many communities and development interests in the second wave see EID as creating a market niche for the type of development product they want to deliver (e.g., Silver Bay, MN; Canastota, NY). Local economic developers understand that they are competing in a worldwide marketplace. In order to stand out in this marketplace they need to develop a brand. Being a 'green' community is one approach to developing brand identity and local development agencies see EIPs as accomplishing this for the larger community. Likewise, amongst the first wave parks, Devens, Massachusetts saw itself competing with the Research Park Triangle in North Carolina, industrial parks in upstate New York and various international sites when it successfully sought to attract Bristol-Myers Squibb (BMS) to locate their bio-pharmaceutical manufacturing plant to Devens. Devens' sustainability message gave it a distinctive image, whilst, significantly, requiring some commitment but little initial action or investment from companies (Deutz and Gibbs, 2008). However, the experience of the first wave sites strongly suggests that whilst green marketing can work, its success is heavily contingent on favourable circumstances (Deutz and Gibbs, 2004).

Environmental Concerns

Concern for the environment, be it biodiversity, resource conservation, or climate change, has been, from the personal experience of the author, a strong motivation for individuals participating in first and second wave EIDs. The author, along with Ray Côté, has called for EIPs to compensate for and enhance the ecosystem services compromised by a park's development (Lowitt and Côté, 2013). EIDs are interested not only in attracting environmental industries, but also in behaving in an environmentally responsible fashion. ReVenture, for example, proposes to preserve Catawba riverfront acreage as part of its redevelopment effort. Seventeen of the 20 second wave parks are deemed 'holistic' (Table 4.2) in that their published plans include a vision of park level environmental operation and potentially eco-industrial engagement between firms, as opposed to co-located but otherwise separate activities. Notably, all 14 projects planned in 2010 had ambitions of a holistic development, but only three of the six operational projects are in this category.

The return of manufacturing to the US alongside the growing importance of corporate social responsibility (CSR) concerns and sustainability initiatives (McKitterick, 2012), may improve the effectiveness of environmental image as a recruitment tool for EIPs.

Academic Support for Industrial Ecology

On the academic side of the equation, the field of industrial ecology has grown over the past decade, which has helped to provide a knowledgeable and enthusiastic workforce to join in the promotion of EID. The International Society of Industrial Ecology's growth worldwide and the number of academic programmes and journals featuring work around EID, industrial symbiosis and by-product exchanges have grown significantly since the first wave of EID. Active programmes at Yale and other academic institutions have produced industrial ecologists prepared to further the goal of creating industrial symbiosis for their employers and clients. These new academics and their students have employed their knowledge for business and industry to bring the opportunity for creating by-product exchanges and EID projects to their new employers. For example, a recent Yale graduate working as a sustainability co-ordinator for Stonyfield Farms, Inc. invited neighbouring businesses to a meeting to discuss by-product exchange possibilities (Fischer, 2012).

Renewable Energy and Energy from Waste

Renewable energy parks including biofuels, solar photovoltaic and wind farm projects have all wrapped themselves in the mantle of EID. Deploying green energy generation in an EIP makes sense from a number of perspectives, including enhancing the green image of the park and providing a renewable or green power source for the firms locating there. Several first wave parks (e.g., Cape Charles and the Green Institute) had green architecture features such as renewable energy generation (Gibbs and Deutz, 2007). The second wave sites, however, are more likely than the first to have, or to be seeking, manufacturers of renewable energy technology. For example, ReVenture Park in Charlotte, NC, hopes to become a leading renewable energy development and manufacturing park, with a bio-waste to energy plant as a key tenant (ReVenture, 2013) reflecting state subsidies for renewable energy technologies.

The infrastructure synergies possible through energy generation have become another driver for EIP development in the US, possibly reflective of advice from the American Planning Association (APA) and a growing knowledge of EID as a means of increasing the efficiency of limited resources. Trends among current parks indicate that biofuels and waste to energy plants are often being proposed as anchors for new EIPs, with four self-identified waste to energy plants, sometimes including Combined Heat and Power (CHP), and six biomass plants (Table 4.2). A broad interpretation of biofuels and waste to energy plants as green energy is part of this appeal. Although the identification of waste to energy is an EID, there are a number of industrial ecology studies on the industrial symbiosis potential of biofuel production (e.g., Martin, 2010).

Restoration of Contaminated Land

The reuse of formerly contaminated industrial lands and bringing that land back to productive use holds an attraction in and of itself. Much of this land is often found in urban areas where there is a scarcity of industrially zoned land. Planners often seek to reuse this land as the infrastructure to support its redevelopment already exists, helping to reduce the need for more infrastructure and discouraging greenfield development. Many EIPs in the initial wave of development in the late 1990s were planned for brownfield locations (e.g., Devens, Front Royal). Brownfield redevelopment remains a driver in this second wave of EIP development, with six of the 30 projects identified as brownfield redevelopments (Table 4.2), but for additional reasons. The Sarbanes-Oxley Act of 2002[1] created an incentive for firms to move highly contaminated brownfield properties off their books or otherwise be responsible for the cost of clean-up. In an effort to mitigate future corporate risk these properties are being sold at a minimal cost to developers with the proviso that they take the responsibility for cleaning up the contaminated site. The effect of this on EIP development is difficult to predict. First wave sites such as Devens and Front Royal benefited from the financial responsibilities on the former owners (the federal government being involved in both cases). Cheap purchase of a contaminated site, but no financial assistance in its clean-up, may prove a decidedly mixed blessing.

Policy

Policy drivers are very influential, albeit often overlooked, factors in setting conditions supportive of EID (e.g., Chapter 6, this volume; Chapter 8, this volume). This section reviews the range of initiatives in the US that lend support to EID.

The US does not have a national economic development policy that embraces EID concepts. Conversely, government policies in Canada, Europe and Asia have supported the development of EID concepts and the European Union (EU) and the United Nations have provided material support for such efforts. In Canada, the Green Municipal Fund of the Canadian Federation of Municipalities has funded a number of EIP planning activities.[2]

In the US, during the Bush (Jnr) presidency, states and local communities developed their own policies and pathways towards a more sustainable economy. Many of these entities joined the International Council for Local Environmental Initiatives (ICLEI; now known as ICLEI – Local Governments for Sustainability) and other organisations with similar goals. International efforts continued to influence US policy. With the election of the Obama Administration, hopes rose that the US would become an active player on the world stage and that a national policy would be put in place to further sustainable development in the US. The US hosted the release of a UN Habitat report (UN Habitat, 2009: v) which called for 'the improvement of eco-efficiency in order to enable the use of waste products to satisfy urban energy and material needs'. However, congressional gridlock has failed to produce any substantive national programmes to support EID and local and state initiatives have had to substitute for lack of a coherent national policy.

The development of the national economic development policy known as the Circular Economy by China, Sweden, the UK and other countries – which calls for the more efficient use of existing resources through reuse, recycling and eco-efficiency – did not escape notice in the US (Koenig and Lowitt, 2009). The Circular Economy, according to Koenig (2005), 'is a holistic economic concept which seeks efficiency in resource use through the integration of cleaner production and industrial ecology into a broader system encompassing industrial firms, networks or chains of firms, eco-industrial parks, and regional infrastructure to support resource optimisation'. This publication was later reprinted and updated for US officials by the APA's Economic Development and Energy, Natural Resources and Renewable Energy Divisions along with a series of case studies of EIPs in the US prepared by Koenig and Lowitt, 2009. However, whilst the idea of an EIP has taken hold in the US, the underlying policy drivers, e.g., diversion of waste from landfill, which are prevalent in the EU (Costa et al., 2010), are missing on a national basis (though individual states such as Massachusetts have these policies). In the UK, for example, the increasing tax on waste sent to landfill provides a strong financial incentive to engage in industrial symbiosis (IS) (Chapter 6, this volume).

At the local scale, most communities in the US do not currently have a policy addressing EID. Many states require communities to update and maintain master or comprehensive plans for their communities' development. As these master plans are updated they are incorporating more and more sustainable development concepts as recommended by APA policy, including EID. Those communities which choose to green their master plans and incorporate sustainable development concepts into their local community's future have very few options when it comes to dealing with economic development. The fact that the APA is recommending EIPs in its policy statements on climate change and sustainable development may lead to their inclusion in future master plans across the country. A local Economic Development section is often a required component of a community master plan. EID and EIPs could become more common as vehicles for achieving the sustainable development goals found in community master plans as a result of these APA policies. Additionally, the APA's policy on climate change, adopted in April 2008 and revised in April 2011, calls for the development of EIPs in a number of instances. Specifically, it calls for 'power generation plants to become anchors of eco-industrial parks' (APA Policy Guide on Climate Change: Energy Policy 8: Energy Generation; American Planning Association, 2011) and for the adoption of a specific EID policy by its chapters, divisions and members (Economic Development Policy 4: Eco-Industrial Development; American Planning Association, 2011).

This concept employs a systems approach to siting industrial development, placing industries that use the by-products of other industries or that can share energy systems and other resources in close proximity, anticipating green construction and infrastructure in industrial park layout and design, and collaborating with the surrounding community for services or resources or to ensure compatibility, amongst other synergistic and environmentally-friendly practices. The goal is to create a node of industrial sustainability that minimises waste, enhances inter-industry co-operation, and more effectively and efficiently utilises local resources. The realisation of this potential, however, may be contingent on financial incentives. The latter could comprise the 'stick' of a landfill tax or the 'carrot' of tax reductions offered by some localities.

The APA's climate change guidelines, though, are not backed by regulatory requirements. Consequently, the USBCSD's vision of climate change regulation fostering interest in IS (Mangan, 2010) has not yet become a reality in the US (Guevarra, 2011). The post Copenhagen fallout in the US has seen a reliance on the first wave driver of eco-efficiency. Greenhouse gas mitigation and climate change remain on the agenda, but emphasis has returned to promoting business efficiency, avoiding politically charged topics for the time being. Andy Mangan noted in a 2010 interview, 'Efficiency sells and attracts business. Climate was a driver up until Copenhagen and still remains a driver for global firms' (Mangan, 2010). This position is supported by results from a survey of sustainability professionals by Globescan Inc. and SustainAbility Ltd, which identified 'climate issues (as) important but less urgent'; further noting a 'frustration with lack of political will to enact effective climate change' and 'the continued economic malaise' as contributing factors (Guevarra, 2011). These drivers for firms to participate in EID, as noted above, would influence their decisions to locate within an EIP in addition to participation in bilateral exchanges.

Funding

Notably, there are more private sector EIP initiatives in this later round of developments addressing the flaws pointed out by Heeres et al. (2004) in their comparison of US and Dutch parks. In fact, 18 of 33 projects are either initiated by private sector players or the USBCSD which focuses on business to business exchanges. All economic development initiatives are the result of cobbling together various funds from various sources, most often with local matching requirements. The point here is that the private sector is creating the parks and accessing the funding sources and providing the local match rather than local or state government. The strength of EIPs, districts and by-product synergy networks is that they take what was once viewed as a waste stream and transform it into a potential revenue stream. Once firms understand their participation as an opportunity they often become willing participants and partners. For example, ReVenture Park and the Pittsboro Biofuels Park in North Carolina have been successful, in part because of their ability to educate investors and park tenants about the economic viability of transforming orphan products (by-products) into feedstock for their operations.

Public sector funding, however, remains an important feature, albeit parks' strategies have adjusted to avail themselves of new funding streams that have become available. New wave EID projects vary from home-grown local economic development efforts (Camden County, North Carolina) to large-scale energy developments with EIPs as a component (e.g., Hillsboro County, Florida [Infinitus Renewable Energy Park, n.d.]). In North Carolina (with three successful and emerging parks), the state legislature passed special legislation to support the redevelopment of a highly contaminated brownfield site (ReVenture Park in Charlotte) by tripling the renewable energy credits generated within the EIP, increasing interest in EIPs as a brownfield redevelopment vehicle.

The lack of a federal energy policy as well as lack of federal policy to support EID and industrial symbiosis means that savvy developers (both public and private) must patch together various state and federal funding sources in order to create an EIP. One reason so many parks include renewable energy components is that the states in which they are located provide financial incentives to support that component of the project. A similar argument can be made for the use of biofuels as components found in this latest round of EIPs.

CONCLUSIONS AND FUTURE POTENTIAL

This chapter has analysed the recent wave of EID developments in the US. The drivers for these developments are primarily the potential to combine economic and environmental benefits. In common with much of the first wave, these projects appear to be primarily economic development initiatives with a green thrust. The latter comprises a varying mixture of place differentiation, environmental protection and accessing of environmental markets (e.g., renewable energy). The initial wave of EIPs mainly failed, and almost all of the new wave projects planned in 2010 had been abandoned by 2015. However, most of the projects active in 2010 (first and second wave) remain so in 2015. There are also a number of new parks which have emerged since the 2010 snapshot in time this chapter represents. These include parks in Bridgeport, CT; Griffin, GA; Hudson, OH; Montgomery, AL (Infinitus moved their project here from Florida); Shawnee, KS; Eco-Commerce park, Rialto, CA; plus other private BPS-type parks designed to feature exchanges and synergies in the biofuel industry including one in Fort Dodge, IA, an Exxon project in Texas and another corporate biofuel park in Nebraska. These last have been featured in the author's EID/IS updates newsletter for the EID/Industrial Symbiosis section of the ISIE (International Society for Industrial Ecology).

Examining the common themes, funding sources (private development versus grant funding), and policy underpinnings may provide some insights into their potential for success. However, as widely noted, EID strategy was of limited success for the early parks (Deutz and Gibbs, 2008). Developments cannot escape from the economic conditions of their location circumstance by employing environmental credentials. Conversely, the USBCSD's by-product synergy programmes continue to have appeal on a regional basis and to raise awareness of the potential to increase the efficiency of a firm's operations by looking outside of its corporate boundaries. It is recommended that states adopt similar reporting requirements for the tracking of 'waste' streams such as those required by the Commonwealth of Pennsylvania in order to further exploit the opportunity to mine resource streams, the effects of which are analysed by Lyons et al. (Chapter 7, this volume).[3]

More generally, though, current policies in the US create a desire for EID yet do not go far enough to make it flourish. The lack of a coherent national policy backed by funding and incentives remains out of reach for the moment, reflective of the political gridlock that surrounds almost all discussions of energy and development policy in the US. EID in all of its varied forms could play a role in that future in the US, as it seems to be emerging in other regions (e.g., Chapter 5, this volume). As the academic field of industrial ecology and the study of cities as urban ecosystems continue to grow both in the US and across the world, more people will be trained to recognise and utilise the vast opportunities our undiscovered resources can provide for us.

Without a national policy in support of industrial symbiosis and EID, the private sector, local communities, states and regions of the US will continue to pursue their own approaches. These local efforts need to be nurtured and supported in a coherent manner. From a planning and practitioner perspective it is important to develop a support network or a coherent policy framework in the next decade to address this need. It is often easier to start small-scale projects and get them off the ground than it is to initiate larger scale change without government support (Feichtinger and Pregernig, 2005). The policy foundations established by the APA will continue to bear fruit over time and more communities across the US will become aware of and supportive of EID. It will become increasingly important to create a network to support these initiatives as they move forward in order to avoid some of the failures from the first round of eco-industrial projects in the late 1990s. An initial gathering of US EIPs was held at Devens in September 2012 to begin this process with a second in the planning stages.

NOTES

1. Sarbanes-Oxley Act 2002 Public Law 104–204 107th Congress, accessed 1 February 2014 at http://www.sec.gov/about/laws/soa2002.pdf.
2. Interview with Tracy Casavant of Eco-Industrial Solutions, Vancouver, BC, Canada, 2010.
3. Côté pushed the idea of a by-products database in Burnside Industrial Park in 1994 and later to the Province of Nova Scotia; an idea Michelle Adams of the Dalhousie Eco-efficiency Centre also championed to the Province.

BIBLIOGRAPHY

American Planning Association (2011), *Climate Change Policy*, accessed 20 November 2011 at https://www.planning.org.

Boons, F., W. Spekkink, R. Isenmann, L. Baas, M. Eklund et al. (2015), 'Comparing Industrial Symbiosis in Europe: Towards a Conceptual Framework and Research Methodology', in P. Deutz, D. Lyons and J. Bi (eds), *International Perspectives on Industrial Ecology*, Cheltenham, UK and Northampton, MA, USA: Edward Elgar, pp. 69–88.

Branson, R. and P. McManus (2015), 'Bilateral Symbiosis in Australia and the Issue of Proximity', in P. Deutz, D. Lyons and J. Bi (eds), *International Perspectives on Industrial Ecology*, Cheltenham, UK and Northampton, MA, USA: Edward Elgar, pp. 126–141.

Chelsea Center (2002), available at http://www.chelseacenter.org/pdfs/RBED_NewBedford.pdf.

Chertow, M. (2007), 'Uncovering Industrial Symbiosis', *Journal of Industrial Ecology*, **11** (1), 11–30.

Chertow, M.R. and D.R. Lombardi (2005), 'Quantifying Economic and Environmental Benefits of Co-Located Firms', *Environmental Science & Technology*, **39**, 6535–6541.

Christianson, R. (2013), 'Huge Vacated G-P Particleboard Mill Being Demolished', accessed 15 March 2015 at http://www.woodworkingnetwork.com/woodworking-industry-management/wood-waste-biofuel/Huge-Vacated-GP-Particleboard-Mill-Being-Demolished-202852221.html#sthash.45vzDQ3w.dpbs.

Cimren, E., J. Fiksel, M.E. Posner and K. Sikdar (2011), 'Material Flow Optimisation in By-product Synergy Networks', *Journal of Industrial Ecology*, **15** (2), 315–332.

Cohen-Rosenthal, E. (ed.) (2000), *Eco-Industrial Development Workbook*, Cornell: Work Environment Initiative Cornell University.

Cohen-Rosenthal, E. (2003), *Eco-Industrial Strategies: Unleashing Synergy between Economic Development and the Environment*, London: Greenleaf Publishing.

Costa, I., G. Massard and A. Agarwal (2010), 'Waste Management Policies for Industrial Symbiosis Development: Case Studies in European Countries', *Journal of Cleaner Production*, **18** (8), 815–822.

Côté, R. and J. Grant et al. (2006), *Industrial Ecology and the Sustainability of Canadian Cities*, Halifax, Nova Scotia: Eco-Efficiency Centre, Dalhousie University.

Deutz, P. and D. Gibbs (2004), 'Eco-Industrial Development: Industrial Ecology or Place Promotion', *Business Strategy and the Environment*, **13**, 347–362.

Deutz, P. and D. Gibbs (2008), 'Industrial Ecology and Regional Development: Eco-Industrial Development as Cluster Policy', *Regional Studies*, **42** (10), 1313–1328.

Dunn, B.C. and A. Steinemann (1998), 'Industrial Ecology for Sustainable Communities', *Journal of Environmental Planning and Management*, **41** (6), 661–672.

Feichtinger, J. and M. Pregernig (2005), 'Participation and/or/versus Sustainability?', *Local Environment*, **10** (3), 229–242.

Fischer, M. (2012), 'Industrial Ecology and Stonyfield', promotional literature.

Gibbs, D. and P. Deutz (2007), 'Reflections on Implementing Industrial Ecology

Through Eco-Industrial Park Development', *Journal of Cleaner Production*, **15**, 1683–1695.

Guevarra, L. (2011), 'Climate Issues Important but Less Urgent for Sustainability Pros', accessed 20 March 2015 at http://www.greenbiz.com/news/2011/09/18/climate-issues-important-less-urgent-sustainability-pros.

Heeres, R.R., W.J.V. Vermeulen and F.B. De Walle (2004), 'Eco-industrial Park Initiatives in the USA and the Netherlands: First Lessons', *Journal of Cleaner Production*, **12**, (8–10), 985–995.

Hewes, A. and D. Lyons (2008), 'The Humanistic Side of Eco-industrial Parks: Champions and the Role of Trust', *Regional Studies*, **42** (10), 1329–1342.

Infinitus Renewable Energy Park (n.d.) accessed 20 November 2011 at http://www.genesisgroup.com/prj/irep/.

Koenig, A. (2005), *The Eco-Industrial Park Development: A Guide for Chinese Government Officials and Industrial Park Managers*, Beijing: EMCP, EU-China.

Koenig, A. and P. Lowitt (eds) (2009), *Eco Industrial Case Studies and Eco-Industrial Park Development: A Guide for US Officials and Industrial Park Managers*, American Planning Association Economic Development Division.

Laybourn, P. and M. Morrissey (2010), *National Industrial Symbiosis Programme The Pathway to a Low Carbon Sustainable Economy*, International Synergies.

Lowitt, P. (2008), 'Something in the Water? The Emergence of a Successful Eco-Industrial Park in the US', *Journal of Industrial Ecology*, **12**, 497–500.

Lowitt, P. (2010), 'Eco Industrial Updates', accessed 27 January 2014 at http://www.devensec.com/sustain/EID-updates.html.

Lowitt, P. and R. Côté (2013), 'Putting the Eco into Eco Parks', *Journal of Industrial Ecology*, **17** (3), 343–344.

Lyons, D. (2007), 'A Spatial Analysis of Loop Closing Among Recycling, Remanufacturing, and Waste Treatment Firms in Texas', *Journal of Industrial Ecology*, **11**, 43–54.

Lyons, D., M. Rice and L. Hu (2015), 'Industrial Waste Management Improvement: A Case Study of Pennsylvania', in P. Deutz, D. Lyons and J. Bi (eds), *International Perspectives on Industrial Ecology*, Cheltenham, UK and Northampton, MA, USA: Edward Elgar, pp. 108–125.

Mangan, A. (2010), 'USBCSD 2010 Annual Report', Austin, Texas, accessed 20 November 2011 at http://www.usbcsd.org/.

Martin, M. (2010), *Industrial Symbiosis for the Development of BioFuel Production*, Thesis No. 1441, Linköping University, Sweden.

McKitterick, T. (2012), 'The Role of the Entrepreneur', Presentation on ReVenture Park at US EIP Networking event, held at Devens, MA, September 2012, accessed 20 March 2015 at http://www.devensec.com/sustain/ReV_Entrepreneur.pdf.

NISP (2014), accessed 1 February 2014 at http://www.nispnetwork.com/.

Nolan, T. (2006), *The Greater Duluth-Superior Area Eco-Industrial Development Initiative: Report to the John S and James L. Knight Foundation*, Minnesota Pollution Control Agency.

Peirce, N.R. and C.W. Johnson (2008), *Century of the City: No Time to Lose*, New York: The Rockefeller Foundation.

Piedmont Biofuels, accessed 11 May 2010 at http://www.locallygrownnews.com/stories/Eco-Industrial-Park-Tour.

ReVenture (2011), accessed 20 November 2011 at http://www.reventure.com.

ReVenture (2013), accessed 18 September 2013 at http://www.reventurepark.com/what-is-reventure/.

UN Habitat (2009), *The UN Habitat Global Report on Human Settlements (2009) Planning Sustainable Cities: Policy Directions*, London and Sterling, VA: Earthscan.

Van Berkel, R. (2010), 'Quantifying Sustainability Benefits of Industrial Symbioses', *Journal of Industrial Ecology*, **14** (3), 371–373.

Veleva, V., S. Todorova, P. Lowitt, N. Angus and D. Neely (2015), 'Understanding and Addressing Business Needs and Sustainability Challenges: Lessons From Devens Eco-Industrial Park', *Journal of Cleaner Production*, **87**, 375–384.

Wang, Q. (2013), 'Knowledge Transfer to Facilitate Industrial Symbiosis: A Case Study of UK–China Collaborators', Department of Geography, Environment and Earth Sciences, University of Hull, UK, accessed 20 February 2015 at https://hydra.hull.ac.uk/assets/hull:7143a/content.

Wang, Q., P. Deutz and D. Gibbs (2015), 'UK–China Collaboration for Industrial Symbiosis: A Multi-Level Approach to Policy Transfer Analysis', in P. Deutz, D. Lyons and J. Bi (eds), *International Perspectives on Industrial Ecology*, Cheltenham, UK and Northampton, MA, USA: Edward Elgar, pp. 89–107.

5. Comparing industrial symbiosis in Europe: towards a conceptual framework and research methodology

**Frank Boons, Wouter Spekkink,
Ralf Isenmann, Leo Baas, Mats Eklund,
Sabrina Brullot, Pauline Deutz, David Gibbs,
Guillaume Massard, Elena Romero Arozamena,
Carmen Ruiz Puente, Veerle Verguts,
Chris Davis, Gijsbert Korevaar, Inês Costa and
Henrikke Baumann**

INTRODUCTION

Industrial symbiosis (IS) continues to raise the interest of researchers and practitioners alike. Individual and haphazard attempts to increase linkages among co-located firms have been complemented by concerted efforts to stimulate the development of industrial regions with intensified resource exchanges that reduce environmental impact. Additionally, there are examples of both spontaneous and facilitated linkages between two or more firms involving flows of materials/energy waste. A striking feature of IS activities is that they are found across diverse social contexts and vary considerably in form (Lombardi et al., 2012); there are substantial differences in the ways in which IS manifests itself. Equally diverse are the activities of policy makers to stimulate such linkages. Such diversity can already be found within Europe, as became apparent in a first meeting among some of the present authors in 2009 (Isenmann and Chernykh, 2009). Researchers present there decided to create a network of European researchers on IS, with the explicit aim to develop a comparative analysis. We can thus provide insight to the relationship between the style of IS and its context and thereby the potential for policy makers in different contexts to learn from each other. Policy learning can be a tempting route to IS, but is fraught with difficulties if the influence of context is not appreciated (e.g., Wang et al., Chapter 6, this volume).

The authors of this chapter first met in Rotterdam in January 2010 as a group of researchers interested in IS, aiming to provide a comparative analysis of European developments in IS. The hope of this large-scale collaborative effort is to enable a systematic comparison of IS in different national contexts, albeit all industrialised, western European nations. Of the nine countries represented, eight are EU members and therefore have the same underlying approaches to waste management and resource recovery governed by the Waste Framework (2008), and other Directives including Producer Responsibility Directives. The ninth country (Switzerland) has a comparable approach to resource management (Costa et al., 2010).

Our initial agenda consisted of the following questions, which we seek to address in this chapter:

1. What are the specific forms in which IS occurs in selected European countries, and how can these forms be compared?
2. What causes IS to emerge and develop in European countries, and to what extent are these causes country specific?

The following section summarises the process we used to bring together empirical material, and the way in which we sought to arrive at consensus about a conceptual framework. We then present our approach to developing a common understanding of IS to enable a comparative analysis. In short, our definition should allow us to identify phenomena that fit our interest (commonality), whilst allowing for the national variability that we seek to study (diversity). We then analyse the data to consider the diversity of IS both within and between countries. Our conceptual model in the following section outlines the three types of IS systems that emerge from our data. Finally, we present preliminary conclusions about the diversity of IS in Europe.

PROCESSES OF COLLABORATION

At the initial meeting (2010) all participants presented a country report in which they provided an overview of definitions of IS that are used in their country, a description of the current state of IS in their country and how this situation evolved, and an inventory of enabling or impeding factors that are relevant in understanding the described developments. These reports indicated a diversity of IS and stimulated a discussion on how to define IS in an inclusive way, i.e. in such a way that it would encompass the cases that each of us, as self-defined IS-researchers, deemed to be manifestations of IS (section 3). We also started to discuss what would be relevant topics for the comparison among countries.

A second meeting was held in September 2010, in Linköping, Sweden. There we discussed two-page documents on the topics for comparison, and started to build a conceptual framework (section 4). At this meeting we also decided to experiment with collaboratively collecting data online using Semantic MediaWiki as a platform. This approach had been employed by Chris Davis at TU Delft on several other projects (Davis, 2012), notably on http://ie.tudelft.nl. In the months that followed, this was set up in such a way that researchers could enter data on IS cases in their country. However, it proved difficult to enter pre-existing data into a format for which it had not been designed and in practice we have relied on a less structured approach to data compilation. We have collected updates based on a survey with broad questions allowing participants to proceed as suited their circumstances. Skype meetings were used for verbal clarification and the resulting summaries/interpretations circulated for confirmation.

Data collection comprised both primary and secondary data, with a non-exhaustive selection of IS examples for each country being selected and described by a researcher based in that country. Primary data (some of which has previously been published by different combinations of the present authors) included document analysis (e.g., national, local government policy or industry statements) and interviews with policy makers, practitioners and/or participating companies. Additional examples have come from the academic literature and internet searches guided by our experience in the field over a number of years. Experience includes working with and/or for industry or government bodies, some of which have been directly engaged in IS projects.

We have discussed and compared the usage of terms such as IS/industrial ecology (IE) and alternatives between countries in order to reduce the possibility of linguistic differences between researchers introducing apparent rather than real variation. The sharing of examples has helped to suggest avenues of exploration for IS that researchers may not have considered. The process of analysis and comparison has been iterative to help ensure that each team is content with the representation of the situation in their own country. The sharing of data helps to ensure that what is presented as IS in each country is not biased by perspectives of the researchers in that country (see following section), in order to achieve a realistic representation of the geographic variability of IS within and between the countries involved.

Defining IS in a Comparative Setting

An early point to emerge in our discussion was the widely different understandings, definitions and usage of the term IS. There are two fundamental ways to approach comparison of a phenomenon among different social contexts. In the *outside-in approach*, the comparison is based on a definition of the phenomenon that is provided by the researcher(s). This definition, and its corresponding indicators, are imposed on the empirical situations that are compared. This approach has the advantage of a high level of consistency, but it risks excluding some of the variability of practice that is of interest. Actors in each context may engage with the concept, in this case IS, in quite distinct ways. The *inside-out approach* aims to capture this aspect of differences in meaning. As a result, the way in which actors in local situations define IS, and the indicators they use to measure success and failure, become part of the investigation.

Our discussion may be best summarised by the position that concepts are small pieces of theory (Stinchcombe, 1968; Toulmin, 1972) that are shaped and evolve as they are confronted with empirical material. Concepts, and the theories of which they are part, form the collectively shared knowledge we have about the outside world. Thus, if we as a group are interested in phenomena that we deem meaningful to compare, then those phenomena are included in the analysis. We may come to the conclusion that not all phenomena under study can be usefully compared, or need to be analysed. Thus our understanding of IS can evolve.

However, a major challenge when adopting the inside-out approach is to define the central concept in such a way that a balance is found between:

1. the high level of diversity among empirical phenomena that researchers, practitioners and policy makers refer to with the label 'industrial symbiosis';
2. the additional circumstance that there are activities resembling those known as 'industrial symbiosis', but which are not thus identified by those involved;
3. the need to come up with a set of empirical phenomena in each country that can be meaningfully compared.

Therefore, it is logically necessary to set some boundary on what is considered a valid object of study. The inductive approach to research is seldom followed to its extreme form (i.e., collection of data without any theoretical preconceptions). Deciding which data to collect, as well as the manner in which it is subsequently organised, draws on prior knowledge and understanding (e.g., Harvey, 1969). The compilation of this group involved making some assumptions about the type of activities entertained as even potentially relevant. For example, initiatives comprising environmental management purely at the level of individual firms were excluded from consideration as IS.

Importantly, IS centres on flows of residue material and energy flows amongst organisations. Such flows, and the extent to which they can be rendered less harmful to the environment, are the core focus of the practitioners and researchers involved in IS. These flows, virtually all IS researchers seem to agree, comprise the heart of IS (e.g., Deutz, 2014). It is from resource efficiencies (whether cascading energy, or use of one firm's residue as another's input) that the environmental and economic benefits of IS as a business practice are derived (Gertler and Ehrenfeld, 1996; Chertow, 2000) and furthermore set it apart from other eco-efficiency practices. Such flows could be seen as the Platonian essence of IS, and thus used as the starting point for identifying manifestations of IS (Deutz, 2014). Practices and phenomena such as exchanges of information, social networking, co-location, shared site management, utility sharing and a network of firms exchanging residues can all be associated with IS. Some of these (e.g., information exchange) are likely necessary or at least helpful in the implementation of IS. It has been a point of debate both in the literature and between us whether any of these phenomena are *necessary* in addition to inter-organisational residue flows to recognise IS in a given situation (e.g., does IS have to be in a network, or can it be bilateral [e.g., Branson and McManus, Chapter 8, this volume])? A second point of debate is whether these phenomena can constitute IS in the absence of residue flows (e.g., Ashton's [2011] study of utility sharing as IS).

Whilst acknowledging that views differ, we delineated our object of study in terms of a shared understanding of the centrality of resource flows to IS. For example, social networking between firms in and of itself does not comprise IS. However, if a social network has been established or adapted with a view to achieving residue synergies, then it is an important part of an IS system. Conversely, residue flows between firms do constitute IS whether or not they have been 'uncovered' (to use Chertow's 2007 term), i.e. identified as such either by one or more of the firms involved or by an external researcher. Empirical examples of activity that could thus be considered to constitute IS were then analysed to determine the practices involved (e.g., policy maker or company-led activity) and to define the system boundary (e.g., based on geographic scale, or supply chain). Thus, we decided to work with an open definition of the form that IS might take in different circumstances.

Given this understanding of the importance of material/energy flows (actual or desired) to IS, we set out to define our object of study as follows:

1. the geographic boundary of the system;
2. the actors involved and relationships between them;
3. policy approaches to IS.

We required that at least some actors in the system are from industry and envisage the wide ecological system as a resource base or sink. In many definitions of IS the criterion of geographical proximity is present; IS revolves around a set of social actors that is seen to have a certain potential because of this proximity. However, it is difficult to set a limit on proximity in any absolute sense, because depending on geo-physical characteristics and the physical residue streams involved, proximity may mean anything from 5 km to 350 km, or indeed loop-closing may have a global scale (e.g., Lyons, 2007). This diversity, with its antecedents and consequences, may be an interesting feature for comparison. Likewise, we keep an open mind as to whether actors use the expression IS/IE and whether they are aware of, or the extent to which they actively seek, ecological benefits. Thus we have kept an open mind regarding the nature of IS systems. Establishing the range and diversity of IS systems is a key purpose of the study.

The set of actors included in the system first of all consists of those responsible for the transformation of material and the use of energy. These are key actors in the sense that without them, there would be no material and energy flows. Whilst these will often be firms, such production facilities may also be owned by governments or other types of actors. The nature of stakeholders involved is an important variable to address in the comparative analysis. In addition to the actors responsible for the transformation of material and use of energy, other actors are involved in the creation and maintenance of symbiotic linkages. Given these system elements, we can then explore the diversity of understandings and manifestations of IS. We seek to enable a common understanding of the phenomenon under study, without trying to define away the diversity that we want to study.

EMPIRICAL DATA AND ANALYSIS

The results of our research are summarised in Table 5.1.[1] A key insight is that the use of the expression 'industrial symbiosis' (or for that matter 'industrial ecology') outside academia is unusual. A data set of self-identified IS projects would be far smaller than this one. Understanding the motivation behind self-identified initiatives would be of interest, but confining attention to them would miss a wide variety of both public and private sector projects exhibiting the type of residue flows central to IS. Perhaps steered by EU policy terminology, the expression Circular

Table 5.1 Characteristics of industrial symbiosis by country

Country	Feature	Comment
Belgium	Terminology	'IS' not used by national scale policy makers; recently appeared at regional scale
	Policy	Policies impacting on IS (environment, innovation and economic affairs) are formulated at the regional scale. IS facilitation schemes have been established since 2012 (in Flanders this has been inspired by the NISP model; but in Wallonia supported by the Ministry of Economy without the international influence)
	Systems	Combination of: 1) local networks, e.g., primarily based around biomass/bio-energy. Some of these are expanding to other types of materials; 2) regional scale facilitated residual exchange
	Actors	Both direct public sector facilitation of residual exchange and promotion of networking opportunities for companies; local IS networks typically private sector led
	Assumptions/priorities	That inter-firm connections generate economic and environmental sustainability
	Sources include	Agentschap Ondernemen (2013); Verguts et al. (in press)
France	Terminology	Policy makers use 'IE' to refer to what academics might term 'IS'. However, 'Circular Economy' preferred as seen as more intuitive and emphasising economic over ecological priorities
	Policy	Institute of Circular Economy founded in 2013; government, industry, NGO, ADEME (the French Environment and Energy Management Agency) and academic partners; Chamber of Commerce and Industry. Territorial ecology (comprising technical aspects of IE, e.g., material flow analysis) also promoted
	Systems	Regional scale, with IS embedded in economic, political, environmental and organisational context (i.e., 'territorial' approach). Co-operation in practice hindered by administrative complexity in crossing jurisdictional boundaries

Table 5.1 (continued)

Country	Feature	Comment
France	Actors	Strong drive from academia; public sector involved in regional initiatives assessing potential IS relationships; private sector can be reluctant to disclose information relevant to IS
	Assumptions/priorities	Economic development and resource efficiency opportunities seen for companies, and as an opportunity to ensure the ecological transition of territories for local and national government
	Sources include	Harpet et al., 2013; Brullot et al., 2014; Massard et al., 2014
Germany	Terminology	Expressions IS and IE typically avoided both inside and outside of academia. Recent flourishing of interest in IS-type activity
	Policy	National policies promoting resource recovery, but not IS specifically
	Systems	Park to regional scale recycling networks, including materials, energy and steam flows. IS is promoted within the context of specific projects; in some cases, the inter-firm links have extended beyond the original geographic boundaries (e.g., of an EIP)
	Actors	Public, private sector, often including universities; companies can be reluctant to disclose information relevant to IS
	Assumptions/priorities	Resource conservation is the priority, with assumed economic and sustainability benefits
	Sources include	Schön et al., 2003; Hasler, 2004; Veiga and Magrini, 2009
Netherlands	Terminology	IS/IE seldom used outside academia; cradle to cradle and Circular Economy are preferred terms. Organisations' definitions, e.g. of EIPs, evolve to current circumstances

	Policy	National policy for sustainable industrial parks (1994–2004), in part inspired by evolved regional scale port-based networks. National government promotes private sector-led Circular Economy initiatives
	Systems	Local scale, e.g. bio-based networks, company driven. EIPs exist in several locations (in accordance with the past national policy). Regional scale IS networks fostered by combination of public and private sector efforts within business agglomerations
	Actors	Public, private actors involved in promoting IS or other collective environmental management; some spontaneous linking. Leadership changes between public and private sector as projects develop. Academic involvement primarily in uncovering links
	Assumptions/priorities	Inter-firm co-operation produces resource efficiencies, economic and ecological benefits. IS is often one aspect of broader developments, such as Circular Economy and bio-based economy
	Sources include	Pellenbarg, 2002; Baas, 2011; Davis, 2012; Spekkink, 2013
Portugal	Terminology	'IS' adopted by policy makers in 2011; used by business as general term for resource recovery
	Policy	National Waste Management plan for 2011–2020 promotes IS
	Systems	Evolved-IS park-based networks; resource recovery parks (RRP), on-line waste brokering. Some RRPs develop synergies; sometimes these extend beyond park boundaries
	Actors	Public and private actors have combined in adaptive 'middle out' approach, each responding to other and with leadership changing between different types of actors
	Assumptions/priorities	Emphasis on resource recovery and waste management
	Sources include	Costa and Ferrão, 2010; Costa et al., 2010; Lopes, 2013
Spain	Terminology	IS and IE of academic and educational importance, and since 2011 also used by policy makers, though 'Circular Economy' becoming key policy term

Table 5.1 (continued)

Country	Feature	Comment
Spain	Policy	National programme to facilitate by-product exchange, via 10 publically-funded regional data bases, the first established in the 1990s
	Systems	Park-scale initiatives to promote sustainable resource consumption and inter-firm co-operation, sometimes including IS; regional scale networks of bilateral exchanges
	Actors	Universities prominent in local to regional IS initiatives, usually via spin-off companies; public sector involvement both in resource exchange networks and to seek potential IS links within existing park-based initiatives
	Assumptions/priorities	IS and IE can result in resource efficiencies, economic savings and thus regional regeneration
	Sources include	Puig et al. 2008; Ecomark Project, 2014; Ruiz Puente et al., 2015
Sweden	Terminology	IS and IE seldom used explicitly in local or national policies
	Policy	Few explicit efforts to promote IS whether by name or not, though heat collaboration and climate investment programmes may have relevant components
	Systems	Numerous local to regional IS networks, largely self-organised; aided by long-term trends, e.g., in forestry industry alongside an interest in energy efficiency. IS also found in petrochemical complexes
	Actors	Public bodies prominently involved, though most IS self-organised; IS opportunities are sought within the context of place-based projects, e.g., by academia and different regional cleantech projects. Public-private collaboration in district heating is common
	Assumptions/priorities	Energy and economic efficiencies along with environmental considerations
	Sources include	Mirata and Emtairah, 2005; Wolf and Petersson, 2007; Baas, 2011; Martin and Eklund, 2011; Linköping University, 2014

Switzerland	Terminology	'IS' and 'IE' and Circular Economy used variously by states/localities similar to academic usages
	Policy	National plan for a green economy supporting resource efficiency of IS type; varying state-level policies to promote IS including directly facilitating and provision of information, through territorial planning
	Systems	Local to regional policy driven exchanges between organisations up to 350 km apart; evolved regional IS network (petrochemical-based evolved network, energy networks, construction industry)
	Actors	IS-facilitators play a significant role (they can variously be public, private or academic sector) given a diverse and dispersed industrial base
	Assumptions/priorities	Resource and energy efficiencies, regional development
	Sources include	Massard and Erkman, 2007; Costa et al., 2010; Massard et al. 2014
United Kingdom	Terminology	IS/IE rare in policy documents; Circular Economy used in policy and press to include related practices
	Policy	National Industrial Symbiosis Programme publically funded 2005–2012; regulations incentivise recovery and encourage Circular Economy practices, but not IS specifically
	Systems	Local networks for resource recovery and/or other environmental co-operation; bilateral exchanges up to national in scale
	Actors	Private sector including as IS facilitator; universities involved in developing resource recovery and refining science
	Assumptions/priorities	Resource efficiency, economic benefits
	Sources include	Mirata, 2004; Penn et al., 2014; Wang et al., Chapter 6, this volume

Economy has taken off in policy circles in several of the countries studied. As in France, this may reflect the fact that the term Circular Economy (which involves extending the productive life span of resources through activity such as recycling, reuse and remanufacturing) is more intuitively obvious in meaning than IE. In Germany there has been a more deep-rooted aversion to the use of biological metaphors (Hauff and Isenmann, 2003). In the spirit of the early industrial ecologists (e.g., Frosch and Gallopoulos, 1989), the Circular Economy is promoted as a route to competiveness alongside improved environmental performance. The expectation, therefore, is for business to lead initiatives (e.g., the Netherlands, the UK).

Notwithstanding the lack of widespread usage of the term IS, IS networks of various kinds can be found in all of the studied countries. The clearest division of these networks is between those with a strong connection to a specific place (whether industrial park, city or region) and those that comprise spatially dispersed inter-linked firms (what might at one time have been referred to as 'virtual' eco-industrial parks [EIPs]). Small-scale initiatives, e.g., a network centring on a specific company (often based on bio-materials), may be entirely private sector driven (e.g., Belgium, the Netherlands, the UK). In Sweden, such IS networks have formed around the forestry industry. Some of these are now regional in scale, often include public sector input (e.g., collaboration in district heating projects) and sometimes with academic involvement to seek additional efficiency savings including symbiotic connections. Larger-scale IS networks resembling the archetypal network at Kalundborg in Denmark have also emerged, e.g., based around port industries (the Netherlands, France, the UK), green chemistry (France) or petrochemicals (Portugal, Sweden, Switzerland). As with Kalundborg, these networks began by private sector actors negotiating each symbiotic link as a separate bilateral arrangement. Also like Kalundborg, both the larger- and the smaller-scale networks evolved in the context of incentivising or at least permissive regulations. Some of these evolved networks (e.g., in the Netherlands) have become self-aware and have taken steps to deliberately increase the connections.

More commonly, though, IS systems comprise a combination of public and private sector bodies, often including NGOs and with academic involvement. These networks tend to be strongly rooted in specific places. This is particularly true in the French case, where IS is strongly linked to regional economic development initiatives, also in conjunction with plans for low carbon energy transitions. In the Netherlands, a number of EIPs survive as a legacy of a former policy to promote sustainable business practices. By contrast, in Germany and Portugal local to regional scale

IS networks are likely found in the context of resource recovery parks (or larger-scale resource recovery initiatives). In all these cases, active effort has been made by a variety of actors to increase the density of the IS network (i.e., to seek additional symbiotic relationships). However, whilst relationships may be sought beyond formal park boundaries, the search is specific to the locality in question. Notably in Portugal and the Netherlands public and private sector-led initiatives are hard to distinguish as leadership can evolve in response to both internal and external stimuli. Costa and Ferrão (2010) termed this a 'middle-out' approach to IS.

Networks comprising a multitude of separate bilateral inter-firm residue flows are present in Belgium, Spain, Portugal, Switzerland and the UK. In all cases (except for the UK), these involve public bodies acting either as facilitators, or funding a database accessible to firms. Partly as a result of austerity post-2008, and partly through political conviction, the UK National Industrial Symbiosis Programme (NISP) is no longer government-funded and free to access. In these countries there is a strong identification of IS with waste reduction, or diversion from landfill. In Spain and Portugal, IS is an explicit component of waste policy. Alongside regulations dis-incentivising the use of landfill as a disposal option, promoting IS alerts firms to an option they may not otherwise have considered (e.g., Wang et al., Chapter 6, this volume, regarding the UK).

All countries studied except Switzerland have the same supra-national context comprising EU resource management regulations. The geographic scale of resource management policies reflects the political organisation of the country, and is typically devised at the national scale (albeit devolved to regions/states in Belgium and Switzerland). Countries such as Germany, France, the Netherlands and the UK have policies encouraging companies to adopt IE practices (generally under the guise of a Circular Economy), e.g., such as design for resource recovery. However, in most cases IS is seen as a policy initiative to be implemented at the local to regional scale. NISP[2] remains the only organisation attempting to facilitate IS on a national scale in the countries studied. The significance of that, however, is related to the distribution and diversity of industry: local to regional scale in practice dominated residue flows in the UK (Jensen et al., 2011). In Switzerland, though, the knowledge and capacity to establish cross-regional synergies is important as potential partners may not exist locally. Public sector involvement appears to be important to facilitate such links. By contrast, in France, co-operation across administrative boundaries is bureaucratically complex. It appears that no attempts at co-operation for IS across sub-national political boundaries have been made, as is the case in most of the countries studied. At the sub-national level, similar types of projects exist in many of these countries.

Actors involved in IS systems are many and varied. They might or might not be aware that the material/energy flows in which they participate in some sense are part of a larger system. Aside from directly participating companies or organisations, actors include other private sector bodies such as maintenance firms and consultants, and also include industry associations, Chambers of Commerce, governmental agencies, NGOs and knowledge institutes. Each has an influence on the actors responsible for material transformations in that they may affect, positively or negatively, the way in which symbiotic linkages are created. The influencing role of other actors indicates that we are not so much interested in an 'atomised' perspective on the actors involved; instead, we see them as tied together in a social network (Granovetter, 1985). As has become clear from several analyses (Ashton, 2009; Paquin and Howard-Grenville, 2012), the structure and evolution of these networks hold clues about the way in which the key actors are able to create symbiotic linkages. In some instances key actors are the knowledge gatekeepers, especially in the waste-oriented networks in Belgium, Spain and elsewhere. In these cases the critical knowledge may comprise the material needs of companies (in terms of both production inputs and outputs). More proactively, though, IS facilitation bodies such as NISP have the technical knowledge to be able to envisage flows that might involve some transformation of materials. In other cases, this knowledge comes from academic actors (e.g., Spain, Sweden, France). Alternatively, networking may be incentivised, or even organised, for companies, but any IS arrangements that may result are their own responsibility (e.g., the Netherlands). For both France and Germany, reluctance amongst firms to disclose their inputs and outputs can be a hurdle to IS. A trusted third-party facilitator may offer a partial solution.

The motivation for involvement in IS may be ecological impact, economic interests, social development, or any combination of these. In each case, it appears that actors involved are aware of both economic and environmental implications of IS. However, the emphasis varies considerably. At the national level, countries can be divided between those emphasising IS as a waste diversion tool (Belgium, Spain, Portugal, the UK), those where it is part of a wider business sustainability agenda (Germany, the Netherlands), and those where the emphasis is on regional economic development (France, Switzerland). Sweden does not seem to fit any of these categories very comfortably; IS seems most indigenous here, i.e. to have evolved with the least conscious effort to stimulate, although a variety of actors have become involved.

CONCEPTUAL MODEL

The above analysis indicates that IS exists in a wide variety of forms within the countries studied. Three types of IS systems emerge from the analysis of our data.

Process-oriented IS

Certain types of industrial activity, such as bio-based activities (e.g., the Swedish forestry IS networks) at the smaller scale or petrochemical activities oriented at the larger scale, appear to lend themselves to the development of IS. Notably, these networks relate to process industries (Lyons, 2007), where the transformation of materials is a standard part of operating procedures, and the existence of in-house expertise therefore likely (whether relating to materials or energy conversion). However, whilst the technical and industrial context greatly facilitate the replicability of these links, the social element in negotiating specific flows, or the significance of the economic and regulatory context constraining those negotiations, may still be important. Indeed, replication even of established IS transactions is contingent on the presence of relevant industries in a pre-existing agglomeration, or the ability of principal actors to attract relevant companies to an emerging network. This type of system is connected to a physical place, though the actual scale will depend on the degree of concentration of companies (as in the Australian examples presented by Van Beers et al., 2007). The principal actors are members of the companies involved, although there may be involvement of other organisations attempting to increase the density of the network within its geographic boundaries, or to extend it to the neighbouring area. Individual companies may have IS linkages further afield, including other countries. The focus is on environmental and economic benefits primarily to the companies, though as observed by van Beers et al. (2007), neighbouring communities may exert an influence on company behaviour.

Residue-oriented IS

This type of IS system is characterised by a network of bilateral residue flows. The distance of individual flows is highly variable; overall the network may extend from local to national scope (not to preclude the possibility of international flows). Participating companies may have little or no concept of the scope of the network of which they are a part. However, other actors in the system may be aware at least of its potential scope and scale. These systems could be divided between those with active facilitation of IS-links (Belgium [in Flanders], Switzerland, the UK), and those where facilitation is restricted to oversight of a database (e.g., Portugal, Spain). The geographic coverage and industrial sectors represented will vary as participants join and leave the network. Resource conservation is the key driver for the initiators, but the primary motivations for participating firms are usually financial savings and regulatory compliance.

Place-oriented IS

Place-oriented IS systems comprise networks at a specific location. Similar to process-oriented systems, there is, or is desired to be, a local network of symbiotic links between companies and other relevant organisations. Unlike the process-based networks outlined above, there is no pre-defined IS network based on specific materials. Another important difference from the IS variants above is that a benefit to the community involved is central to the intentions behind the development of the network. Efforts to engage companies are therefore confined to the locality of the network, whose boundaries are therefore more rigid than in the other cases. Companies are highly likely to be aware of their membership of the network, although their aspirations may differ from those of the network initiators. IS is likely to be just one of a number of environmental and/or economic initiatives being implemented locally. Local authorities, Chambers of Commerce, universities and other bodies with a connection to the place are likely to be involved; participation, and leadership, can change as the network develops (e.g., Costa and Ferrão, 2010; Ruiz, 2014; Ruiz et al., 2015).

CONCLUSIONS

This chapter has provided an empirical analysis of IS from nine European countries. Based on our shared experience and discussions it is apparent that IS exists in a wide variety of systems. Although national characterisations can be made, variability within countries is almost as great as between countries. Of significance, however, our analysis has been confined to varied, but on a global scale, all industrialised, prosperous countries which are highly regulated in terms of resource management.

We observe that whilst IS systems can be closely tied to specific places, this is not necessarily the case. A key difference between countries was whether or not IS is used as a deliberate tool for diverting industrial residues from landfill, which may reflect a country's historic landfill dependence (diverting waste from landfill was an urgent priority in the UK in the light of EU targets). However, having this type of IS system does not preclude the development of more local, spontaneous arrangements. These appear to be driven by the opportunities inherent in certain types of industry. A third type of IS system is one that deliberately seeks to capture the economic/environmental benefits of IS for specific places. These types of systems are likely to have been initiated by public organisations connected to the places, but in the more successful cases they have engaged company involvement to the point where leadership may transfer to the private sector.

An important characteristic of all these systems is that they are dynamic. Individual members can join or leave, possibly significantly altering the geographic scale or industrial scope of a network. The geographic scale is highly variable, but seldom greater than regional, even in diffuse networks. The members of a network might or might not be aware of it, but ongoing efforts are required to preserve individual links, to increase the density of the network, or to increase the spread of connections. Social networks and information flows are important to all these types of IS, although the way they are used, the types of actors involved, and the motivations of the actors involved can vary. There is overlap between the IS variants in terms of both potential technical/scientific issues encountered in achieving residue flows and social, cultural, or regulatory constraints and approaches. Excluding any of these variants from our definition of IS would have limited understanding of the phenomenon of IS as well as risk potential for co-operation and learning between participants of different types of IS.

The approach employed by this chapter could be used by other groups of researchers to facilitate large-scale comparisons without the level of financial support typically implied by such efforts. The aim of our approach is to promote the contextualised study of IS, in search of a better understanding of the dynamics involved in the emergence and development of IS systems. Comparative research can help to uncover similarities and differences in these underlying dynamics and relate these patterns to networks of IS linkages as outcomes. In addition, it can help us determine the extent to which these patterns are rooted in the places in which they occur.

ACKNOWLEDGEMENTS

The UK contribution to this research was partially funded by the Natural Environment Research Council (with the Economic and Social Research Council and Defra: NE/I019468/1).

NOTES

1. The full list of examples of IS in participating countries is available online at https://www.e-elgar.com/international-perspectives-on-industrial-ecology-companion-site. Table 5.1 contains a non-exhaustive list of identified cases of industrial symbiosis, providing a short description, current status, and initiating actors.
2. See https://www.nispnetwork.com/, accessed on 23 December 2014.

REFERENCES

Agentschap Ondernemen (2013), Projecten fabriek van de toekomst, Brussels, Belgium: Agentschap Ondernemen, 64.

Ashton, W.S. (2009), 'The structure, function, and evolution of a regional industrial ecosystem', *Journal of Industrial Ecology*, **13**, 228–246.

Ashton, W.S. (2011), 'Managing performance expectations of industrial symbiosis', *Business Strategy and the Environment*, **20**, 297–309.

Baas, L. (2011), 'Planning and uncovering industrial symbiosis: comparing the Rotterdam and Östergötland regions', *Business Strategy and the Environment*, **20**, 428–440.

Branson, R. and P. McManus (2015), 'Bilateral symbiosis in Australia and the issue of geographic proximity', in P. Deutz, D. Lyons and J. Bi (eds), *International Perspectives on Industrial Ecology*, Cheltenham, UK and Northampton, MA, USA: Edward Elgar, pp. 126–141.

Brullot, S., M. Maillefert and J. Joubert (2014), 'Stratégies d'acteurs et gouvernance des démarches d'écologie industrielle et territoriale', *Développement durable et territoires*, [online], **5** (1), February 2014.

Chertow, M.R. (2000), 'Industrial symbiosis: literature and taxonomy', *Annual Review of Energy and Environment*, **25**, 313–337.

Chertow, M.R. (2007), '"Uncovering" industrial symbiosis', *Journal of Industrial Ecology*, **11**, 11–30.

Costa, I. and P. Ferrão (2010), 'A case study of industrial symbiosis development using a middle-out approach', *Journal of Cleaner Production*, **18** (10), 984–992.

Costa, I., G. Massard and A. Agarwal (2010), 'Waste management policies for industrial symbiosis development: case studies in European countries', *Journal of Cleaner Production*, **18**, 815–822.

Davis, C.B. (2012), *Making Sense of Open Data – From Raw Data to Actional Insight*, PhD thesis, TU Delft.

Deutz, P. (2014), 'Food for thought: seeking the essence of industrial symbiosis', in R. Salomone and G. Saija (eds), *Pathways to Environmental Sustainability: Methodologies and Experiences*, Switzerland: Springer, pp. 3–11.

Ecomark Project (2014), *Case Studies*, accessed 20 March 2015 at http://www.ecomarkproject.eu/en/casestudies/view/23.

Frosch, R.A. and N.E. Gallopoulos (1989), 'Strategies for manufacturing', *Scientific American*, **261**, 94–102.

Gertler, N. and J.R. Ehrenfeld (1996), 'A down-to-earth approach to clean production', *Technology Review*, **99** (2), 48–54.

Granovetter, M. (1985), 'Economic action and social structure: the problem of embeddedness', *The American Journal of Sociology*, **78**, 1360–1380.

Harpet, C., E. Gully, C Blavot, J. Bonnet and J. Mehu (2013), 'Seeking industrial synergies and cooperations research program on a territory: the case of Chemichal Valley in France', *Progress on Industrial Ecology*, special issue, **8**, 92–113.

Harvey, D. (1969), *Explanation in Geography*, London: Arnold.

Hasler, A. (2004), 'Kommunikative Verwertungsnetze – innovative Instrumente nachhaltiger Wirtschaft', in E. Schwarz (ed.), *Nachhaltiges Innovationsmanagement. Heinz Strebel zum 65. Geburtstag*, Wiesbaden, pp. 451–475.

Hauff, M. von and R. Isenmann (2003), 'Industrial ecology – emerging field of research, (but why) neglected in Germany?', *Business Strategy and the Environment Conference 2003*, ERP Environment (ed.), Shipley: ERP, 62–71.

Heeres, R.R., W.J.V. Vermeulen and F.B. de Walle (2004), 'Eco-industrial park initiatives in the USA and the Netherlands: first lessons', *Journal of Cleaner Production*, **12** (8–10), 985–995.

Isenmann, R. and K. Chernykh (2009), 'Environmental ICT applications for eco-industrial development', in V. Wohlgemuth, B. Page and K. Voigt (eds), *Environmental Informatics and industrial environmental protection, 23rd International Conference on Informatics for Environmental Protection*, Aachen: Shaker, **2**, pp. 231–242.

Jensen, P.D., L. Basson, E.E. Hellawell, M.R. Bailey and M. Leach (2011), 'Quantifying "geographic proximity": experiences from the United Kingdom's National Industrial Symbiosis Programme', *Resources, Conservation and Recycling*, **55**, 703–712.

Linköping University (2014), 'Industrial symbiosis in Sweden', accessed 20 March 2015 at http://www.industriellekologi.se/symbiosis/.

Lombardi, R.D., D. Lyons, H. Shi and A. Agarwal (2012), 'Industrial symbiosis: testing the boundaries and advancing knowledge', *Journal of Industrial Ecology*, **16**, 2–7.

Lopes, M. (2013), 'Industrial symbiosis potential of the Sines Oil Refinery – environmental and economic evaluation', Dissertation for MSc degree in Environmental Engineering, Lisbon: New University of Lisbon, accessed 20 March 2015 at http://run.unl.pt/bitstream/10362/11189/1/Lopes_2013.pdf.

Lyons, D.I. (2007), 'A spatial analysis of loop closing among recycling, remanufacturing and waste treatment firms in Texas', *Journal of Industrial Ecology*, **11**, 43–54.

Massard, G. and S. Erkman (2007), 'A regional industrial symbiosis methodology and its implementation in Geneva, Switzerland', Paper presented at the 3rd International Conference on Life Cycle Management, Irchel, University of Zurich, 27–29 August 2007, accessed 24 February 2015 at http://www.lcm2007.org/paper/51_2.pdf.

Massard G., O. Jacquat and D. Zürcher (2014), 'International survey on eco-innovation parks. Learning from experiences on the spatial dimension of eco-innovation', Federal Office for the Environment and the ERANET ECO-INNOVERA, Bern, *Environmental Studies*, **1402**.

Martin, M. and M. Eklund (2011), 'Improving the environmental performance of biofuels with industrial symbiosis', *Biomass and Bioenergy*, **35**, 1747–1755.

Mirata, M. (2004), 'Experiences from early stages of a national industrial symbiosis programme in the UK', *Journal of Cleaner Production*, **12**, 967–983.

Mirata, M. and T. Emtairah (2005), 'Industrial symbiosis networks and the contribution to environmental innovation: the case of the Landskrona industrial symbiosis programme', *Journal of Cleaner Production*, **13**, 993–1002.

Paquin, R.L. and J. Howard-Grenville (2012), 'The evolution of facilitated industrial symbiosis', *Journal of Industrial Ecology*, **16**, 83–93.

Pellenbarg, P.H. (2002), 'Sustainable business sites in the Netherlands: a survey of policies and experiences', *Journal of Environmental Planning and Management*, **45**, 59–84.

Penn, A.S., P.D. Jensen, A. Woodward, L. Basson, F. Schiller and A. Druckman (2014), 'Sketching a network portrait of the Humber Region', *Complexity*, **19**, 54–72.

Puig, R., A. Rius, E. Marti, M. Solé, J. Riba and P. Fullana (2008), 'Industrial ecology in the Catalan paper industry', *Afinidad*, **65**, 262–268.

Ruiz Puente, M.C. (2014), 'Planning for urban growth and sustainable industrial development', in K.M. Reynolds, P.F. Hessburg and P.S. Bourgeron (eds), *Making Transparent Environmental Management Decisions*, Berlin: Springer-Verlag Berlin Heidelberg, 253–276.

Ruiz Puente, M.C., E. Romero Arozamena and S. Evans (2015), 'Industrial symbiosis opportunities for small and medium sized enterprises: preliminary study in the Besaya region (Cantabria, Northern Spain)', *Journal of Cleaner Production*, **87**, 357–374.

Schön, M.F., H. Delahaye, C. Hiessl, U. Kotz, A. Kuntze, P. Matuschewski, P. Schunke and P. Zoche (2003), *CuRa: Cooperationen für umweltschonenden Ressourcenaustausch zur Nutzung von Kostenreduktionspotenzialen*, Endbericht, Karlsruhe: Fraunhofer Institut für Systemtechnik und Innovationsforschung (ISI), [online], accessed 26 February 2015 at http://www.isi.fraunhofer.de/isi-w Assets/docs/n/de/publikationen/cura-ges.pdf.

Spekkink, W. (2013), 'Institutional capacity building for industrial symbiosis in the Canal Zone of Zeeland in the Netherlands: a process analysis', *Journal of Cleaner Production*, **52**, 342–355.

Stinchcombe, A.L. (1968), *Constructing Social Theories*, Chicago and London: University of Chicago Press.

Toulmin, S. (1972), *Human Understanding: The Collective Use and Evolution of Concepts*, Princeton: Princeton University Press.

Van Beers, D., G. Corder, A. Bossilkov and R. van Berkel (2007), 'Industrial symbiosis in the Australian minerals industry: the cases of Kwinana and Gladstone', *Journal of Industrial Ecology*, **11**, 55–72.

Veiga, L.B.E. and A. Magrini (2009), 'Eco-industrial park development in Rio de Janeiro, Brazil: a tool for sustainable development', *Journal of Cleaner Production*, **17**, 653–661.

Verguts, V., J. Dessein, A. Dewulf, L. Lauwers, R. Werkman and C.J.A.M. Termeer (in press), 'Industrial symbiosis as sustainable development strategy: adding a change perspective', *International Journal Sustainable Development*.

Wang, Q., P. Deutz and D. Gibbs (2015), 'UK-China collaboration for industrial symbiosis: a multi-level approach to policy transfer analysis', in P. Deutz, D. Lyons and J. Bi (eds), *International Perspectives on Industrial Ecology*, Cheltenham, UK and Northampton, MA, USA: Edward Elgar, pp. 89–107.

Wolf, A. and K. Petersson (2007), 'Industrial symbiosis in the Swedish forestry industry', *Progress in Industrial Ecology*, **4**, 348–362.

6. UK–China collaboration for industrial symbiosis: a multi-level approach to policy transfer analysis

Qiaozhi Wang, Pauline Deutz and David Gibbs

INTRODUCTION

Over the last two decades there has been substantial research on both the potential and promotion of industrial symbiosis (IS) as a means to improve the efficiency of resource use. IS comprises the use of under-utilised resources (including by-products, waste and energy streams) as a means of promoting sustainable industrial development (Deutz, 2014). Attracted by IS exemplars such as the network at Kalundborg in Denmark and the UK's IS facilitation programme, policymakers in numerous countries have attempted to initiate IS activities in a wide range of different economic, social and policy contexts (Lombardi et al., 2012).

Whilst the study of IS as a policy initiative is not new (see for example Gibbs and Deutz, 2005; Costa et al., 2010; Laybourn and Lombardi, 2012), this area of research has taken on a new momentum (see Jiao and Boons [2014] for a review). Existing work points to the significance of waste regulations that are at least 'enabling' of IS (in the European context: Costa et al., 2010; Salmi et al., 2012). In the Asian context, national government commitment to IS is part of a wide range of environmental initiatives (Mathews, 2012). Other research examines the potential of IS development in a given institutional context (Simboli et al., 2014 in Italy) or evaluates the environmental benefits of IS (Dong et al., 2013). These are rich and detailed case studies, in some cases incorporating international comparison (e.g., Costa et al., 2010), or employing case studies from multiple countries (Dong et al., 2013). However, the literature is often missing a critical analysis of policy (Jiao and Boons, 2014) and an explicit attention to the potential for application of findings across geographic contexts. This is particularly important as attention extends to developing countries (e.g. Ashton and Bains, 2012; Alfaro and Miller, 2013).

Policy efforts to emulate the implementation of IS are frequently rooted in the assumption that it is possible to apply initiatives outside the context in which they have been successful. The IS literature has not interrogated that assumption and could therefore usefully draw on lessons from the policy transfer (PT) literature. PT refers to the attempt to use knowledge about policies, administrative arrangements and institutions from one place in the development of policies, administrative arrangements and/ or institutions elsewhere (Evans, 2009; Stone, 2012). Whilst learning from the experience of others is a time-honoured approach to policymaking, extracting applicable lessons involves disentangling key policy elements from a likely complex array of cultural, institutional, political and economic factors deeply embedded in their geographic setting (Evans, 2004; Swainson and de Loe, 2011). Despite, or because of, this, analysis of actual and planned attempts at PT can provide both academic understanding and useful insight for policymakers (Evans, 2009).

This chapter draws on ideas from the PT literature to present an analytical approach to a case study of IS collaboration. Analysis considers both spatial influences (e.g., the impact of multiple geographic scales of governance) and temporal influences (e.g., the unfolding process of policy development and implementation). The case study concerns an international collaboration that is attempting to transfer a particular form of IS facilitation from the UK to China. In order to study this collaborative arrangement, policy and regulatory documents affecting IS development in the UK and China were collected through online searches and the policy transfer initiative was then investigated through in-depth interviews with both UK and Chinese partners involved in the collaboration. Interviews focused on the exploration of factors affecting the implementation of IS programmes in the UK and China. In addition, the first author spent a one-month internship assisting with the inauguration of the collaborative venture and spent three months with International Synergies Ltd (ISL) (see Wang, 2013 for details). This ethnographic approach provided additional insights beyond those gained through interviews and documentary analysis.

POLICIES AND POLICY TRANSFER

A policy is the purposeful course of action of a governmental body, covering interrelated set of goals and decisions in response to a problem (UNEP, 2007). It commonly involves instruments such as regulations, economic incentives (e.g., levies and financial support) and informational tools (e.g., guidance) to accomplish particular policy goals (UNEP, 2007; Costa et al., 2010). The present era of global flows of finance, resources, products, people and information has seen a proliferation of policy exchange at all scales of governance (e.g., Stone, 2012) and across highly diverse policy areas (Evans, 2004) including environmental regulation (e.g., water management) (Swainson and de Loe, 2011) and promotion of green jobs (Ladi, 2004). This flourishing of PT has happened in geo-political contexts including the Europeanisation of EU accession countries, imposed modernisation schemes in developing countries and also developing countries initiating learning from elsewhere (e.g., Evans, 2009; Dolowitz and Marsh, 2012).

The search for a ready-made solution, or a partial solution, can be viewed by politicians as a cost-effective answer to a policy problem (Marsden and Stead, 2011). The underlying assumption is that a policy successful in one place can also be successful in another. PT researchers, however, have cautioned that the suitability of a policy for transfer between contexts needs to be considered before the initiation of the transfer (Dolowitz and Marsh, 2000; Swainson and de Loe, 2011). Contextual factors include variations in political, cultural and historical elements between locations. For example, the attempt to transfer a Danish programme for the creation of green jobs to Piraeus in Greece stalled both because of the lack of a relevant regional/ local scale body to lead the implementation and a lack of tradition of SME networking, on which the Danish programme was built (Ladi, 2004). Perhaps most notably, though, the Danish assumption that SMEs could be assisted to exploit a market for green goods and services did not hold in Greece. Despite having comparable (EU) environmental regulations as Denmark, these are not as well ingrained in practice or attitude in Greece as in Denmark (Ladi, 2004). Consequently, the Danish need, or opportunity, for an organisation to train companies for a green market did not exist in Greece.

Given such constraints, policies are seldom successfully transferred in their original form, but rather 'translated' to the receiving context (Stone, 2012). They may be directly copied, adapted, combined with other elements or simply serve as inspiration for a substantially different approach to a similar goal (Rose, 2005; Evans, 2009). Critical to policy transfer is understanding the problem being tackled and assessing the suitability of a proposed policy to tackle it. To help judge suitability, Rose (2005) advocates the development of a model abstracting generic elements (e.g., relevant regulations, organisations, skills, finance) necessary for success. This process of abstraction needs to identify the elements critical to the success of the policy in its original setting (Luo et al., 2009). Questions have been posed as to the extent to which policymakers are operating in this idealised setting of bounded rationality under which systematic searches are made for optimal solutions to well constrained policy problems. More likely, options are constrained by the time and budget available, and policymakers themselves are guided by political economic constraints and agendas (e.g., pervasive belief in recent decades in neoliberalism, which can result in certain policy options appearing inevitable, whilst others are not acknowledged) (Peck, 2011).

Notwithstanding such constraints, there are policymakers with discretion in decision making who are undertaking what Evans (2009: 244) refers to as 'action-oriented intentional learning'. Policymakers, having identified a problem, initially search for potential solutions and sources of advice, based on which a policy transfer network may be formed. The second stage involves the exploration of potential actions and setting of the policy agenda. The third stage is the operational delivery and evaluation, which informs further policy evolution in a process of ongoing learning. Whilst this process is unfolding in time, there are spatial scalar constraints on the policy transfer network. The actions (and judgements) of the network are constrained by national regulatory and institutional factors, and international circumstances, though these are not well defined.

Although clearly a simplification of the multi-scalar process of governance within which environmental policies are formulated and implemented, the combined elements of a temporal decision making process within geographic constraints provides a useful framework for the analysis of IS projects. Authors have commented on the significance of national level policies (Costa et al., 2010) and/or the economic-geographic limitations on policy-driven IS projects (Deutz and Gibbs, 2008). To what extent are decision makers taking these factors into account in their problem definition? IS is fundamentally a problem of resource efficiency, and the properties of materials and energy are independent of political economic context. The technically viable options for recovery of a residue stream are also similar wherever that stream may be generated. Viable options, however, depend on potential recipients, technology and expertise available to identify and implement exchanges. Whilst some of these issues have been analysed in specific settings, there tends to be an implicit assumption that the lesson from one setting transfers to another. In this chapter we explicitly explore this assumption.

A CASE STUDY OF POLICY TRANSFER FOR INDUSTRIAL SYMBIOSIS

In this chapter we examine the collaborative arrangements between the UK's National Industrial Symbiosis Programme (NISP), operated by ISL, and the Tianjin Economic-Technological Development Area (TEDA) Administrative Commission in China to replicate NISP's approach to IS in the TEDA area (Table 6.1).

Table 6.1 *Policy transfer network for the ISL–TEDA collaboration*

Partners	Tianjin Economic-Technological Development Area (TEDA), China	International Synergies Ltd (operators of NISP), UK
Motivation	• Saw IS as tool for resource efficiency *Problem* • Lacked expertise in identifying potential for materials recovery • Lacked networking expertise, i.e., to identify and bring together potential partners	• Opportunity for international collaboration *Expertise* • Track record of material recovery by facilitating symbiotic relationships between companies
Implementation bodies	TEDA Eco-Centre	ISL
Funding	EU Switch-Asia Programme	
Object of transfer	NISP's method of facilitating industrial symbiosis	

Policy Problem and Policy Transfer Network

Founded in December 1984, TEDA is one of the first 14 national economic development zones in China (TEDA, 2011). For TEDA, the policy problem was to aid the development of a Circular Economy (CE) by recovering value from unwanted substances via the construction of resource synergies between companies. Problems with implementing IS in TEDA were identified as a lack of effective pre-existing networks for SMEs, through which potential synergies for efficient resource management could be identified, and insufficient expertise to support the implementation of potential synergies (TEDA AC, 2009). According to one interviewee from TEDA, local Chinese policymakers saw a potential solution to these problems through the adoption of NISP's third-party facilitator approach, which they were aware of through previous collaborative efforts elsewhere in China.

ISL's NISP was established in the mid-2000s as the first national programme specifically aiming to facilitate symbiotic links between companies; NISP utilised a particular set of practices devised by its predecessor regional bodies (Mirata and Emtairah, 2005). Until 2012, NISP was a UK government funded programme working on collecting information on excess or required resources from businesses through networking events, identifying resource exchange opportunities and facilitating the implementation of the IS concept free of charge. NISP compiled a database of 12 500 companies and diverted 7 million tonnes plus of waste from landfill (Laybourn and Morrissey, 2009). The waste diversion and financial achievements of NISP have attracted considerable international attention from academics (Chertow and Ehrenfeld, 2012; Paquin and Howard-Grenville, 2012) and policymakers. ISL is involved in collaborative efforts to promote its approach in Romania, Hungary, Turkey, Mexico and South Africa, in addition to the current and other attempts to transfer the practices to China.

TEDA entered into collaboration with ISL to access advice on how to establish the technical support required for the identification of residues with the potential for value recovery, and to identify and introduce potential synergy partners. Funding from the EU SWITCH-Asia programme[1] was accessed in 2010. The collaborative programme with ISL is seen as a step towards introducing the facilitation approach nationwide in China (TEDA Eco-centre, 2012).

Operational Delivery

Thus there appeared to be an excellent match between the problem that the TEDA local authority needed to solve and the expertise that ISL offered.

Instead of implementing the IS programme by its own staff, the TEDA local government established an eco-centre in March 2010 and the learning process proceeded with ISL sending a team of consultants to explain and demonstrate their operating policies to the eco-centre staff in 2010. In brief, the NISP approach to facilitating IS involves the collection of information from companies on both the residues they have for disposal and the materials they require as inputs. In the UK, a national database alongside the regional knowledge and materials expertise of delivery partners enables the identification of companies with potentially matching 'haves' and 'wants' (Laybourn and Morrissey, 2009). To overcome initial limitations in the size of the database, companies were invited to 'Quick-win' workshops at which NISP practitioners endeavoured with some success to identify potential matches.

However, when this same practice was replicated at TEDA, the level of interest of companies was much less than it had been in the UK; advertised workshops were cancelled due to insufficient participants. The slow level of company engagement left the ISL staff limited opportunities to apply their materials knowledge. To understand both why the collaboration was less immediately successful than expected and the positive lessons that can nonetheless be learned, it is necessary to examine the multi-level context of this PT.

MULTI-LEVEL ANALYSIS OF POLICY TRANSFER

The main features of the PT collaboration across different levels of analysis are shown in Figure 6.1. It is the supranational to global scale structures and processes (Level 1 in Figure 6.1) that enable this UK–China collaboration to take place. The context includes the industrialisation and opening up of China, which has brought a willingness to consider external solutions, alongside the appreciation of environmental problems (Liu et al., Chapter 10, this volume). Likewise the operation of NISP by a non-governmental body is part of the process of a growing withdrawal of the state in the UK from service delivery. ISL has been able to take part in this type of international policy transfer activity, even though it is outside the remit of NISP. The EU funding for the project comes from a programme which itself rests on the assumption of the validity of transferring environmental practice across continents.

As discussed, the policy problem perceived by TEDA eco-centre (Level 4) is a good match for the skills and experience offered by ISL. The TEDA eco-centre appears to offer an appropriate body for implementing a NISP-like approach, having local knowledge of industry, and a specific resource

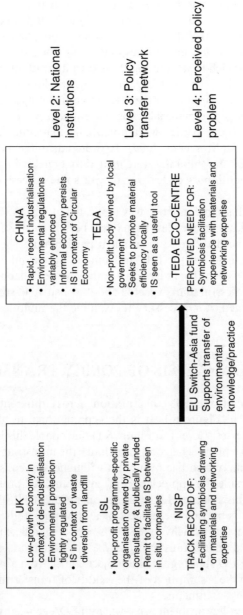

Level 1: Global, International and Transnational Structures

UK
- Low-growth economy in context of de-industrialisation
- Environmental protection tightly regulated
- IS in context of waste diversion from landfill

ISL
- Non-profit programme-specific organisation owned by private consultancy & publically funded
- Remit to facilitate IS between in situ companies

NISP
TRACK RECORD OF:
- Facilitating symbiosis drawing on materials and networking expertise

EU Switch-Asia fund Supports transfer of environmental knowledge/practice

CHINA
- Rapid, recent industrialisation
- Environmental regulations variably enforced
- Informal economy persists
- IS in context of Circular Economy

TEDA
- Non-profit body owned by local government
- Seeks to promote material efficiency locally
- IS seen as a useful tool

TEDA ECO-CENTRE
PERCEIVED NEED FOR:
- Symbiosis facilitation experience with materials and networking expertise

Level 2: National institutions

Level 3: Policy transfer network

Level 4: Perceived policy problem

Scientific, technical issues: 'constant in space'

International industrial symbiosis networks

Figure 6.1   ISL–TEDA collaboration analysed as an exercise in multi-level policy transfer

efficiency remit. The apparent deficiencies in the eco-centre to deliver such a programme were precisely the areas with which ISL was engaged to help (Level 3). Arguably, therefore, to some extent the success of the initiative would stand on the abilities of the individuals involved to respectively teach and learn the required skills. However, potentially TEDA's analysis of its policy problem was coloured by previous knowledge of ISL, rather than a detailed appreciation of their respective national policy contexts (Level 2). In the following section we outline how these different policy contexts influence the policy transfer process and its relative success and failure.

IS IN UK NATIONAL POLICY CONTEXT

At the national level, the UK's waste policy is issued by Defra periodically through the waste strategy documents. The domestic waste strategy is constrained by EU requirements such as the Waste Framework Directive (2008), which stipulates the prioritisation of waste prevention and the Landfill Directive (1999) which set targets for the diversion of biodegradable waste from landfill. Within the UK, IS has been shaped by the waste policy targeting resource efficiency and landfill diversion for moving towards a Zero Waste Economy (ZWE). The ZWE has been proposed as the government's overarching goal for waste management, and is described as a longer-term vision to shift the current throwaway society towards waste prevention, reuse, recycling and recovery, where disposal is the last resort (Defra, 2011). A twofold strategy has been adopted (Table 6.2) to improve resource efficiency, comprising disincentives to landfill and support for IS.

Disincentives to Landfill

Key to disincentivising landfill, the UK landfill tax has increased annually since its introduction in 1996 (Seely, 2009). Landfill site operators pay the landfill tax for every tonnage of waste that is landfilled. However, the tax is passed to businesses and local councils on top of their normal landfill fees. In addition, value added tax (VAT) is charged on the landfill fees and the landfill tax. Although the tax does not encourage any specific alternative to landfill, it has reached a level (GBP£80/tonne in 2014: HMRC, 2014) where alternative technologies become financially viable (MT Waste Management, 2011). This tax has been an important incentive to implement IS in the UK (Costa et al., 2010). Indeed one representative from NISP commented that many environmental observers in the UK would

Table 6.2   The comparison of industrial symbiosis-related policy assemblages in England and China

Approach to IS	England	China
Regulations incentivising alternatives to landfill	Producer responsibility regulations (WEEE, packaging, waste batteries and vehicles)	The Circular Economy Promotion Law
Regulations restricting use of landfill	Landfill bans (e.g., tyres)	NA
Economic instruments disincentivising landfill	Landfill tax and escalator	NA
Provision of information relevant to IS	Quality protocols	Catalogue of promoted Circular Economy technology, technique and equipment (Promotion Catalogue). List of Technically Innovative Pilot Circular Economy projects
Directly promoting and/or subsidising IS	Resource efficiency facilitation programmes (e.g., WRAP, NISP)	Subsidies for corporate income tax and value-added tax for specified activities on resource comprehensive re-utilisation. Funding pilot projects (e.g., individual energy/water conservation, eco-industrial parks/agricultural industrial park development, waste disposal, utilising large solid waste streams) (NDRC, 2011c)
Disincentives to IS	Duty of care; waste handling regulations	Lack of enforcement

point to the creation of the landfill tax 'as the most important piece of environmental legislation in recent UK history'. In addition, the UK has landfill bans on specific substances, including used whole and shredded tyres since 2006. Types of waste banned from landfill are increasing as the government has examined the feasibility to restrict landfilling biodegradable wastes and recycled materials (Defra, 2007). This type of coercion can potentially drive businesses to find alternative options, such as engaging in IS activities, for waste management.

Support for IS

Critically, alongside the landfill tax, support and advice has been provided directly to assist business resource efficiency activities and programmes, some delivered by non-governmental organisations (Seeley, 2009). The Waste Resource and Action Programme (WRAP) was launched in 2000 to support recycling by developing markets for recycled materials (WRAP, 2015). Funded through WRAP, NISP had a complementary role of promoting cross-industry resource efficiency, i.e., IS (Defra, 2009) via its facilitation strategy outlined above. Given the financial incentive of the landfill tax for companies to consider alternatives to disposal, NISP could recruit members via a business case, rather than an environmental one. Once the reputation of NISP had spread, the number of companies that could be assisted was constrained by the level of funding, not any difficulty in recruitment.

Additional regulatory factors supportive of NISP's approach to IS (Table 6.2) include the liability ('duty of care', Gov.UK [2015]) that companies have for their residues even when passed on, whether for disposal or recovery. Use of facilitators such as NISP provides some assurance that the recipient company is legitimate. Finally, there are quality protocols (Environment Agency, 2014) available for an increasing range of materials which provide guidance standards for recovered materials being used as inputs. Thus, although the impact of NISP should not be overstated, it appears to operate in a well-defined policy niche. NISP is part of a package of measures designed to improve resource recovery (e.g., by research into materials recycling, or providing advice to companies on alternatives to landfill). Critically, there is a corresponding array of measures disincentivising, even banning, the use of landfill. The various schemes and regulations are both part of the context of NISP and provide the tools on which the organisation can draw to achieve its waste diversion and other targets.

TEDA IN CHINESE NATIONAL POLICY CONTEXT

In China, IS has been shaped by national resource policies targeting resource efficiency. The government has promoted development models such as resource comprehensive reutilisation (RCR)[2] and the CE.[3] The Chinese national resource strategy is formulated in the national government's policy documents by the State Council and its subordinate department commanding national economic development, the National Development and Reform Commission (NDRC). The strategy is presented in *The Guidance on Resource Comprehensive Re-utilisation for the 11th Five-year Plan* (NDRC, 2006a) and stresses the need to utilise valuable by-products through developing a number of pilot projects.[4] The latest resource strategy (NDRC, 2011a) confirmed the improvement in the RCR, regulatory and stimulus policies, and pointed out problems such as insufficient large enterprises engaging with resource utilisation and insufficient advanced technologies to support resource utilisation.

The CE Promotion Law issued in 2008 was developed based on the central government's two decades of experience of promoting resource utilisation, and was believed to be the first law in the world to legislate for a CE as a national strategy (Mathews and Tan, 2011). The law introduces a range of resource conserving and utilising activities which are encouraged by the central government. It assigns multiple government departments' responsibilities to plan, supervise and assess national CE development through setting up national targets and building indicator systems to quantify the effectiveness of the CE development.

Promotion of IS

As part of the above regulations, the Chinese government provided funds for a range of technical, innovative individual RCR activities, developing the infrastructure for waste treatment and projects utilising large solid waste streams (NDRC, 2011b). The Promotion Catalogue (Table 6.2) lists a number of RCR technologies, techniques and equipment that can receive preferential tax policies (NDRC, 2006b) and thus incentivise capable enterprises to engage in IS. In addition, the List of Technically Innovative Pilot CE projects aims to compile good technical practices working on building production chains for resource utilisation in heavy industrial networks and in industrial parks (MIIT, 2011). The first list was issued in 2012 covering 23 pilot CE projects (MIIT, 2012). The Catalogue can potentially guide inter-business IS activities. However, policies favouring large-scale operations and technological developments in promoting RCR potentially overlook the group of small businesses lacking the financial capacity to introduce these practices. Whilst these promoted RCR initiatives could support IS, that is not a primary intention and is almost incidental.

Disincentives to Landfill

There are few disincentives to landfill in China. In the absence of a landfill tax, landfill is by far the cheapest waste disposal option. The average landfill cost is around the equivalent of GBP£4 per tonne (Zhang et al., 2012). According to Wang and Zhang (2010), due to the limited level of RCR capacities, large quantities of industrial solid waste in China are directly transported to municipal solid waste landfill sites and have caused secondary pollution. Although the Restriction Catalogue is issued periodically to ban outdated techniques and equipment in several industries (MIIT, 2010, 2013), there are no bans on specific products in landfill. Instead of setting up targets for diverting waste from landfill, attention is paid to the broader target of preventing pollution as mentioned in the national Law on Prevention and Control of Environmental Pollution by Solid Waste (2004).

In addition, during the collaboration exercise, NISP officials found that there was an active informal waste disposal sector:

> They [scavengers in TEDA] don't have a permit to take waste. So, they'll take electronic waste and they'll charge less than the company who takes electronic waste legally. So, they take out the expensive bits, and then throw the other away but they aren't allowed to, but the proper company will have to dispose the waste that has no use, and they have to do something to it before it gets to landfill. For other companies, they just throw it away. So, they can be cheaper than the companies who are legitimate. (Interviewee 16 from NISP)

These informal operators continue to practice despite the existence of waste management guidelines requiring a permit and certain procedures.

When the eco-centre's policy context is considered, the mismatch with the NISP facilitation model becomes apparent. Unlike in the UK, the disposal of unwanted substances does not constitute a problem for companies in China. Formal disposal is extremely cheap, and informal recovery options are readily available, despite regulations prohibiting them. Lack of strict implementation of waste regulations is part of the context of informal IS and potentially inhibits the process of implementing the NISP approach in TEDA. However, a significant, but likely unmeasurable, amount of IS is happening at TEDA. The problem therefore is not the lack of know-how in bringing companies together, rather the lack of incentives for companies to engage in formal waste recovery operations.

CONCLUSIONS

This chapter has analysed a collaborative attempt to transfer a UK-derived approach to IS facilitation to China drawing on concepts applied in the policy transfer literature. The analysis framework has both a scalar element (level of governance) and temporal element (stage of the PT process). We have argued that the TEDA administrative committee defined its policy problem based on the local scale situation, but then sought to transfer a solution from another national context. The facilitation approach the administrative committee tried to adopt was found to be a poor match in terms of the national institutions governing industrial waste management. The choice of solution, and potentially the definition of the problem, were influenced by prior experience, i.e., knowledge of an IS-facilitation scheme successful in its own national context. This could be an example of an attempted 'quick fix' resulting from the global scale networking and the commercialisation of policy transfer (Prince, 2010; Peck, 2011). However, the situation includes all the elements of formal policy transfer process (Evans, 2009). Policymakers unsurprisingly are influenced by global-level pressures whilst attempting to solve local-scale problems within national policy constraints. This does not preclude the learning of valuable lessons from this case study.

In particular, the case study underscores the importance of the national-scale context in supporting local-scale implementation of IS (e.g., Mathews, 2012). The UK, unlike China, appears to have a useful balance of disincentives to landfill alongside advice and support for IS practices. The need for an economic case for participating in IS is shown to be important, but equally critical is the enforcement of waste management regulations. Even if a landfill tax is introduced in China, without comparable levels of enforcement it could have very different outcomes than in the UK.

Clearly, therefore, both the policy problem and potential solutions need to be considered in a multi-level context. There are often constraints beyond the scope of policymakers to directly shape policy (Dolowitz and Marsh, 2012), as the TEDA eco-centre found. Policymakers (and other IS practitioners) should appraise international options in the light of local- and national-level constraints. Avoiding 're-inventing the wheel' in a policy situation (Marsden and Stead, 2011: 493) is only helpful if your vehicle matches the wheel on offer. Significantly, as in this case, an apparently technical problem (materials knowledge and networking skills) could not be solved by a purely technical solution (collaborating with an organisation rich in relevant experience). Thus even apparently non-spatial knowledge is rooted in a geographic context. Moreover, analysis of policies on paper may not be sufficient; a key lesson for organisations exporting a policy is that standards of implementation and enforcement may differ from expectations. Furthermore, although the collaboration did not bear immediate fruit, it is possible that the light cast on Chinese national policies by this collaboration might have been lent an authority by the technical credibility of the international input. Ideally, the policy learning process from this experience would happen at both the local and national scale in China, and also inform ISL.

Finally, implications can be drawn for the study of IS. The implicit assumption that lessons on IS derived in a given location can be applied elsewhere did not withstand explicit examination. This is not to say that a third-party facilitation approach to IS could only work in a UK-style policy context. Rather, that the approach and expectations need to match the given context. Geographic context is important and should not be overlooked even in studies where the social/policy context is not the primary concern. Analysis of that context should include multi-level dimensions and analysis of policy as part of a dynamic learning process. Further research is needed to apply and interrogate this framework at different scales of policy formation/transfer and in different geographic contexts.

ACKNOWLEDGEMENTS

We thank Paul Jensen and Zengwei Yuan for comments; any errors are ours. The research was funded by the China Scholarship Council and the University of Hull with additional support from the UK Natural Environment Research Council (with the Economic and Social Research Council and Defra: NE/I019468/1).

NOTES

1. The SWITCH-Asia programme involved the EU providing funding to projects focusing on promoting sustainable consumption and production across the Asia region (SWITCH-Asia, 2012).
2. In the concept of RCR, resource refers to mineral by-products, waste residues (water or gases) and various waste or outdated products. Comprehensive reutilisation means recycling, regenerating and reusing activities (The Former State Economic and Trade Commission, 1996).
3. CE development mainly refers to the promotion of resource conservation, cleaner production, RCR and environmental protection industries (State Council, 2005).
4. Pilot projects supposed to be developed have covered developing systems to recycling discarded household appliances, scrap tyres, plastic wastes, etc. (NDRC, 2006a).

REFERENCES

Alfaro, J. and S. Miller (2013), 'Applying industrial symbiosis to smallholder farms: modelling a case study in Liberia, West Africa', *Journal of Industrial Ecology*, **18**, 145–154.

Ashton, W.S. and A.C. Bains (2012), 'Assessing the "short mental distance" in eco-industrial networks', *Journal of Industrial Ecology*, **16**, 70–82.

Chertow, M. and J. Ehrenfeld (2012), 'Organizing self-organizing systems', *Journal of Industrial Ecology*, **16**, 13–27.

Costa, I., G. Massard and A. Agarwal (2010), 'Waste management policies for industrial symbiosis development: case studies in European countries', *Journal of Cleaner Production*, **18**, 815–822.

Defra (2007), *Waste Strategy for England 2007*, London: Defra.

Defra (2009), *Resource Efficiency Delivery Landscape Review*, London: Defra.

Defra (2011), *Government Review of Waste Policy in England 2011*, London: Defra.

Deutz, P. (2014), 'Food for thought: seeking the essence of industrial symbiosis', in R. Salomone and G. Saija (eds), *Pathways to Environmental Sustainability: Methodologies and Experiences*, Switzerland: Springer, pp. 3–11.

Deutz, P. and D. Gibbs (2008), 'Industrial ecology and regional development: eco-industrial development as cluster policy', *Regional Studies*, **42**, 1313–1328.

Dolowitz, D.P. and D. Marsh (2000), 'Learning from abroad: the role of policy transfer in contemporary policy-making', *Governance*, **13**, 5–23.

Dolowitz, D.P. and D. Marsh (2012), 'The future of policy transfer research', *Political Studies Review*, **10**, 339–345.

Dong L., H. Zhang, T. Fujita, S. Ohnishi, L. Huiquan, M. Fujii and H. Dong (2013), 'Environmental and economic gains of industrial symbiosis for Chinese iron/steel industry: Kawasaski's experience and practice in Liuzhou and Jinan', *Journal of Cleaner Production*, **59**, 226–238.

Environment Agency (2014), *Environmental Management – Guidance*, accessed 20 February 2015 at https://www.gov.uk/turn-your-waste-into-a-new-non-waste-product-or-material.

Evans, M. (2004), *Policy Transfer in Global Perspective*, Aldershot, UK: Ashgate.

Evans, M. (2009), 'Policy transfer in critical perspective', *Policy Studies*, **30**, 243–268.

Gibbs, D. and P. Deutz (2005), 'Implementing industrial ecology? Planning for eco-industrial parks in the USA', *Geoforum*, **36**, 452–464.

Gov.UK (2015), *Business and Commercial Waste: Duty of Care*, accessed 22 February 2015 at https://www.gov.uk/managing-your-waste-an-overview/duty-of-care.

HMRC (2014), *Rates and Allowances: Landfill Tax*, accessed 20 February 2015 at https://www.gov.uk/government/publications/rates-and-allowances-landfill-tax/rates-and-allowances-landfill-tax.

Jiao, W. and F. Boons (2014), 'Toward a research agenda for policy intervention and facilitation to enhance industrial symbiosis based on a comprehensive literature review', *Journal of Cleaner Production*, **67**, 14–25.

Ladi, S. (2004), 'Environmental policy transfer in German and Greece', in M. Evans (ed.), *Policy Transfer in Global Perspective*, Aldershot, UK: Ashgate.

Laybourn, P. and D.R. Lombardi (2012), 'Industrial symbiosis in European policy', *Journal of Industrial Ecology*, **16**, 11–12.

Laybourn, P. and M. Morrissey (2009), *The Pathway to a Low Carbon Sustainable Economy*, International Synergies Ltd, Birmingham, UK.

Liu, L., B. Zhang and J. Bi (2015), 'Institutional context of eco-industrial parks development in China: environmental governance in industrial parks and zones', in P. Deutz, D. Lyons and J. Bi (eds), *International Perspectives on Industrial Ecology*, Cheltenham, UK and Northampton, MA, USA: Edward Elgar, pp. 157–174.

Lombardi, D.R., D. Lyons, H. Shi and A. Agarwal (2012), 'Industrial symbiosis', *Journal of Industrial Ecology*, **16**, 2–7.

Luo, Q., P. Catney and D. Lerner (2009), 'Risk-based management of contaminated land in the UK: lessons for China?', *Journal of Environmental Management*, **90**, 1123–34.

Marsden, G. and D. Stead (2011), 'Policy transfer and learning in the field of transport: a review of concepts and evidence', *Transport Policy*, **18**, 492–500.

Mathews, J.A. (2012), 'Green growth strategies – Korean initiatives', *Futures*, **44**, 761–769.

Mathews, J.A. and H. Tan, (2011), 'Progress toward a circular economy in China', *Journal of Industrial Ecology*, **15**, 435–457.

MIIT (2010), *Catalogue of Eliminating Outdated Techniques, Equipment, and Products in Several Industries* (in Chinese), accessed 2 June 2014 at http://www.gov.cn/zwgk/2010-12/06/content_1760311.htm.

MIIT (2011), *Notice about Organising and Recommending Technically Innovative Pilot Circular Economy Projects* (in Chinese), accessed 22 February 2015 at http://www.miit.gov.cn/n11293472/n11295091/n11299329/13569639.html.

MIIT (2012), *The 1st Batch of Technically Innovative Pilot Circular Economy Projects*, accessed 22 February 2015 at http://www.miit.gov.cn/n11293472/n11293832/n12843926/n13917012/n14541528.files/n14541231.pdf.

MIIT (2013), *The List of Enterprises in 19 Industries with Outdated Techniques in 2013*, accessed 22 February 2015 at http://www.gov.cn/zwgk/2013-07/26/content_2455751.htm.

Mirata, M. and T. Emtairah (2005), 'Industrial symbiosis networks and the contribution to environmental innovation', *Journal of Cleaner Production*, **13**, 993–1002.

MT Waste Management (2011), *New Landfill Tax Makes Energy from Waste More Attractive*, accessed 2 June 2014 at http://www.mtwaste.co.uk/news-and-information/new_landfill_tax_makes_energy_from_waste_more_attractive/.

NDRC (2006a), *The Guidance on Resource Comprehensive Re-utilisation for the 11th Five-year Plan* (in Chinese), accessed 22 February 2015 at http://www.sdpc.gov.cn/fzgggz/fzgh/ghwb/115zxgh/200709/P020071010364235664907.pdf.

NDRC (2006b), *The Administrative Measures for the Determination of the Resource Comprehensive Re-utilisation Encouraged by the State* (in Chinese), accessed 22 February 2015 at http://www.gov.cn/zwgk/2006-09/13/content_387619.htm.

NDRC (2011a), *The Guidance on Resource Comprehensive Re-utilisation for the 12th Five-year Plans* (in Chinese), accessed 20 February 2015 at http://zfs.mep.gov.cn/gz/bmhb/gwygf/201112/W020111230555251585919.pdf.

NDRC (2011b), *Notice about the Organisation of Applying for 2012 Central Budget Supported Resource Conservation and Environmental Protection Projects* (in Chinese), accessed 2 July 2014 at http://www.sdpc.gov.cn/zcfb/zcfbtz/2011tz/t20111229_453571.htm.

NDRC (2011c), *Notice about the Organisation of Applying for 2012 Central Budget*

Supported Resource Conservation and Environmental Protection Projects (in Chinese), accessed 28 May 2015 at http://www.tjdpc.gov.cn/dtzx/tzgg/201308/t20130804_34202.shtml.

Paquin, R.L. and J. Howard-Grenville (2012), 'The evolution of facilitated industrial symbiosis', *Journal of Industrial Ecology*, **16**, 83–93.

Peck, J. (2011), 'Geographies of policy: from transfer-diffusion to mobility-mutation', *Progress in Human Geography*, **35**, 773–797.

Prince, R. (2010), 'Policy transfer as policy assemblage: making policy for the creative industries in New Zealand', *Environment and Planning A*, **42**, 169–186.

Rose, R. (2005), *Learning from Comparative Public Policy: A Practical Guide*, Abingdon, UK: Routledge.

Salmi, O., J. Hukkinen, J. Heino, N. Pajunen and M. Wierink (2012), 'Governing the interplay between industrial ecosystems and environmental regulation', *Journal of Industry Ecology*, **16**, 119–128.

Seely, A. (2009), 'Landfill tax : recent developments', House of Commons Library, Standard Note SN/BT/237, accessed 20 February 2015 at file:///C:/Users/ggspd/Downloads/SN00237.pdf.

Simboli A., R. Taddeo and A. Morgante (2014), 'Analysing the development of industrial symbiosis in a motorcycle local industrial network: the role of contextual factors', *Journal of Cleaner Production*, **66**, 372–383.

State Council (2005), *Several Opinions of the State Council on Speeding up the Development of the Circular Economy Development* (in Chinese), accessed 22 February 2015 at http://www.gov.cn/zwgk/2005-09/08/content_30305.htm.

Stone, D. (2012), 'Transfer and translation of policy', *Policy Studies*, **33**, 1–17.

Swainson, R. and R.C. de Loe (2011), 'The importance of context in relation to policy transfer: a case study of environmental water allocation in Australia', *Environmental Policy and Governance*, **21**, 58–69.

SWITCH-Asia (2012), *Implementing Industrial Symbiosis and Environmental Management Systems in Tianjin Binhai New Area*, accessed 16 November 2012 at http://www.switch-asia.eu/switch-projects/project-impact/projects-on-improving-production/industrial-symbiosis.html.

TEDA (2011), *TEDA Overview*, accessed 22 February 2015 at http://www.chn-sourcing.com/outsourcing-news/parks/tianjin_teda/.

TEDA AC (2009), *Switch-Asia Promoting Sustainable Consumption and Production Grant Application Form: Implementing Industrial Symbiosis and Environmental Management Systems in Tianjin Binhai New Area* (internal document).

TEDA eco-centre (2012), *Implementing Industrial Symbiosis and Environmental Management System in Tianjin Binhai New Area: Progress Report, June 2012* (internal), TEDA IS team presentation to NISP headquarters in Birmingham.

The Former State Economic and Trade Commission (1996), *Clarifying Several Questions about the Opinions on Further Promoting Resource Re-utilisation*, accessed 22 February 2015 at http://www.cnki.com.cn/Article/CJFDTotal-BUIL199701001.htm.

UNEP (2007), *GEO Resource Book – Module 5: Integrated Analysis of Environmental Trends and Policies*, accessed 20 February 2015 at http://geodata.rrcap.unep.org/ieatraining/module-5.pdf.

Wang, Q. (2013), *Knowledge Transfer to Facilitate Industrial Symbiosis: A Case Study of UK-China Collaborators*, Hull, UK: Department of Geography, Environment and Earth Sciences, University of Hull, accessed 20 February 2015 at https://hydra.hull.ac.uk/assets/hull:7143a/content.

Wang, S. and S. Zhang (2010), 'Exploring the environmental monitoring of projects of general industrial solid waste landfill sites' (in Chinese), *Environmental Protection and Circular Economy*, **6**, 38–41.

WRAP (2015), accessed 20 February 2015 at http://www.wrap.org.uk/content/about-us.

Zhang, X., L. Li, H. Hu and Y. Song (2012), 'Comparisons and analysis on international resource recycling: a case study of waste disposal and recycling between China and Japan', in M. Matsumoto, Y. Umeda, K. Masui and S. Fukushige (eds), *Design for Innovative Value Towards a Sustainable Society*, Netherlands. Springer, pp. 246–250.

7. Industrial waste management improvement: a case study of Pennsylvania

Donald I. Lyons, Murray Rice and Lan Hu

INTRODUCTION

Industrial symbiosis (IS), one of the major strategies put forward by industrial ecology for dealing with the perennial issue of waste, argues that industrial production and consumption must close the loop on materials and products in a manner that mimics the material efficiency of natural ecosystems. By substituting virgin material inputs with wastes and by-products, extraction is minimised, waste is minimised, material use is maximised, while also reducing energy use (Frosch and Gallopoulos, 1989).

IS practices, particularly eco-industrial parks (EIPs) (planned or organically formed) and various forms of non-'park'-based IS have demonstrated considerable success across the world at a variety of spatial scales from the facilitated programmes of the UK (i.e., NISP) to the more top-down approaches adopted in China (Shi et al., 2012; Tian et al., 2014). Scrap materials also move over large geographic areas (Lyons, 2007; Lyons et al., 2009), mainly driven by differential regulations between countries and regions, imbalances of supply and demand, and the existence of declining transport and transaction costs (Lyons et al., 2009; Chen et al., 2012; Zhuang et al., 2012). In the US, planned EIPs have a more chequered history of success (Deutz and Gibbs, 2008; Lowitt, Chapter 4, this volume), although there are signs that regional-scale symbiosis networks are now in development in several locations (Lowitt, Chapter 4, this volume).

Much of the prominent empirical evidence for IS is based on a limited number of case studies of local to regional networks such as the classic case of Kalundborg and other similar local-to-regional-scale networks such as the Kwinana Industrial Area in Western Australia (MacLachlan, 2013), Tianjin EIP in China (Shi et al., 2010), Ulsan EIP in South Korea, and so on (Ehrenfeld and Gertler, 1997; Van Beers et al., 2007; Park et al., 2008; Shi et al., 2012). In addition, in the UK context the evolution and geographic pattern of IS resource flows within a network of firms up to national in scale has been widely studied (e.g., Paquin and Howard-Grenville, 2009; Jensen et al., 2011). However, in the US relatively little attention has been paid to overall levels of by-product and waste flows occurring in the marketplace – in part perhaps owing to the challenge of identifying IS in situations where it has not been facilitated by either a public or private sector body, and given the lack of comprehensive data-bases of residue flows from which estimates can be made.

While there are substantial databases regarding the generation and treatment of municipal and hazardous waste, very little is known about non-hazardous industrial waste (Chertow and Park, 2011). Yet the US Environmental Protection Agency (EPA) estimates that, yearly, the US alone generates approximately 6.6 billion tons (1 US ton = 2000 pounds or 907 kg) of non-hazardous industrial waste (NHIW) (Eckelman and Chertow, 2009). As such, the sheer volume and potential impacts of NHIW make investigation of its characteristics and geography an important pri-ority for research. Furthermore, developments in chemical and process engineering are emerging that can capture ever-larger amounts of NHIW, allowing them to be used in newly productive ways in the manner suggested by IS (see for example, Dippenaar, 2005; Malik and Thapliyal, 2009).

Most states in the US have relatively little and generally imprecise data on NHIW. NHIW is typically stored and treated on site in surface com-pounds, or discarded in industrial waste piles, land disposal units and municipal landfills (Dernbach, 1993; Eckelman and Chertow, 2009). An important exception is the Commonwealth of Pennsylvania in the US. Since 1992, The Pennsylvania Department of Environmental Protection (PA DEP) has required facilities producing more than 13 tons of non-hazardous industrial waste/year (referred to as residual waste) to report the type, weight, industrial sector, generators' geographic location, treat-ment/disposal strategies and final destination for their wastes. However, although by-products are not considered to be residual waste under the regulation, many facilities chose to report cases where by-products were used on site or sold to another facility. In addition, an unknown quantity of by-products may not have been reported and may be missing from the dataset, while newer production techniques may be emerging that are changing the characterisation of a waste to a by-product. To avoid costly and constant litigation over definitions, there are multiple rules governing resource recovery. Some materials are excluded altogether, others are regu-lated under beneficial use permits with specific conditions. So while some by-products may be missing from the dataset, it is nonetheless useful for determining what happens to NHIW over time and the beneficial reuses that are emerging (Eckelman and Chertow, 2009).

In an effort to develop long-term waste management planning, the principle aims of the programme were to help the PA DEP ascertain the correct facilities to inspect, and to encourage waste sharing among Pennsylvania industries as a waste reduction strategy (Dernbach, 1993). As such, this dataset is highly unusual and allows us to ask more systematic questions regarding the management and nature of NHIW reuse (including IS-type practices) in a heavily industrialised state of the US. Specifically, this chapter examines what type of NHIW is being generated within Pennsylvania, where it is being generated and treated or disposed of and how that pattern has changed over time. Second, it examines the evolution of the dominant treatment strategies for Pennsylvania's NHIW waste. Finally, it asks if scale economies, in terms of both generation and management/treatment of NHIW influence the extent to which waste is reprocessed rather than disposed of in landfills or surface impoundments. Throughout, there is a focus on Combustion Residues, which dominate the NHIW waste streams by weight throughout the study period.

NON HAZARDOUS INDUSTRIAL WASTE (NHIW)

NHIW is a highly diversified waste stream distinct from either Municipal Solid Waste (MSW) or hazardous waste as defined by the US Resource Conservation and Recovery Act (RCRA) Subtitle C. In Pennsylvania, the major categories of NHIW include Combustion Residues (e.g., bottom ash, fly ash and flue gas desulphurisation residue), Metallurgical Wastes (e.g., foundry sand and slag), Sludges and Scales (e.g., industrial wastewater treatment sludge and food processing sludge) and Generic Manufacturing Wastes (e.g., wood and paper wastes, polyethylene, polystyrene, polyurethane). According to the PA DEP, the 20 million tons of solid NHIW was almost twice the combined total of Pennsylvania's municipal wastes (11.7 million tons per year) and hazardous wastes (4 million tons) in 2008 (PA DEP, 2012).

The total amount of NHIW produced per year has remained close to 14 million tons over the study period. This study therefore investigates changes to waste practices in terms of relative proportions. The largest component of NHIW in Pennsylvania is Combustion Residues which accounted for 51% of total solid NHIW in 1992, rising to 81% of the total in 2008.

MANAGEMENT OF NHIW COMBUSTION RESIDUES

Combustion Residue (coal ash) is a generic term referring to several very distinct residues produced from using a variety of different types of coal to produce electricity and includes coal-derived bottom ash, coal-derived fly ash, boiler slag and flue gas desulphurisation residues. Although the beneficial reuse of Combustion Residues began with the use of fly ash in the concrete mix for the Hoover Dam in the 1930s, until recently most coal ash was landfilled in specialised landfills or stored on site in containment ponds built to prevent trace elements from leaching into drinking water supplies (Glazer et al., 2011). Various forms of beneficial reuse have increased over the years and both the US EPA and the American Coal Ash Association (ACAA) now refer to Coal Combustion Residues as Coal Combustion Products (CCP) to promote their reuse and to emphasise their commercial value (ACAA, 2014; US EPA, 2014a). Still, unlike Japan and the European Union (EU) where 80–90% of coal ash is reused (Park, 2014a), the majority of coal ash generated in the US is not reused. For example, of the 131 million tons of coal residues produced in the US in 2007, nearly 75 million tons were disposed of, with the remaining 43% beneficially reused. Such beneficial reuse, however, has led to a multibillion-dollar industry over the past 50-plus years, with the production and use of CCPs contributing more than US$4 billion to the US economy each year (ACAA, 2014).

Fly ash in concrete accounts for the largest volume of Combustion Residues reused annually in the US. Fly ash and bottom ash can be used to produce road base materials, manufactured aggregates, flowable fills, structural fills and embankments. Coal ash is also used to replace virgin materials (cement and lime) in the production of Portland cement. Other applications for Combustion Residues include wallboard manufacturing, roofing tiles and shingles, waste stabilisation, snow and ice control, soil modification, as mineral fillers, in agriculture and mining, and for very specialised uses. For example, some Combustion Residues have properties suitable for metal castings in the aerospace and automotive industries (see Park, 2014b). As such, there are clear economic and 'substitutable' reasons (see Deutz, 2014) to expect flows of CCPs across entities to increase overtime.

Beneficial reuse of Combustion Residues can have environmental savings as well. For example, fly ash used in the production of concrete, is estimated to save approximately 13 million tons of carbon dioxide from entering the earth's atmosphere each year, reducing landfill space requirements and transport emissions. Using coal ash instead of natural soil in the construction of highway fills or embankments eliminates the need to remove soil from undisturbed areas, thus saving energy. Land application of fly ash is also used to stabilise clayey soils (Malik and Thapliyal, 2009). While Deutz (2014) argues that such environmental benefits are contingent characteristics of IS, other definitions (e.g., Chertow and Ehrenfeld, 2012) place environmental benefit at the core of their definition. In this case, land application appears to be an environmentally beneficial disposal route, and can be seen as preferable to landfill.

However, some question the release of Combustion Residues into the environment. Glazer et al. (2011) argue that there is still no clear scientific evidence regarding the environmental or human impact on the use of CCPs, while Lombardi (2014) points to a number of instances where CCPs have been detected in local environments after use as structural fill. In addition, leachate seeping from fly ash landfills has caused groundwater and surface river contamination at a number of sites (Environmental Integrity Project and Earth Justice, 2010), and ash spills from storage sites (e.g., Kingston plant, Tennessee Valley Authority, 2010) are an additional cause for concern. In addition, while earlier (1993, 2000) US EPA rules determined that the management and use of coal combustion products did not warrant regulation as a hazardous waste, the US EPA began to revise this decision in 2010 and is currently in the final stages of publishing new rules on the disposal and reuse of coal ash (US EPA, 2014b).

POLICY CONTEXT FOR IS IN PENNSYLVANIA

At the heart of the initial PA DEP's NHIW strategy was an effort to move industries in Pennsylvania to examine their operations and to switch their perception of their wastes and by-products as disposal issues to potential resources that were being discarded (Dernbach, 1993). Generators of NHIW must prepare a source-reduction strategy for each type of waste generated in volumes of more than one metric ton per month. Generally, the plan must document the source reduction strategy to reduce waste, when the action will be done, and must include a quantitative estimate of the level of source reduction. More importantly, if no source reduction action is proposed, the facility is required to submit an even more detailed justification for each waste stream, the potential source reduction options evaluated, the technical and economic barriers that prohibit reduction, and why they were not chosen. Violation of permitting and operational requirements can result in civil penalties assessed on the basis of the wilfulness of the violation, the costs avoided by the operator by incurring the violation, and the extent of any environment or health damage done (The Pennsylvania Code, 2014).

National-scale regulations effectively began with the Clean Air Act of

1970 and other environmental regulations of the time, which required electricity producers to account for all their Combustion Residues (Ward, 2010). But by the 1990s air quality had improved considerably and the influence of federal environmental policies surrounding Combustion Residues became less important. The drivers of new residue uses were more market oriented. However, Park (2014a) argues that in the absence of federal regulations requiring the reuse of coal combustion by-products (CCPs), state-level regulations have indirectly affected innovation by controlling the overall management and disposal of Combustion Residues and by changing their generation and quality.

As an example of this, the PA DEP sought to create incentives for disposal alternatives. While initially utilities were disposing of all the ash, a Combustion Residue industry soon emerged to begin finding new uses for the residues (Ward, 2010). By issuing general permits for processing and beneficial use of NHIW the PA DEP has hoped to encourage large-scale residual waste recycling in a uniform and environmentally protective way since any number of firms could operate under the same permit if they meet the requirements of that permit and either register with the PA DEP or obtain its approval (Dernbach, 1993). For utilities, revenue from coal ash sales, in general, constitutes an insignificant portion of the overall revenue stream and coal ash sales are viewed more as a means to reduce disposal costs (Park, 2014b). As such there is little incentive other than disposal costs for generators to reuse their Combustion Residues. Rather it is the end users who have generated most of the technologies to reuse Combustion Residues, and a primary motivator here is also cost. For example, in 2005, the price of Portland cement was approximately US$80 dollars per ton, but the price of concrete-quality fly ash was in a range between US$0 and US$45 dollars per ton (Park, 2014b). Park (2014b) also found that knowledge sharing among power plants owned or operated by the same utility had an important effect on a plant's decision to reuse fly ash.

METHODS

Data for this research were obtained from the PA DEP. Given this database, Pennsylvania provides an ideal and unique window into waste management practices. Additionally, Pennsylvania has long been a highly industrialised state, and while much of its manufacturing base has declined in recent years it has continued to increase its coal-fuelled electricity generation with much of the excess exported to surrounding states (Rose et al., 2005). The NHIW reports are readily accessible via the PA DEP website, providing access to comprehensive industrial waste information for the state.

The PA DEP dataset for this research comes from the solid NHIW residual waste biennial reports from 1992 to 2008 (see below also), which comprise 109 069 observations and 18 variables. The dataset identifies 4146 generators and 3808 processors participating in NHIW flows in Pennsylvania with the amount of wastes produced/processed per firm per year ranging from 1 ton to 4.9 million tons. Although there are a large number of small firms generating NHIW, a relatively small number of firms account for the great majority of NHIW (Table 7.1). Forty-five per cent of residue generators appear in the database for just one year. Only 10% of firms are present in the database for more than five years and those are generally the largest generators.

Table 7.1 *Size distribution of firms in the Pennsylvania Department of Environmental Protection NHIW dataset by amount and proportion of residue generated*

	Small generators (less than 1000 tons)	Medium-sized generators (1000 to 5000 tons)	Large generators (5000 to 10000 tons)	Very large generators (greater than 10000 tons)
% of total generators	64.2	19.1	5.3	11.4
% of total NHIW	0.4	1.3	1.1	97.2

As is the case with many self-reported datasets there are issues with accuracy and continuity over time. There have been some significant reporting changes over the years, not all of which are documented. Most importantly, records of discharges to Publicly Owned Treatment Works (POTWs) and to the National Pollutant Discharge Elimination System (NPDES) were no longer reported after 2004 so this entire category was removed from the study (Finkel, personal communication 2011). For some NHIW categories it was not possible to identify when changes in reporting took place since there is limited official documentation associated with the dataset. For example, the weight of chemical NHIW reported during the study period varies from a high of 1 million tons in 1992 to a low of approximately 50 000 tons in 1998, and returns to approximately 1 million tons in 2008. Clearly, such data is 'suspect' in terms of a continuous time series and was therefore removed from the analysis.

Of the ten major categories of wastes remaining after the removal of POTWs, NPDES and chemical wastes, four waste types (Combustion Residues, Metallurgical Process Residues, Sludges and Scales, and Generic Manufacturing Wastes) constitute 89.3% of the remaining total and form the basis for this study. The remaining minor categories (special handling wastes, industrial maintenance waste/scrap, non-coal mining wastes, and miscellaneous) were also removed from the analysis. Robert Finkel of the PA DEP is gratefully acknowledged for access to the dataset and advice on its use. With some minor adjustments (e.g., inferring county from the name and location of city), the Pennsylvania dataset becomes almost entirely unproblematic. Only 0.08% of records cannot be linked to a valid disposal state or receiving location.

NHIW and Industrial Symbiosis

The PA DEP database records 13 treatment strategies for residual wastes. They are divided into beneficial reuses and treatment/disposal. Beneficial strategies include composting, industrial kiln, land application, recycle/ reuse and other (non-conventional reuse). According to Eckelman and Chertow (2009), non-conventional reuse generally refers to industrial ecology type practices. Of the five reuse strategies, three (land application, recycling/reuse and other non-conventional reuse) dominate beneficial reuse strategies. These constitute IS in that they represent use of a residue by another entity, thereby saving the use of a new material (Deutz, 2014). Disposal strategies include incineration, underground injection, landfill, surface impoundment, on site treatment, storage, on site and off site wastewater treatment. Of the seven potential disposal methods, two (surface impoundment and landfilling) dominate disposal strategies. Thus for ease of analysis, only those two disposal strategies were examined. In total, IS residue uses and the two dominant disposal strategies constitute 98% of the total weight of residues in the dataset.

THE GEOGRAPHY OF PENNSYLVANIA'S NHIW MANAGEMENT

Although NHIW is generated by firms across the state the major source areas are concentrated in three regions: Philadelphia, Pittsburgh and Alleghenies (Figure 7.1 and Table 7.2), with considerable variation at the county level within each region. Over the time frame of the study, the proportion of NHIW generated in both the Philadelphia and Alleghenies regions has declined substantially (Table 7.2). In contrast, the Pittsburgh

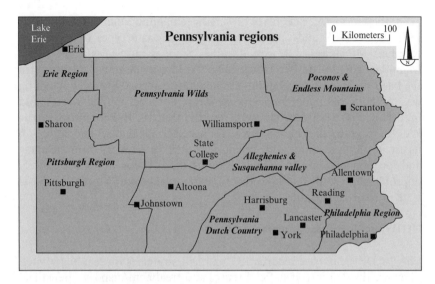

Figure 7.1　Map of Pennsylvania showing its regions

region has increased its proportion of total NHIW for the state from 39% to 62% over the study period. In large part this reflects the changing evolution of Pennsylvania's manufacturing economy and the consequent declines in traditional manufacturing (e.g., heavy manufacturing) since the 1970s (Deitrick and Beauregard, 1995; Pennsylvania's Industrial Resource Centers, 2009).

The total weight of solid NHIW generated in Pennsylvania has remained relatively stable at approximately 14 million tons per year. This pattern reflects substantial increases in Combustion Residues or CCPs (from 51% of the total in 1992 to 81% in 2008) and decreases in the proportional contribution of the other NHIWs (Metallurgical Residues, Sludge and Scales, and Generic Manufacturing) over the study period (Table 7.3).

For most categories of NHIW examined, wastes generally remain within the county or metropolitan region in which they are generated. For example, during the study period over 95% of Combustion Residues or CCPs consistently remained within the region in which they were generated with increasing proportions remaining within the county in which they were produced over time. This pattern of localisation of waste generation and treatment/disposal or treatment/reuse is also true for the other NHIW produced in the Pittsburgh area but less so beyond that region. In particular, Metallurgical Process Residues and Sludges and Scales are being shipped increasingly beyond the region of production, while Generic Manufacturing Wastes produced in the Philadelphia region are increasingly concentrated there.

Table 7.2 *Regional distribution of NHIW generation in Pennsylvania by year, 1992–2008*

Region	Percentage of yearly total of NHIW									Total (000 000 tons) 1992–2008	% of total NHIW 1992–2008
	1992	1994	1996	1998	2000	2002	2004	2006	2008		
Pittsburgh	39.2	55.1	57.7	44.4	44.4	47.8	56.0	60.2	62.0	73.8	51.9
Erie	3.0	1.6	4.6	4.5	5.6	4.0	0.9	0.9	1.0	42.0	3.0
Pennsylvania Wilds	7.7	5.7	7.0	13.1	7.5	7.0	4.8	4.9	5.6	10.1	7.1
Poconos	3.5	5.5	1.8	5.2	4.3	2.0	2.4	1.7	1.8	4.5	3.2
Philadelphia	17.3	15.4	7.1	8.8	6.9	6.7	8.0	7.2	7.0	13.4	9.4
Pennsylvania Dutch	8.5	5.1	5.1	6.9	9.6	8.8	7.3	5.1	6.9	9.9	6.9
Alleghenies	20.7	11.6	16.7	17.1	21.6	23.7	20.5	20.1	15.8	26.2	18.5
Total per year	100	100	100	100	100	100	100	100	100	142.2	100

Table 7.3　Total residue produced per year and proportion represented by each major residue type

Year	Combustion Residues %	Metallurgical Process Residues %	Sludges and Scales %	Generic Manufacturing Wastes %	Total (000 000 tons)
1992	51.05	11.8	24.69	12.11	14.7
1994	52.23	8.49	28.77	10.19	17.7
1996	53.97	14.47	26.46	4.81	17.4
1998	65.69	12.75	12.19	9.07	17.2
2000	65.82	12.92	12.68	8.31	15.6
2002	73.86	10.55	7.44	7.9	14.8
2004	71.32	11.52	9.02	8.04	13.3
2006	83.66	3.55	6.63	5.94	16.3
2008	81.04	4.38	7.92	6.36	14.8

Source:　Authors' analysis of Pennsylvania DEP NHIW dataset.

The increasing concentration of industry in the Pittsburgh area and the concomitant decrease in industrial concentration in other areas of Pennsylvania suggest that the Pittsburgh area continues to have the infrastructure to absorb its NHIW (either via treatment/disposal or reuse) while deindustrialising areas are losing that capacity.

While Jensen et al. (2011) found no general relationship between distance travelled and the quantity or weight of materials being exchanged, it is likely that for Combustion Residues the relationship between distance moved and cost of movement is likely associated since shipment of CCPs is constrained by transport costs to approximately a 50–150 mile (80–241 km) radius of the power plants (ACCA, 2014). In contrast, the distance over which Metallurgical Process Residues and Sludges and Scales is travelling is increasing which may indicate, as Jensen et al. (2011) suggest, that more problematic wastes need to travel further since there are fewer local options to absorb such wastes. This certainly seems to be the case for Sludges and Scales which over the study period have increased both distance travelled and the extent to which they are being reused.

Overall, IS activities have increased substantially over the period of the study from 33.4% to 56.5% (Table 7.4). However, there is considerable variation across the different NHIW categories (Table 7.4). Land application is the most common form of IS for Sludges and Scales, followed by other Non-Conventional Uses, while Recycling/Reuse is the dominant strategy for Generic Manufacturing Waste. The declining proportion of Metallurgical and Generic Manufacturing Wastes taken up by IS

Table 7.4   Proportion of selected NHIW residue streams redirected to treatment and utilisation strategies comprising IS, 1992–2008

	Land application %		Non-conventional %		Recycle/ reuse %		Total % treated/ utilised	
	1992	2008	1992	2008	1992	2008	1992	2008
Combustion Residues (CCPs)	15.7	5.3	10.8	54.9	1.2	0.2	27.7	60.4
Metallurgical Wastes	0.5	0.3	31.6	0.4	15.1	34.5	47.3	35.2
Sludges and Scales	4.6	20.0	15.7	10.3	0.4	4.8	22.3	39.8
Generic Manufacturing Wastes	2.1	9.4	56.0*	2.7	8.1	30.2	66.8	44.8
Total selected NHIW	9.4	6.5	19.9	45.3	3.6	4.0	33.4	56.3

Note: * Caution should be used in reference to this value. This number may be a result of a coding error or other reclassification and 1992 is the only year where the value is greater than 10%.

exchanges during the study period reflects a marked drop in the proportion undergoing non-conventional recovery. By contrast, the proportion undergoing Recycling and Reuse has more than doubled (Table 7.4).

The increased use of non-conventional reuses can be seen clearly if we examine patterns of beneficial reuse in the Pittsburgh Region (Table 7.5).

Table 7.5   Reuse patterns in the Pittsburgh region, showing the percentage of the specified residue stream diverted to the reuse activity in the specified year

	Land application		Non-conventional reuse		Recycle/ reuse	
	1992	2008	1992	2008	1992	2008
Coal-Derived Bottom Ash	23.7	9.3	7.4	78.0	1.3	0.3
Coal-Derived Fly Ash	3.1	4.8	16.2	58.0	1.5	0.3
Flue Gas Desulphurisation Residue	0	0	0	16.3	0	0
Other Ash	78.2	14.0	1.8	32.4	0	6.6

Fully 78% of Coal Derived Bottom Ash and 58% of Coal-Derived Fly Ash were beneficially reused via non-conventional practices in Pittsburgh by 2008. The proportion of Flue Gas Desulphurisation Residues and Other

Ash beneficially reused is considerably lower, but their total contribution to Combustion Residues is also considerably lower than the other components (20.7% and 1.0% respectively).

ECONOMIES OF SCALE AND REUSE CAPACITY

The fact that a large proportion of NHIW is generated by a relatively small number of very large firms raises the question of a generator's capacity to deal with its NHIW. On the one hand, very large generators are likely to have the necessary technologies, and are more likely to be under regulatory scrutiny and to have greater economic incentives to find alternatives to disposal given the very large weight of NHIW to be dealt with. On the other hand, for small firms the effort required to find suitable alternatives to disposal may be too great. Table 7.6 presents data on the proportion of NHIW redirected to various IS strategies by firm size in 2008.

In almost every case, larger firms redirect their NHIW to IS type flows in greater proportions than smaller firms. In particular, for example, very large generators of Combustion Residues or (CCPs) redirect over half of their residues to IS flows. Similarly, large and very large generators of Metallurgical Wastes recycle/reuse much higher proportions of their wastes to IS strategies. In only one case, that of Generic Manufacturing Wastes, do medium-sized firms redirect their wastes in greater proportion that large and very large generators. The greater propensity of larger firms for IS strategies may reflect greater expertise and/or access to necessary equipment for equipment for coal ash reuse (Park, 2014b). Accordingly most generators form partnerships with Combustion Residue users to manage and reuse coal ash, either on or off site. Additionally, however, smaller generators may not be able to access institutional support such as industrial associations (e.g., the ACAA), nor the research support to meet product standards for Combustion Residues (Park, 2014a).

CONCLUSION

This study examined the evolution of the management of NHIW in Pennsylvania between 1992 and 2008 to assess whether IS practices are taking hold. The results suggest that the PA DEP NHIW strategies are working and that IS-type strategies are taking hold. The impact of Pennsylvania's NHIW regulations challenges the idea that industrial development must come at the expense of the environment. Although the motivation for IS is not apparent in the dataset, it appears that the

*Table 7.6   Major industrial symbiosis strategies by firm size, 2008, showing
the percentage of the specified residue category diverted to the
given strategy by the specified category of firm size*

NHIW type	Land application			
	Small firms	Medium-sized firms	Large firms	Very large firms
Combustion Residues (CCPs)	0	0	18.5	5.2
Metallurgical Wastes	0	1.4	0	0
Sludges and Scales	4.7	24.1	24.0	19.9
General Manufacturing wastes	0.9	9.9	30.5	3.1
Total selected NHIW	1.7	11.9	17.5	6.0
NHIW Type	Non-conventional			
	Small firms	Medium-sized firms	Large firms	Very large firms
Combustion Residues (CCPs)	15.3	12.9	21.6	55.1
Metallurgical Wastes	1.5	1.7	0	0
Sludges and Scales	2.9	1.8	0	13.3
General Manufacturing wastes	1.1	4.6	7.9	0
Total selected NHIW	2.0	3.8	5.7	48.9
NHIW Type	Recycle/reuse			
	Small firms	Medium-sized firms	Large firms	Very large firms
Combustion Residues (CCPs)	3.3	5.1	44.4	0
Metallurgical Wastes	15.0	24.0	31.0	40.9
Sludges and Scales	4.5	3.7	0	5.5
General Manufacturing wastes	22.9	44.3	31.8	24.7
Total selected NHIW	18.5	27.0	25.3	2.3

state may have begun to change the perception of waste as a nuisance to
that of waste as a resource, as they intended (Dernbach, 1993). This is
an important finding for IS, especially given the US context, where park-
based IS has had some difficulty taking off as a dominant strategy (but see
Lowitt, Chapter 4, this volume). It also strongly suggests that the type of

regulatory signals employed in the EU (Costa et al., 2010; Q. Wang et al., Chapter 6, this volume) can have an impact in the US context.

The increased localisation of NHIW management for the largest generating sectors (Combustion Residues) suggests increased local accountability of waste management, but it may also be a result of the costs of movement for Combustion Residues, particularly of the more difficult categories of waste such as Sludges and Scales. This may reflect, as Jensen et al. (2011) suggested, that industrialised nations have sufficiently diverse agglomerations of industry at the urban scale to absorb a range of residues. Regions outside Pittsburgh with decreasing waste generation may have lost their ability to absorb NHIW too. Localisation of residue use could also indicate that new economic capacity that has been generated in the various IS strategies is located in the same regions where industrial production remains. There have also been shifts between different IS options, e.g., as with Metallurgical Waste, possibly reflecting fluctuations in the market price for recovered metals.

However, even though the trends are generally in the right direction, fully 44% of Pennsylvania's solid NHIW are disposed of. This presents challenges to incentivise greater levels of reuse. Such incentives must be derived from a combination of market, government and technological advances and an understanding of the motivations of the different actors involved. Other research suggests that generating companies are likely to respond to disposal regulations while companies utilising wastes are more likely to respond to technological improvements and market signals (e.g., Park, 2014b).

At the same time, thorough risk assessments are necessary since some reuse strategies are likely risker than others both financially and environmentally. CCBs can contain toxic elements (e.g., arsenic and lead) which are more appropriate for uses such as cement, and plastics, where CCBs are retained in a matrix that hinders leaching of any toxic constituents. Whereas in CCBs other categories such as snow and ice control, or agricultural applications, are still controversial (Park and Chertow, 2014).

This study has provided a first step towards a spatial analysis of NHIW in the US context. Further research should attempt to map flows to examine movements at a finer spatial and temporal resolution, with additional data to indicate the relationship to production levels. In particular, qualitative research to investigate the motivations of both residue providers and recipients, the environmental implications of the various technologies and the effects on employment need to be investigated.

REFERENCES

ACCA (2014), 'About coal ash – what are CCPs?', American Coal Combustion Association, accessed throughout 2014 at http://www.acaa-usa.org/What-are-CCPs.

Chen, X., T. Fujita, S. Ohnishi, M. Fujii and Y. Geng (2012), 'The impact of scale, recycling boundary, and type of waste on symbiosis and recycling', *Journal of Industrial Ecology*, **16**, 129–141.

Chertow, M. and J. Ehrenfeld (2012), 'Organizing self-organizing systems', *Journal of Industrial Ecology*, **16**, 13–27.

Chertow, M. and J. Park (2011), 'Reusing nonhazardous industrial waste across business clusters', in T. Letcher and D. Vallero (eds), *Waste: A Handbook for Management*, New York: Elsevier.

Costa, I., G. Massard and A. Agarwal (2010), Waste management policies for industrial symbiosis development: case studies in European countries', *Journal of Cleaner Production*, **18** (8), 815–822.

Deitrick, S. and R.A. Beauregard (1995), 'From front runner to also ran – the transformation of a once dominant region: Pennsylvania, USA', in P. Cooke (ed.), *The Rise of the Rustbelt*, London: Routledge, pp. 52–71.

Dernbach, J. (1993), 'The other ninety-six percent', *Environmental Forum*, 10–15.

Deutz, P. (2014), 'Food for thought: seeking the essence of industrial symbiosis', in R. Salomone and G. Saija (eds), *Pathways for Environmental Sustainability: Methodologies and Experiences*, Switzerland: Springer, pp. 3–11.

Deutz, P. and D. Gibbs (2008), 'Industrial ecology and regional development: eco-industrial development as cluster policy', *Regional Studies*, **42**, 1313–1328.

Dippenaar, R. (2005), 'Industrial uses of slag (the use and re-use of iron and steelmaking slags', Advances in Materials and Processing Technologies (AMPT) Conference, **32**, 35–46.

Eckelman, M.J. and M. Chertow (2009), 'Quantifying life cycle environmental benefits from the reuse of industrial materials in Pennsylvania', *Environmental Science & Technology*, **43**, 2550–2556.

Ehrenfeld, J. and N. Gertler (1997), 'Industrial ecology in practice: the evolution of interdependence at Kalundborg', *Journal of Industrial Ecology*, **1**, 67–79.

Environmental Integrity Project and Earth Justice (2010), 'In harm's way: lack of federal coal ash regulations endangers Americans and their environment', accessed January 2015 at http://media.cleveland.com/business_impact/other/Coal%20Ash%20Study.pdf.

Frosch, R. and N. Gallopoulos (1989), 'Strategies for manufacturing', *Scientific American*, **261**, 144–152.

Glazer, B., C. Graber, C. Roose, P. Syrett and C. Youssef (2011), 'Fly ash in concrete', accessed December 2014 at http://transparency.perkinswill.com/assets/Whitepapers/FlyAsh_WhitePaper.pdf.

Jensen, P.D., L. Basson, E.E. Hellawell, R.B. Bailey and M. Leach (2011), 'Quantifying "geographic proximity": experiences from the United Kingdom's National Industrial Symbiosis Programme', *Resources, Conservation and Recycling*, **55**, 703–712.

Lombardi, K. (2014), 'Beneficial use of coal ash in question as EPA mulls regulation', The Centre for Public Integrity, accessed December 2014 at http://www.publicintegrity.org/2010/11/24/2291/beneficial-use-coal-ash-question-epa-mulls-regulation.

Lowitt, P.C. (2008), 'Devens redevelopment', *Journal of Industrial Ecology*, **12**, 497–500.

Lowitt, P.C. (2015), 'Eco-industrial development in the United States: analysing progress from 2010–2015', in P. Deutz, D. Lyons and J. Bi (eds), *International Perspectives on Industrial Ecology*, Cheltenham, UK and Northampton, MA, USA: Edward Elgar, pp. 46–68.

Lyons, D.I. (2007), 'A spatial analysis of loop closing among recycling, remanufacturing, and waste treatment firms in Texas', *Journal of Industrial Ecology*, **11**, 43–54.

Lyons, D., M. Rice and R. Wachal (2009), 'Circuits of scrap: closed loop industrial ecosystems and the geography of US international recyclable material flows 1995–2005', *The Geographical Journal*, **175**, 286–300.

MacLachlan, I. (2013), 'Kwinana Industrial Area: agglomeration economies and industrial symbiosis on Western Australia's Cockburn Sound', *Australian Geographer*, **4**, 383–400.

Malik, A. and A. Thapliyal (2009), 'Eco-friendly fly ash utilization: potential for land application', *Critical Reviews in Environmental Science and Technology*, **39**, 333–366.

PA DEP (2012), 'What is residual waste fact sheet', accessed January 2014 at http://www.portal.state.pa.us/portal/server.pt/community/residual_waste/14093/what_is_residual_waste_fact_sheet/589699.

Paquin, R.L. and J. Howard-Grenville (2009), 'Facilitating regional industrial symbiosis: network growth in the UK's National Industrial Symbiosis Programme', in F.A. Boons and J. Howard-Grenville (eds), *The Social Embeddedness of Industrial Ecology*, Cheltenham, UK and Northampton, MA, USA: Edward Elgar.

Park, J.Y. (2014a), 'The evolution of waste into a resource: examining innovation in technologies reusing coal combustion by-products using patent data', *Research Policy*, **43**, 1816–1826.

Park, J.Y. (2014b), 'Assessing determinants of industrial waste reuse: the case of coal ash in the United States', *Resources, Conservation and Recycling*, **92**, 116–127.

Park, J.Y. and M. Chertow (2014), 'Establishing and testing the "reuse potential" indicator for managing wastes as resources', *Journal of Environmental Management*, **137**, 45–53.

Park, H.S., E.R. Rene, S.M. Choi and A.S.F. Chiu (2008), 'Strategies for sustainable development of industrial park in Ulsan, South Korea – from spontaneous evolution to systematic expansion of industrial symbiosis', *Journal of Environmental Management*, **87**, 1–13.

Pennsylvania's Industrial Resource Centers (2009), *Pennsylvania's True Commonwealth: The State of Manufacturing – Challenges and Opportunities Executive Summary*, accessed November 2014 at http://www.dvirc.org/wp-content/uploads/Pennsylvania-State-of-Manufacturing-Challenges-and-Opportunities-Executive-Summary.pdf.

Rose, A., R. Neff, B. Yarnal and H. Greenberg (2005), 'A greenhouse gas emissions inventory for Pennsylvania', *Journal of the Air & Waste Management Association*, **55**, 1122–1133.

Shi, H., M. Chertow and Y. Song (2010), 'Developing country experience with eco-industrial parks: a case study of the Tianjin Economic-

Technological Development Area in China', *Journal of Cleaner Production*, **18**, 191–199.

Shi, H., J. Tian and L. Chen (2012), 'China's quest for eco-industrial parks, Part I: history and distinctiveness', *Journal of Industrial Ecology*, **16**, 8–10.

The Pennsylvania Code (2014), *Subchapter F. Civil Penalties and Enforcement*, accessed 8 December 2014 at http://www.pacode.com/secure/data/025/chapter271/subchapEtoc.html.

Tian, J., W. Liu, B. Lai, X. Li and L. Chen, (2014), 'Study of the performance of eco-industrial park development in China', *Journal of Cleaner Production*, **64**, 486–494.

US EPA (2014a), *Coal Ash (Coal Combustion Residuals, or CCR*, accessed February 2015 at http://www2.epa.gov/coalash.

US EPA (2014b), *Final Rule: Disposal of Coal Combustion Residuals from Electric Utilities*, accessed February 2015at http://www2.epa.gov/coalash/coal-ash-rule.

Van Beers, D., G. Corder, A. Bossilkov and R. van Berkel (2007), 'Industrial symbiosis in the Australian minerals industry: the cases of Kwinana and Gladstone', *Journal of Industrial Ecology*, **11**, 55–72.

Wang, Q., P. Deutz and D. Gibbs (2015), 'UK–China collaboration for industrial symbiosis: a multi-level approach to policy transfer analysis', in P. Deutz, D.I. Lyons and J. Bi (eds), *International Perspectives on Industrial Ecology*, Cheltenham, UK and Northampton, MA, USA: Edward Elgar, pp. 89–107.

Ward, J. (2010), *The Value of Coal Combustion Products: An Economic Assessment of CCP Utilization of the U.S. Economy*, Washington, DC: American Coal Council.

Zhuang, Z., L. Ding and H. Li (2012), *China's Pulp and Paper Industry: A Review*, Georgia Institute of Technology, Atlanta, GA: Center for Paper Business and Industry Studies.

8. Bilateral symbiosis in Australia and the issue of geographic proximity

Robin Branson and Phil McManus

INTRODUCTION

The central topic of this chapter is the spatial dimension of industrial symbiosis, applied particularly to the use of waste for environmental and commercial benefit. In it we examine the significance of geographic proximity and the related features of a network and short mental distance in establishing relationships in practice. Reference to waste raises the question of how waste is defined and what distinguishes it from a by-product. This and the other issues mentioned below are also addressed.

Chertow (2000) described industrial symbiosis as separate organisations collectively exchanging materials, energy and water to their mutual advantage. Key features are inter-firm collaboration and geographic proximity. She subsequently developed the concept by stating a minimum criterion of a '3–2 heuristic'. This means that 'at least three different entities must be involved in exchanging at least two different resources to be counted as a basic type of industrial symbiosis' (Chertow, 2007, 12). In this article also, Chertow emphasises the criticality of geographic proximity as a prerequisite for industrial symbiosis.

The feature of close geographic proximity was described originally in relation to the famous example of industrial symbiosis at Kalundborg in Denmark. Early accounts (Engberg 1993; Gertler 1995; Gertler and Ehrenfeld 1996) focused on transactions between the four organisations at the 'core' of the symbiosis. The sites were no more than 3–4 miles apart, that is, less than 7 km. All three authors, however, alluded to arrangements that involved distances of more than 100 km. Research by Jensen et al. (2011) on quantifying geographic proximity records that although 75% of synergies facilitated by the National Industrial Symbiosis Programme (NISP) in the UK took place over distances of up to 70 km (39.1 miles), some extended for almost 500 km. In Australia, waste has been transported between sites that are over 900 km apart (Branson, 2011). In light of these experiences in Kalundborg and the UK, the influence of geographic proximity on industrial symbiosis is reassessed in the Australian context. The notion of 'commercial proximity', as explained below, is suggested as a more comprehensive determinant of successful symbiosis than geographic proximity alone.

The structural concept of a network of organisations and the notion of a short mental distance between managers are features of industrial symbiosis that are thought to be closely associated with geographic proximity. These notions are also reassessed with reference to circumstances in Australia. For reasons mentioned later, extensive eco-industrial systems, such as exist in Kalundborg, are rare in Australia. Where industrial symbiosis has been successful beyond the geographic limits of such eco-systems as do exist in Australia, it is based on a structure consisting solely of an arrangement between an organisation that produces waste and another that uses it, a structure described as bilateral symbiosis (Branson, 2011). Discussion in this chapter corroborates the view that neither close geographic proximity nor the notion of a short mental distance is a prerequisite for originating transactions.

Manufacturing in Australia is the practical context in which this study is situated. The underlying issues are readily exemplified but, perhaps more usefully, a perspective is presented from which to consider industrial symbiosis in practice, especially in countries with configurations of industrial activity similar to those in Australia.

Particular questions are brought into focus: What constitutes close geographic proximity? What is bilateral symbiosis and what distinguishes it from other forms of trading? Do these issues have a bearing on theory? Are there implications for applying industrial symbiosis in practice? Section 3 deals with the first of these questions; it summarises the early literature and its reference to close geographic proximity. The notion of bilateral symbiosis is developed in Section 4, based on a temporal deconstruction of the eco-industrial system at Kalundborg, which although not the only example of industrial symbiosis in existence is widely recognised as the archetype of industrial symbiosis and is the origin of modern academic interest in the topic. It provides a foundation for the discussions that ensue. The setting in which issues are addressed is manufacturing in Australia; described in Section 5 with specific reference to the state of New South Wales (NSW). In relevant aspects of the discussion, conditions in NSW are broadly similar to those in the other mainland states and territories. Insights derived from experience in Australia and related observations are presented in Section 6. The final section summarises the issues covered in this chapter and draws conclusions about their significance. This agenda starts, however, with a commentary on waste. It is the core issue in this chapter and arguably of industrial symbiosis itself.

IT'S ALL ABOUT WASTE

Controversy over what constitutes waste might arise for various reasons but one in particular is seemingly that there is no single, universally accepted definition. The absence of such a definition is understandable, given that waste is usually defined for a particular purpose, such as government regulation (see below) or in a specific context such as public health and safety. Definitions may be incompatible with one another and may also be antithetical to the objectives of industrial symbiosis. Phrases like 'by-product' (Chertow, 2000) or 'resources' (Baas, 2008) are used as epithets for waste, possibly to counter any pejorative sense of the word or to convey a perception that waste may in fact be useful.

The perspective of this chapter is that waste is entirely defined with reference to only two factors: one is the holder of the waste, whether or not also the producer, and the other is the (legal) boundary of the site on which the material is held. Building on the form of definition given, for example, by Knight (2009), which is similar to that used in the European Union (EU, 2008), waste means any substance, matter, thing or energy (referred to collectively in this chapter as material) that is not wanted by the holder and is therefore to be discarded from the site or might escape from the site on which it is held. This definition includes material that is required to be removed from site under relevant regulations, whether or not it is wanted by the holder. It also includes material that the holder wants to discard but must nevertheless be retained on site pending an authorised means of disposal. The (legal) boundary of the site is a critical factor in determining what constitutes waste. The reason is that discarding is deemed to occur when material classified as waste within the boundary of a site on which it is held actually crosses that boundary. Beyond it, the material could cease to be waste, provided a subsequent holder intends to use it for a purpose approved by the relevant authorities.

Given that a principal objective of industrial symbiosis is to use material previously designated as waste, it is appropriate to distinguish between this category of material and others, especially those that might be conflated with it. The term 'by-product' is a particular case in point. It has a specific commercial meaning in practice, which, ironically, is opposite to its use as a euphemism for waste. Deconstructing the iconic symbiosis at Kalundborg, which is an inspiration and a model for attempts to create industrial symbiosis in other locations (Branson, 2011), provides details that illustrate the distinction between categories. Of the 30 projects established before 2010, only 16 involved the use of waste, as defined above. The remaining 14 projects involved four other, distinct forms of supply: raw material, that is, water from Lake Tisso; the provision of a service, such as Kalundborg municipality treating effluent from Novo Nordisk; the sale of a product such as steam for community heating and industrial processes. Notably, several projects involve the sale of what we refer to as a 'true by-product' such as gypsum and fertiliser. In commercial practice, a by-product is material which results incidentally from a manufacturing process intended to create some other product. The material is not wanted by the producer and is therefore to be discarded. Thus far, it is comparable to waste but there is a crucial distinguishing factor: a genuine by-product has what might be thought of as intrinsic value that enables the producer to sell it in an established market on commercial trading terms typical of product supply. As such, a by-product is indistinguishable from a product created deliberately.

The distinction between waste and a 'true by-product' may be subtle, perhaps illusive, and a discussion of relevant academic theory to elucidate it is beyond the scope of this chapter. Nevertheless, distinguishing between the various categories of supply does have a bearing on what might be considered the ambit of industrial symbiosis. Whether or not projects that share the pipeline from Lake Tisso constitute industrial symbiosis is moot but projects involving the provision of services, the sale of true by-products or normal products are commercial transactions, subject to normal terms of trade and as such are not, we believe, within the purview of industrial symbiosis, despite being included in some of the relevant literature. Given this re-evaluation of the emblematic example of industrial concentration at Kalundborg, a process that could also be undertaken in other locations which may not conform to, but are often inspired by the Kalundborg model, the issue of what does actually constitute industrial symbiosis is pertinent.

ATTRIBUTES OF INDUSTRIAL SYMBIOSIS

Since 1961, various organisations in and around Kalundborg had made arrangements among themselves to use waste and resources. Aggregation of these arrangements was not done until 1989 when a 'structure of relationships' was revealed by a high-school project. The phrase 'industrial symbiosis' was used originally to describe this structure; one that could otherwise have been called an 'industrial ecosystem' (Frosch and Gallopoulos, 1989, 144). Interpretations of industrial symbiosis have been suggested from a range of academic perspectives, mainly in relation to areas of extensive industrialisation or dense configurations of industrial sites. As outlined below on p. 134, much of the manufacturing in Australia is not densely configured, which raises the issue of whether or not industrial symbiosis is applicable. In addressing this issue, we identify attributes of industrial symbiosis that serve as a reference for comparison between configurations and as a guide to its application in practice.

Early Accounts of Kalundborg

Probably the first academic study was done by Engberg in 1993, perhaps inspired by a presentation on the topic given by Jorgen Christensen at the International Conference on Sustainable Development, Rio de Janeiro, in 1992. Engberg refers to the relationships at Kalundborg interchangeably as an 'industrial ecosystem' or 'industrial symbiosis', as in 'this industrial ecosystem, or industrial symbiosis, as it often is referred to . . .' (Engberg, 1993, 1). He also states that 'the key to an industrial ecosystem is the con-ceptualization of industrial wastes as raw materials that can be used as inputs in other industrial processes' (Engberg, 1993, 1).

Engberg identified two overarching factors that 'drove' the industrial symbiosis at Kalundborg: the existence or threat of environmental regula-tions and the economic justification for any given project. 'The Danish government's increasingly strict environmental regulations with respect to smoke emissions and waste discharge were important in setting in motion planning processes and managerial decisions that otherwise might have been postponed' (Engberg, 1993, 26). Other characteristics described by Engberg include the necessity for dissimilar participants, which are:

> . . . in close geographical proximity. Together with the municipality, they [the principal participants in the symbiosis] are all located within a radius of three-to-four miles' [less than 7 km]. This, of course, is essential when steam and waste heat are piped from one place to another. The location factor may be overcome for other products, such as hot and liquid sulphur, which is trucked nearly a hundred miles . . . (Engberg, 1993, 25)

Engberg recognised that: 'The key managers of the four Kalundborg companies and the municipality are also in close "mental distance"' (p. 25) (see discussion below). Nicholas Gertler visited Kalundborg in July 1994, to conduct research for his Master's thesis on industrial ecosystems (Gertler, 1995). His descriptions of the various transactions were similar to Engberg's, with one significant exception. Whereas Engberg only once used the word 'network' in his case study, and even then seemingly inci-dentally, the notion of a 'network' pervades Gertler's thesis. For example:

> An industrial ecosystem is what results from the repeated implementation of industrial symbiosis . . . [it] is a community or network of companies and other organizations in a region who chose to interact by exchanging and making use

of byproducts and/or energy in a way that provides one or more . . . benefits over traditional, nonlinked [sic] operations . . . (Gertler, 1995, 16)

The concept of industrial symbiosis as comprising a network of organisations exchanging by-products is challenged in this chapter on the grounds discussed in Sections 4 and 6.

An article published in early 1996 (Gertler and Ehrenfeld, 1996) probably made the industrial ecosystem at Kalundborg more widely known than did the two unpublished academic papers mentioned above. The inaugural issue of the *Journal of Industrial Ecology (JIE)* contained an article (Ehrenfeld and Gertler, 1997), which depicted the system graphically as a complete network of relationships and noted that 'symbiosis in economic systems is manifest in the exchange of materials and energy between individual firms located in close proximity' (Ehrenfeld and Gertler, 1997, 69). They further state that 'although not a necessary condition for all loop-closing exchanges, in particular those for commodity materials like scrap paper or steel, proximity is a hallmark of industrial symbiosis' (Ehrenfeld and Gertler, 1997, 69). Proximity is seen as a way to 'avoid large transportation costs and energy degradation during transit' (Ehrenfeld and Gertler, 1997, 75). Although close geographic proximity is a recurring characteristic in these early descriptions of industrial symbiosis, not all transactions at Kalundborg involved short distances.

A Particular View of Industrial Symbiosis

Four features of Kalundborg identified in the early literature have a particular bearing on industrial symbiosis in Australia. They are: the construct of a 'network' of relationships within a group of organisations; the exchange of waste or degraded resources between participants in the network; close geographic proximity between the industrial sites; and a short 'mental distance' between managers involved with the network.

The concept of a network is a recurring theme in more recent literature as seen for example in Chertow's influential work on 'uncovering' industrial symbiosis (Chertow, 2007) and features in a range of diverse contexts represented, for example, by Korhonen (2004); Zhu et al. (2007); Chen et al. (2012); Lombardi and Laybourn (2012); Paquin and Howard-Grenville (2012). Furthermore, two basic manifestations of industrial symbiosis can be identified from the literature. One is the physical manifestation, which involves the transfer of material and energy between sites. The other we described as the social manifestation, represented by the notion of a 'short mental distance' in which people communicate informally by various means to exchange ideas, information and knowledge.

To the extent that the concept of a network concatenates the notion of exchange and the attributes of proximity in relation to both these manifestations, the phrase 'network symbiosis' is used here to denote a form of industrial symbiosis prevalent in the literature on eco-industrial systems, of which Kalundborg is the archetypical example. It is widely referenced in this body of work, represented for example by Schwarz and Steininger (1997); Korhonen et al. (1999); Chertow (2000); Heeres et al. (2004); Van Berkel (2005). Using network symbiosis as a model for improving industrial sustainability risks the possibility that viable opportunities in other circumstances might be overlooked in practice. Not all existing manufacturing sites are densely configured. As we outline in Section 5, much of the manufacturing in Australia takes place at remote locations, in circumstances that are not represented by network symbiosis. Nevertheless, bilateral arrangements have been successful in transferring industrial waste from its producer to a user. Since this achieves the overarching objectives of industrial symbiosis, the notion of 'bilateral symbiosis' is explored in the following section.

BILATERAL SYMBIOSIS

Using Kalundborg again as the starting point, it is noted that Ehrenfeld and Gertler (1997) depict the system graphically as a network of boxes connected by arrows representing the various relationships. An almost identical diagram is shown in Chertow (2000). Although most diagrams in this genre provide information about the state of Kalundborg at any given time, the temporal dimension of its evolution is not made clear, if represented at all. A Gantt chart recording each transaction (e.g., Branson 2011), shows the significance of bilateral symbiosis. Each of the 30 projects that had been established by 2009, when the most recent began operating, was arranged between two organisations only. Each began completely independently of all the others and those that ended did so without impacting the longevity of any other. Ehrenfeld and Gertler point out that: 'Each link in the system [at Kalundborg] was negotiated . . . as an independent business deal and was established only if it was [sic] expected to be economically beneficial' (Ehrenfeld and Gertler 1997, 73). Such arrangements have been alluded to, for example, by Chertow (1999) and Jacobsen (2006), however, the characteristic of independence between projects illustrated by the temporal deconstruction of Kalundborg emphasises the role of bilateral symbiosis in its evolution and in other eco-industrial systems, e.g., Schwarz and Steininger (1997); Korhonen et al. (1999); Posch (2010). Paradoxically, Chertow (2007) specifically excludes bilateral arrangements from her concept of industrial symbiosis, while simultaneously recognising their embryonic role: 'The words "kernel" and "precursor" have been chosen to describe instances of bilateral or multilateral exchange of these types that have the potential to expand, but do not yet meet the fuller 3–2 definition of industrial symbiosis' (Chertow, 2007, 12).

Chertow also specifically excludes from her heuristic the participation of organisations whose primary business is recycling and may be thought of, therefore, as 'third parties' in the process of industrial symbiosis. Chertow reiterates the heuristic in the context of developing a theory of industrial symbiosis (Chertow and Ehrenfeld, 2012), which has a bearing on literature that includes descriptions of 'third-party' facilitation of bilateral symbiosis as a commercially viable strategy. There is increasing interest in NISP, established in the UK by International Synergies Limited in this context (Mirata, 2004; Jensen et al., 2011; Lombardi et al., 2012; Paquin and Howard-Grenville, 2012). In Australia, Qubator Pty Ltd has been facilitating bilateral symbiosis as a third party since 1989.

Bilateral symbiosis can be summarised as an arrangement between two organisations which may not necessarily be in close geographic proximity to one another, whereby one of them uses the material discarded as waste by the other. In this view, arrangements facilitated by an intermediary unequivocally constitute industrial symbiosis. In fact, it is highly likely that facilitated bilateral symbiosis will be the dominant approach supported by governments in various parts of the world that introduce industrial symbiosis as part of a national or regional development strategy (e.g. European Industrial Symbiosis Association, 2013). We believe this to be so because not every industrial setting conforms to the conditions pertaining at Kalundborg. Developing commercially viable arrangements to maximise beneficial disposal of waste may therefore depend on intervention by 'third parties', as evidenced by the evolution of NISP (e.g., Wang, 2103). We now turn to the situation in Australia, being potentially one country in which to apply the insights derived from this reassessment of industrial symbiosis at Kalundborg.

MANUFACTURING IN AUSTRALIA

Australia covers an area of approximately 7.69 million km^2 (Geosciences Australia, n.d.) and has a population of about 22.7 million (ABS, 2012). The population is concentrated in five major cities of over one million people; the two closest being Adelaide and Melbourne, which are 725 km apart (RAA, 2013). The country has a federal political system comprising six state governments, two territory governments and one federal (Commonwealth) government.

Two features of manufacturing in Australia particularly influence the viability of industrial symbiosis: one is its geographic dispersion; the other is the political structure and history of the country, particularly with respect to environmental legislation. For the purposes of this chapter the term 'manufacturing' includes activities such as steel production, power generation and food processing. Industries such as agriculture, mining and forestry are not considered here, for want of space, but they certainly come within the general ambit of industrial symbiosis.

Several areas in Australia resemble the structure of eco-industrial systems where manufacturing sites are within close geographical proximity to one another. These include Kwinana in Western Australia and Gladstone in Queensland, which evolved over decades, as had Kalundborg (Van Berkel, 2005). Eco-industrial systems have also been designed such as Synergy Park, west of Brisbane in Queensland (Roberts, 2004). These areas represent a 'proximate configuration' of manufacturing and to varying extent exhibit the characteristics of network symbiosis.

Manufacturing more generally in Australia does not conform to this configuration. Considering NSW as an example, heavy industry is predominantly located in the regions of Greater Sydney, the Illawarra (approximately 80 km south of Sydney) and the Hunter (approximately 180 km north of Sydney). Manufacturing beyond these regions generally occurs in the vicinity of transport hubs: towns such as Albury (570 km south of Sydney), Broken Hill (1160 km west of Sydney) and Tamworth (460 km north of Sydney). Manufacturing also occurs in smaller country towns, perhaps by a single enterprise, which might be the only one of its type in the state, if not in Australia. This scenario represents a 'remote configuration' of manufacturing, characterised by widely dispersed, isolated sites and a sparse number of manufacturers in a given industrial sector.

The remote configuration presents formidable obstacles to achieving industrial symbiosis. Long distances mean long transit times, which have a bearing on the transportation of putrescible waste such as arises from fermentation processes. Isolation significantly restricts opportunities to consolidate supplies of waste to large-scale users. For example, although technically feasible, it remains at the time of writing economically unviable to accumulate sufficient quantities of clean, scrap timber discarded from a wide range of sources on the eastern seaboard of NSW for supply as 'furnish' to the only two particle board manufacturers in the state, whose sites are located 250 km away, immediately adjacent to harvestable forests. Notwithstanding the difficulties, bilateral symbiosis has been successful in Australia. For more than 15 years, scrap therapeutic confectionary produced in Sydney was transported approximately 900 km for use as stock food at a piggery in Victoria. Scrap yeast arising in Sydney was transported 630 km, also to be used as stock food. At least 1500 kilolitres per month of effluent arising in Toowoomba, Queensland, is supplied for soil conditioning to farms within a 40 km radius of the factory and occasionally to a destination 140 km distant (Branson, 2011).

INSIGHTS FROM AUSTRALIA

Analysis of the transactions at Kalundborg and the experience in Australia indicate that close geographic proximity is not a prerequisite for bilateral symbiosis. Similar findings in relation to NISP in the UK have been recorded by Jensen et al. (2011) and by Lombardi and Laybourn (2012). The evidence suggests that proximity other than what may be represented by Euclidian geography needs to be taken into account. The following sections explore the notion of social proximity (as short mental distance) and the concept of commercial proximity, meaning the commercially viable distance over which a particular waste can be transported.

Social Proximity

Short mental distance has been described by Christensen (personal correspondence) in the context of Kalundborg as informal business and social communication, especially face to face, between the employees of different organisations participating in network symbiosis. Principal benefits include the sharing of knowledge about each other's processes and discovering opportunities for projects; see also Doménech and Davies (2011). Although a thorough discussion of social proximity is beyond the scope of this chapter, it is addressed briefly to show that its relevance in bilateral symbiosis is significantly less than perhaps it might be in network symbiosis.

Some projects in Kalundborg apparently succeeded without the benefits of short mental distance. For example, after inspecting cement plants in the UK, Mogens Olesen, director of Asnaes power station at the time, persuaded the Aalborg Portland Cement Company to use fly ash. Aalborg is approximately 170 km from Kalundborg, on a different island. Similarly, projects disposing of liquid sulphur, effluent to farms and yeast to piggeries did not depend on short mental distance of the type that might have facilitated the supply of industrial steam or district heating, for example. As all the arrangements at Kalundborg were bilateral, short mental distance is clearly not necessarily a factor in successful bilateral symbiosis.

Rarely, if ever, is it a feature of the experience in Australia, owing principally to the conditions described in Section 5. In the context of conflating the notion of short mental distance with those of trust and risk, it is noted that Christensen used the phrase precisely to mean the personal relationship formed as a direct result of close geographic proximity. In practice, the notions of trust and risk are characteristic of commercial arrangements between corporations (or their legal equivalents) and as such do not formally reflect the informal relationships between individuals, in the way that short mental distance does. Trust between corporations is dealt with by various forms of contract; risk is assessed by reference to corporate risk profiles and managed by relevant strategies. Since industrial symbiosis exists between corporations and not between individuals, even though individuals may have arranged it, transactions are undertaken from the corporate perspective and neither trust nor risk depends on short mental distance.

The absence of social proximity raises the question of how do the participants in industrial symbiosis even know about each other, far less collaborate? Almost invariably bilateral symbiosis in Australia is established through introduction by an intermediary. It is rare that manufacturers have the knowledge, resources or the capability to develop projects themselves. Opportunities may arise through happenstance or from supply chain relationships but, generally, bilateral symbiosis requires facilitation by an intermediary (Branson, 2011). This analysis aligns with that of Roberts (2004), who highlighted the importance of an intermediary in the Australian context (and more generally) in relation to the development of eco-industrial parks.

Commercial Proximity

As noted previously, manufacturing waste has been transferred over long distances in Australia, as indeed it has in Denmark. Gertler wrote that: 'Close geographical proximity is not an absolute requirement even in Kalundborg ... The Kalundborg example indicates that geographical closeness is very important for the sharing of physical energy, such as heat and pressure, and only helpful in the transportation of material resources' (Gertler 1995, 38–39). The assumption underlying these comments is that the viability of bilateral symbiosis is a function of cost. Even physical energy or large-volume, low-value materials such as water can technically be transported over long distances; doing so is simply a matter of cost. It is suggested that a determining criterion for bilateral symbiosis is the 'total cost' of transferring waste from holder to user, rather than geographic proximity. Total cost includes freight plus related costs such as cargo temperature control, cargo security or special equipment that may be required for handling and storage. Total cost also includes anything the holder is willing to pay (or receive) for disposal of its waste and anything a user is willing to receive (or pay) for accepting the material. It might also happen that assessing a transaction involves consideration of qualitative factors such as company policies or perceptions of corporate social responsibility. Although such factors may be non-monetary in themselves, they may influence management decisions on funding and should, therefore, be recognised. Yet another possibility is that an independent body such as a government department or a philanthropic organisation is willing to help fund an arrangement. The notion of commercial proximity is derived from this reasoning and may be defined as the maximum distance that material can be transferred from one site to another, according to a given arrangement, determined by combining the funds that each party to the arrangement is willing to contribute to finance the transfer. While geographic proximity is likely to be a significant consideration, commercial proximity is a more inclusive determinant of viable arrangements in practice.

Regulation of Waste

However waste may be defined, what really matters to manufacturers in practice is how the authorities treat the issue of waste. The symbiosis in Kalundborg evolved primarily in response to environmental initiatives by the authorities. Similarly, when bilateral symbiosis occurs in Australia, it is generally in response to environmental regulations. The location of a site producing waste is a crucial factor in relation to disposal and subsequent use because the state and territory governments have primary responsibility for the environment. The regulations differ significantly between jurisdictions.

Regulation of waste in NSW is the most stringent of any jurisdiction in Australia (e.g., Bates, 2002). It restricts the options for disposal, such as banning specified substances etc., from landfill and it imposes the highest costs for landfill. For example, the levy in the Sydney Metropolitan Region for dry landfill in the 2012/2013 financial year was approximately AUS$95/tonne. Annual increases of approximately 10% have been legislated until 2015. Landfill levies in other jurisdictions, where they exist at all, are about one-third of this rate. Disparity between jurisdictions is starkly illustrated when NSW is compared with the adjacent state of Queensland, where landfill levies were introduced on 1 December 2011, ranging from AUS$35/tonne to AUS$150/tonne, depending on the type of waste. For political reasons, a new government in Queensland, elected in March 2012, reduced all landfill levies to zero, effective 30 June 2012.

The NSW government strategy is intended to create an incentive for manufacturers to find uses for their waste. This approach assumes that a use exists for all manufacturing waste, and that given sufficient economic 'encouragement' manufacturers will find an alternative to dumping. Research in NSW (Branson, 2011) has shown that manufacturers typically lack the necessary management resources and infrastructure within their own organisations to do so. These limitations in NSW highlight the importance of not just regulating the disposal of waste through market mechanisms, but underline the necessity to have a viable strategy in place to facilitate alternative approaches to landfill, including the development of industrial symbiosis, rather than simply leaving it to individual corporations to dispose of waste in a manner that best meets their current needs. Unfortunately, this strategy has been inadequate, to date, in NSW. Despite such limitations and the difficulties of making trans-jurisdictional arrangements, the evidence presented above of facilitated business transactions founded on industrial symbiosis principles shows that it is possible in Australia. This success, the dispersal of industrial activity in Australia, and the revaluation of emblematic forms of industrial activity such as Kalundborg, and NISP, point to the need to develop the bilateral form of industrial symbiosis in order to reduce the amount of waste going to landfill and thereby foster sustainability.

CONCLUSIONS

The underlying theme of this chapter has been a review of spatial proximity as it relates to industrial symbiosis. The issue is particularly significant in reconciling the theory with practice in Australia where manufacturing predominantly occurs in circumstances which do not reflect those associated with network symbiosis. Bilateral transactions over long distances have been successful, essentially because they are commercially viable.

Although it may seem that close geographic proximity is necessary for transfers of low-value, high-volume substances such as water or degraded energy, the limitation is commercial. A decision may be influenced by the geographic dimension, as it relates to technological factors and transport cost. Other business considerations, however, may also influence a decision. Inducements to go beyond compliance, anticipated environmental benefits or corporate social responsibility may have significant influence from a commercial perspective. The notion of commercial proximity encompasses all these considerations. It reflects the sort of decisions likely made by organisations that must discard waste and of those that intend to use the materials made available thereby. It is seen as a realistic determinant in practice of bilateral symbiosis.

It has been suggested in this chapter that bilateral symbiosis is the basic mechanism by which eco-industrial systems evolve, whether naturally or by design. Some researchers since the mid-2000s have identified social attributes of industrial symbiosis that seem to be associated predominantly with the notion of network symbiosis. Reflecting these developments, a distinction between the two principal forms of industrial symbiosis is suggested. On one hand, there is the physical transfer of substances etc., accomplished through bilateral symbiosis in both the proximate and the remote manufacturing configurations. On the other hand, there are the social relationships facilitated by network symbiosis, whether business, communal or recreational. Thinking of industrial symbiosis as comprising a physical dimension manifested as bilateral symbiosis and a social dimension manifested as network symbiosis facilitates its adaptation to circumstances such as exist in Australia. This has profound implications for both theory and practice, especially with the need to focus on industrial symbiosis rather than trying to create industrial networks or emphasise geographic proximity in the formation of eco-industrial parks.

It is hoped that the ideas discussed in this chapter will contribute to the theory of industrial symbiosis but, more importantly, will also advance its application in practice. After all, what happens in practice will ultimately determine the extent of industrial sustainability.

ACKNOWLEDGMENTS

The authors are grateful to Dr Pauline Deutz for originally suggesting this chapter, for her guidance in its development and for her commentary on previous versions.

REFERENCES

ABS (2012), accessed April 2013 at http://www.abs.gov.au/ausstats/abs@.nsf/mf/3101.0.

Baas, L. (2008), 'Industrial symbiosis in the Rotterdam Harbour and industry complex: reflections on the interconnection of the techno-sphere with the social system', *Business Strategy and the Environment*, **17** (5), 330–340.

Bates, G. (2002), *Environmental Law in Australia*, Oxford: Butterworth.

Branson, R. (2011), 'Bilateral industrial symbiosis, 2011', University of Sydney, unpublished thesis available at http://hdl.handle.net/2123/8287.

Chen, X., T. Fujita, S. Ohnishi, M. Fujii and Y. Geng (2012), 'The impact of scale, recycling boundary and type of waste on symbiosis and recycling: an empirical study of Japanese eco-towns', *Journal of Industrial Ecology*, **16** (1), 129–141.

Chertow, M.R. (1999), 'The eco-industrial park model reconsidered', *Journal of Industrial Ecology*, **2** (3), 8–10.

Chertow, M.R. (2000), 'Industrial symbiosis: literature and taxonomy', *Annual Review Energy Environment*, **25**, 313–337.

Chertow, M.R. (2007), '"Uncovering" industrial symbiosis', *Journal of Industrial Ecology*, **11** (1), 11–30.

Chertow, M.R. and J. Ehrenfeld (2012), 'Organizing self-organizing systems: toward a theory of industrial symbiosis', *Journal of Industrial Ecology*, **16**, 13–27.

Christensen, J. (1992), 'The industrial symbiosis in Kalundborg, Denmark', Presented at the International Conference on Sustainable Development, Rio de Janeiro, 1992.

Doménech, T. and M. Davies (2011), 'Structure and morphology of industrial symbiosis networks: the case of Kalundborg', *Procedia Social and Behavioral Sciences*, **10**, 79–89.

Ehrenfeld, J. and N. Gertler (1997), 'Industrial ecology in practice: the evolution of interdependence at Kalundborg', *Journal of Industrial Ecology*, **1** (1), 67–79.

Engberg, H. (1993), 'Industrial symbiosis in Denmark' (unpublished), New York University, pp. 1–27.

EU Directive 2008/98/EC (Waste Framework Directive) Official Journal of the European Union **L312** 3-30 22.11.2008.

European Industrial Symbiosis Association (2013), accessed at http://www.international-synergies.com/media-centre/press-releases/154-global-green-growth-forum-welcomes-industrial-symbiosis.

Frosch, R.A. and N.E. Gallopoulos (1989), 'Strategies for manufacturing', *Scientific American*, **261**, 94–102.

Geosciences Australia (n.d.), accessed 20 March 2015 at http://www.ga.gov.au/education/geoscience-basics/dimensions/area-of-australia-states-and-territories.html.

Gertler, N. (1995), 'Industrial ecosystems: developing sustainable industrial structures', Massachusetts Institute of Technology, unpublished thesis.

Gertler, N. and J.R. Ehrenfeld (1996), 'A down-to-earth approach to clean production', *Technology Review*, **99** (2), 48–54.

Heeres, R.R., W.J.V. Vermeulen and F.B. de Walle (2004), 'Eco-industrial park initiatives in the USA and the Netherlands: first lessons', *Journal of Cleaner Production*, **12**, 985–995.

Jacobsen, N.B. (2006), 'Industrial symbiosis in Kalundborg, Denmark: a quantitative assessment of economic and environmental aspects', *Journal of Industrial Ecology*, **10** (1–2), 239–255.

Jensen, P.D., L. Basson, E.E. Hellawell, M.R. Bailey and M. Leach (2011), 'Quantifying "geographic proximity": experiences from the United Kingdom's National Industrial Symbiosis Programme', *Resources, Conservation and Recycling*, **55** (7), 703–712.

Knight, L. (2009), 'What is waste that we should account for it? A look inside Queensland's ecological rucksack', *Geographical Research*, **47** (4), 422–433.

Korhonen, J. (2004), 'Industrial ecology in the strategic sustainable development model: strategic applications of industrial ecology', *Journal of Cleaner Production*, **12**, 809–823.

Korhonen, J., M. Wihersaari and I. Savolained (1999), 'Industrial ecology of a regional energy system: the case of the Jyvaskyla region, Finland', *GMI*, **26**, 57–67.

Lombardi, R.D. and P. Laybourn (2012), 'Redefining industrial symbiosis: crossing academic-practitioner and disciplinary boundaries', *Journal of Industrial Ecology*, **16** (1), 28–37.

Lombardi, R.D., D. Lyons, H. Shi and A. Agarwal (2012), 'Industrial symbiosis: testing the boundaries and advancing knowledge', *Journal of Industrial Ecology*, **16** (1), 2–7.

Mirata, M. (2004), 'Experiences from early stages of a national industrial symbiosis programme in the UK', *Journal of Cleaner Production*, **12**, 967–983.

Paquin, R.L. and J. Howard-Grenville (2012), 'The evolution of facilitated industrial symbiosis', *Journal of Industrial Ecology*, **16** (1), 83–93.

Posch, A. (2010), 'Industrial recycling networks as starting points for broader sustainability-oriented cooperation?', *Journal of Industrial Ecology*, **14** (2), 242–257.

RAA (2013), accessed at http://www.raa.com.au/download.aspx?secid=294&file=documents\document_125.pdf.

Roberts, B. (2004), 'The application of industrial ecology principles and planning guidelines for the development of eco-industrial parks: an Australian case study', *Journal of Cleaner Production*, **12**, 997–1010.

Schwarz, E.J. and K.W. Steininger (1997), 'Implementing nature's lesson: the industrial recycling network enhancing regional development', *Journal of Cleaner Production*, **5** (1–2), 47–56.

Van Berkel, R. (2005), 'Industrial symbiosis for sustainable resource processing: the cases of Kwinana and Gladstone (Australia)', in 6th Asia Pacific Roundtable on Sustainable Production and Consumption, Melbourne.

Wang, Q. (2013), 'Knowledge transfer to facilitate industrial symbiosis: a case study of UK–China collaborators', Hull, UK: Department of Geography, Environment and Earth Sciences, University of Hull, accessed 20 February 2015 at https://hydra.hull.ac.uk/assets/hull:7143a/content.

Zhu, Q., E.A. Lowe, Y.-A. Wei and D. Barnes (2007), 'Industrial symbiosis in China: a case study of the Guitang Group', *Journal of Industrial Ecology*, **11** (1), 31–42.

9. Varieties of industrial symbiosis

Wouter Spekkink

INTRODUCTION

The concept of industrial symbiosis was first introduced into the industrial ecology literature by Lowe and Evans (1995) to depict the web of material and energy exchanges that was developed at Kalundborg in Denmark. While the exchanges among firms in Kalundborg may be interpreted as a form of economic coordination among many others, what made them appealing to advocates of industrial ecology was the combination of economic and environmental benefits that resulted from the exchanges. Since the introduction of the concept of industrial symbiosis numerous efforts have been made to identify other existing occurrences of industrial symbiosis or to plan new ones, which is illustrated by the many case studies presented in the literature on industrial symbiosis (e.g., Eilering and Vermeulen, 2004; Chertow, 2007; Deutz and Gibbs, 2008).

An interesting feature of these developments that has received relatively little academic attention is that industrial symbiosis unfolds in very different ways in different places of the world. In the UK, the NISP programme emerged as a government funded programme for the brokerage of waste streams. Based on regional experiences, the programme was extended to cover the whole of the UK. Many of the symbiotic exchanges concern the exchange of existing waste streams, but over time NISP facilitators have sought to help firms in their network to develop more innovative linkages (Paquin and Howard-Grenville, 2012). In the Netherlands the Dutch government has provided subsidies for sustainability projects on industrial parks, which in some cases has led to, or catalysed, the development of symbiotic exchanges (Boons and Janssen, 2004; Boons and Spekkink, 2012). By contrast, cases such as Kalundborg and the Rotterdam Harbour area are examples where firms have developed larger networks of symbiotic exchanges without the active stimulation of outside actors (Ehrenfeld and Gertler, 1997; Baas and Boons, 2007).

In this chapter I present a conceptual framework of industrial symbiosis that may serve as a basis for explanations for the different ways in which industrial symbiosis unfolds in different places of the world. The conceptual framework is grounded in an understanding of industrial symbiosis as a process. As a consequence the framework is focused in the first place on identifying and explaining differences in the dynamics through which networks of symbiotic exchanges emerge and develop over time. The structural features of the networks of symbiotic exchanges are understood as outcomes of these dynamics and are of secondary concern. Industrial symbiosis is defined as the process through which firms and other relevant actors within regional industrial systems increase their connectedness in terms of material, energy and information flows in order to lower the ecological impact of their regional industrial system (Boons et al., 2011). The framework distinguishes between dynamics of industrial symbiosis at three levels: (1) the project level at which actors prepare and implement symbiotic exchanges and engage in other relevant types of interactions, (2) the regional industrial system at which actors develop the institutional capacity that enables them to coordinate their activities in a collaborative fashion,[1] and (3) the institutional context which is the source of institutional pressures and conditions the opportunities that actors have for different courses of action in the process of industrial symbiosis.

In addition to the conceptual framework I introduce several mechanisms through which dynamics at the three levels of the framework are connected. These mechanisms are '... frequently occurring and easily recognisable causal patterns that are triggered under generally unknown conditions or with indeterminate consequences' (Elster, 2007: 36). The purpose of the conceptual framework is to offer a set of concepts relevant to the investigation of the coming about of industrial symbiosis and the purpose of the mechanisms is to link the concepts into partial theories about typical patterns in the emergence and development of industrial symbiosis.

I introduce the conceptual framework in the next section. Then I identify several mechanisms that link together the dynamics at the different levels of the framework and discuss how these shape the networks of symbiotic exchanges that emerge from them. Finally, I conclude the chapter with a brief discussion on how the mechanisms might be investigated.

THE CONCEPTUAL FRAMEWORK

The framework breaks down the process of industrial symbiosis into dynamics at three different levels: the project level, the regional industrial system, and the institutional context (see Figure 9.1). The framework suggests several linkages between the concepts and these are further

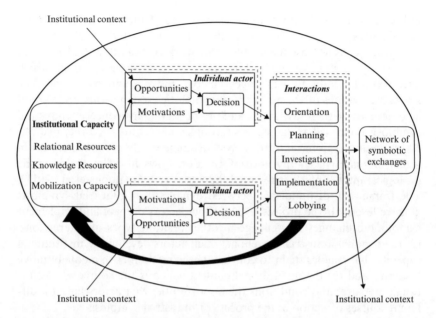

Figure 9.1   The conceptual framework

elaborated in the discussion on mechanisms (below). The outcome of the process of industrial symbiosis is conceptualised as the emergence and development of a network of symbiotic exchanges in the regional industrial system.

Based on the work of Van Berkel et al. (2007) I distinguish between two types of symbiotic exchanges. First, by-product synergies concern the exchange between firms of previously disposed by-products to replace other business inputs. By-products can originate from process operations (e.g., residues, wastes, leftovers) and non-process operations (e.g., maintenance, warehousing, administration, etc.). Second, utility synergies concern the shared use of utility infrastructures for the production of energy carriers, process water and for the joint treatment of wastes and emissions.

I propose that the emergence and development of networks of symbiotic exchanges can be explained, in the first place, by interactions between actors in the regional industrial system. The implementation of symbiotic exchanges is a type of interaction that contributes to the development of the network of symbiotic exchanges directly, but other types of interactions such as orientation on possibilities for symbiotic exchanges, planning of symbiotic exchanges, investigations on the feasibility of symbiotic exchanges, and lobbying for support may also be important parts of the process through which industrial symbiosis comes about. Such interactions are often project based and their scope does not necessarily cover the entire regional industrial system. Therefore, they are included in the project level of the framework.

The interactions themselves are shaped by the decisions that individual actors involved in the interactions make. I propose that to a large extent industrial symbiosis revolves around the decisions made by particular people at particular moments (Andrews, 2000; Posch, 2010). However, these decisions should not be taken as the ultimate building blocks for explanations of the different ways in which industrial symbiosis comes about. Decisions are shaped by the motivations (i.e., beliefs and desires) and the opportunities of actors. Although decisions should always be understood as a function of both motivations and opportunities, opportunities are of special importance because it is through opportunities that the dynamics at the other levels of the framework influence the decisions that actors make. The opportunities that an actor sees for different courses of action are conditioned by the institutional context in which s/he is embedded and by dynamics of institutional capacity building that unfold at the level of the regional industrial system.

The institutional context represents '. . . the rules of the game in society . . . that shape human interaction' (North, 1990: 3). It consists of regulatory structures, governmental agencies, laws, courts, professions, cultural norms, etc. (Scott, 1987). There are many ways in which the institutional context of actors conditions the opportunities they see for different actions, ranging from subtle influences, such as taken-for-granted cultural norms, to palpable influences, such as laws and regulations (Oliver, 1991). The institutional context can act to limit the opportunities that actors see for different courses of action, for example, when institutional pressures make the costs of choosing for particular types of exchanges prohibitive. The institutional context may also provide actors with increased opportunities; this can happen when institutions provide the basis for increased trust among actors that enables them to engage in more lengthy and strategic types of exchanges.

The opportunities that actors see for different courses of action are also shaped by dynamics of institutional capacity building at the level of the regional industrial system. Institutional capacity is the capacity of a community of actors to coordinate their actions toward issues of common concern in a collaborative fashion (Healey, 1998; Innes and Booher, 1999; Healey et al., 2003). Based on the work of Healey and colleagues (2003) I distinguish three dimensions along which institutional capacity develops in a regional industrial system:

1. Relational resources: through repeated interactions actors may develop bonds of trust and mutual recognition which contribute to the development of stronger personal and professional relationships.
2. Knowledge resources: the stronger relationships between actors serve as a basis for the exchange and joint production of knowledge, including shared conceptions of issues, problems and opportunities.
3. Mobilisation capacity: increases in relational resources and knowledge resources increase the capacity of actors to mobilise for joint initiatives by providing a social network which they can draw upon and by providing shared conceptions around which actors may mobilise (strategic visions). In addition, the mobilisation of resources often depends on one or more actors to take initiative in mobilising others.

Institutional capacity builds up through interactions between the actors in the regional industrial system. These interactions may concern the implementation of symbiotic exchanges themselves but institutional capacity also builds up through other types of projects in which actors orient themselves on the possibilities for symbiotic exchanges, develop concrete plans for symbiotic exchanges, or investigate the technical, organisational and economic feasibility of symbiotic exchanges (e.g., Boons and Spekkink, 2012). Such interactions at the project level set the stage for future developments by contributing to the development of institutional capacity at the level of the regional industrial system.

MECHANISMS OF INDUSTRIAL SYMBIOSIS

I use a mechanism-based approach to elaborate on the linkages between the concepts introduced in the previous section. This is an approach in sociology which acknowledges that explanation of social phenomena should not strive towards generic theories, but should consist of understanding why certain social mechanisms operate in specific situations (Stinchcombe, 1991; Hedström and Swedberg, 1998; Mayntz, 2004; Elster, 2007; Gross, 2009). This approach leads to the development of multiple (often alternative) partial theories that link two or more concepts of the framework together, rather than one coherent theory that accounts for all concepts and relations.

Based on this approach a process such as the emergence and development of industrial symbiosis can be studied as a concatenation of mechanisms. In doing so, it is important to take into account sequence effects; mechanisms may influence the course of the process as a whole in a path-dependent way and thus the order in which they occur is relevant (cf., Poole et al., 2000).

A large variety of mechanisms may be identified based on this conceptual approach that may influence the way industrial symbiosis unfolds and, more specifically, the network of symbiotic exchanges that develops throughout the process. My aim is not to provide an exclusive list of all mechanisms that may be relevant to the development of industrial symbiosis, but to describe a small number of mechanisms that I believe to be central to many examples of industrial symbiosis. Also, to keep the discussion simple and concise I restrict my discussion to mechanisms that link dynamics at the level of the institutional context to dynamics at the project level and mechanisms that link dynamics at the level of the regional industrial system to the project level. Where possible, I clarify the mechanisms by offering empirical examples.

Mechanisms Linking the Institutional Dynamics to Dynamics at the Project Level

The first mechanisms I discuss are those that link dynamics at the level of the institutional context to dynamics at the project level. As I discussed before, the opportunities that actors see for different courses of action form the conceptual link between the dynamics at these two levels. Here I present two mechanisms that illustrate how the actions of actors are influenced by institutional dynamics that are mediated by opportunities. The two mechanisms I discuss here are closely linked to the motivations that an actor may have to engage in symbiotic exchanges. The first mechanism is linked to legitimacy seeking behaviour and the second mechanism is linked to behaviour driven by conventional business motivations.

In the case of the first mechanism the actions of actors can be understood as responses to different types of institutional pressures that actors face (cf., Oliver, 1991). A type of institutional pressure that is easy to grasp is regulatory pressure (i.e., legislative and regulatory requirements). Although regulatory pressures are likely to play a role in any variant of industrial symbiosis, their role is probably most evident in Chinese variants, where regulatory pressures traditionally play an important role in the promotion of eco-industrial developments (Shi and Zhang, 2006; Geng and Doberstein, 2008). However, legitimacy-seeking behaviour often goes beyond simply following governmental regulations. It also involves attempts to meet expectations that are set by the general public (i.e., societal pressures). Ashton (2010) demonstrates how certain changes in the practices of firms on the island of Puerto Rico resulted from a combination of regulatory and societal pressures. In this case societal pressures took the form of expectations with regard to the health impact and environmental impact of the firms' activities.

The opportunities for different courses of action that actors should follow to attain legitimacy are often encoded in the institutional pressures themselves. For example, in support of its circular economy programme the Chinese government published specific guidelines for the development of eco-industrial parks (Yuan et al., 2006; Geng and Doberstein, 2008). Similarly, in the Netherlands the government published a handbook that suggests possible approaches to the sustainable development of industrial parks. Also, actors could only be subsidised for such activities if they performed certain types of projects in a specific order (Boons and Spekkink, 2012).

If industrial symbiosis activities are the consequence of institutional pressures, their results (in terms of the types of symbiotic exchanges that emerge) are likely to reflect those pressures. For example, many of the more than 200 projects that were subsidised by the Dutch stimulation programme for sustainable parks (1999–2004) followed the logic prescribed in the handbook that the government had published earlier (Boons and Spekkink, 2012). Differences in the structure of different networks of symbiotic exchanges may thus be partly explained by differences in the institutional pressures faced by actors involved in their development.

A mechanism alternative to the one introduced above is based on the observation that many industrial symbiosis initiatives are driven by business motivations, such as cutting costs and resource security (Chertow, 2007). With this mechanism the institutional context shapes industrial symbiosis in a different way than it does with initiatives that are driven by legitimacy-seeking behaviour. Here, the actions of actors can be understood to reflect their attempts to reduce the risks entailed by the symbiotic exchanges they engage in, which is the topic of transaction cost economics (Williamson, 1975, 1985, 1996; see also Shi, 2011). The opportunities that actors have to mitigate the risks of exchanges are determined by the types of economic coordination that are supported by the institutional context in which they are embedded (e.g., contract laws). This type of reasoning is central to the varieties of capitalism approach of Hall and Soskice (2001). The varieties of capitalism approach draws a core distinction between liberal market economies where actors typically rely on hierarchies and competitive market arrangements for coordination and coordinated market economies where actors typically rely on relational and incomplete contracting for coordination.

Although this distinction is rather idealised (Peck and Theodore, 2007; Gertler, 2010) it serves well to illustrate that there may be systematic differences in the forms of economic coordination that actors choose for their exchanges. For example, in China some firms have the possibility to set up an intra-firm network of symbiotic exchanges such as in the case of the Guitang Group (Zhu and Côté, 2004; Zhu et al., 2007). Such arrangements do not entail the risks entailed by exchanges between two or more independent firms. In an institutional context where such elaborate intra-firm arrangements are unfeasible, bilaterally dependent actors typically rely on complexes of contracts and alliances such as in the case of Kalundborg (Ehrenfeld and Gertler, 1997).

To summarise, the opportunities actors have to mitigate the risks of symbiotic exchanges depend on the institutional context in which they are embedded and, more specifically, the forms of economic coordination it supports. Differences in the structure of different networks of symbiotic exchanges can thus be partially explained by differences in the types of economic coordination available to the actors involved in their development.

Both types of mechanisms discussed above are likely to be at play in the evolution of any network of symbiotic exchanges and additional mechanisms are conceivable. The development of symbiotic exchanges involves multiple actors that often have more than one motivation for engaging in industrial symbiosis. Also, their motivations may change over time. The fact that different mechanisms can link the institutional context to actor decisions means that empirical research should also focus on the conditions under which one or the other mechanism comes into play.

Building Institutional Capacity

So far I have presented mechanisms that explain how the decisions of actors are linked to institutional dynamics by the opportunities that these dynamics generate for different courses of action. As I mentioned above, the opportunities that actors see for different courses of action are also shaped by dynamics that occur within the boundaries of the regional industrial system. Here, I discuss a set of mechanisms that link the dynamics at the level of the regional industrial system to dynamics at the project level. I conceptualise the dynamics at the level of the regional industrial system in terms of institutional capacity building (Boons and Spekkink, 2012). Before I introduce the mechanisms that link institutional capacity building to actor behaviour a further explanation of the concept of institutional capacity building is required.

In the process of industrial symbiosis the actions and interactions at the project level are not all directly dedicated to the development of symbiotic exchanges. There are many activities that may precede the actual development of symbiotic exchanges, such as the exploration of possibilities to cooperate, the gathering of knowledge on the economic, organisational and technical feasibility of exchanges, the bargaining of agreements, the development of plans and strategic visions, etc. Examples of such activities can be found in the case of the INES project in the Rotterdam Harbour industrial area as described by Baas and Boons (2007). Long before firms in this area engaged in symbiotic exchanges they were involved in other initiatives concerning environmental performance such as the reduction of Hydrocarbons, the reduction of Chlorine Fluor Carbon implementation and the implementation of environmental management systems. The INES project itself consisted of four phases that together span a period from 1992 to 2002, after which the INES project became included in the ROM-Rijnmond project (Baas and Boons, 2007). Throughout the process the actors engaged in workshops, performed feasibility studies and made attempts to implement symbiotic exchanges.

I propose that such interactions contribute to the development of institutional capacity at the level of the regional industrial system. Through recurring interactions actors develop stronger personal and professional relationships, which contribute to the growth of social networks in the regional industrial system (Deutz and Gibbs, 2008). These social networks also offer actors better opportunities to exchange and jointly produce knowledge, including shared conceptions of problems and solutions. The combination of a growing social network and the development of shared visions around which actors can mobilise offers actors better opportunities to mobilise for collaborative action and engage in new projects together (Healey, 1998; Innes and Booher, 1999; Healey et al., 2003).

The development of institutional capacity continuously feeds back on the process of industrial symbiosis by influencing the opportunities that actors see for further interactions. This occurs through at least three mechanisms. First, as the personal and professional relationships between actors strengthen they are less likely to perceive relational risks in further interactions, including symbiotic exchanges. This mechanism was also observed in the INES project: 'Thanks to the historical development within several programmes the strategic platform could build on the built-up trust between the members of the different organizations and the conditions for successful projects that earlier failed' (Baas and Boons, 2007: 559). Second, by producing and exchanging knowledge actors may develop a better view on the feasibility of symbiotic exchanges and identify new possibilities for symbiotic exchanges. In this regard, Baas and Boons (2007) describe a learning process that occurred in the INES project. Finally, the availability of the social network, the development of knowledge in addition to the presence of key actors and a strategic vision around which to mobilise increase the opportunities that actors have to actually engage in further joint action. In the INES project the industrial association Deltalinqs repeatedly played a key role in mobilising others. Also, throughout the project multiple strategic platforms were developed as well as a strategic vision in the later stages of the project. For the platforms and the strategic vision it is less clear to what extend they actually contributed to further initiatives.

It is important to note that a positive influence of institutional capacity on symbiotic exchanges does not necessarily involve an enlarged opportunity set. Symbiotic exchanges may also become more feasible as a result of a diminished opportunity set, for example by excluding actions such as opportunistic behaviour. As the case of the INES project illustrates, the development of institutional capacity is a gradual process that may span a period of many years. It may take a very long time before these dynamics result in actual symbiotic exchanges. In addition, institutional capacity may have built up through earlier interactions that were not specifically related to the development of industrial symbiosis. In the literature on industrial symbiosis this is sometimes referred to as shared histories or pre-existing organisational relationships (Eilering and Vermeulen, 2004; Heeres et al., 2004; Gibbs and Deutz, 2007).

One question that remains to be answered is how these dynamics at the level of the regional industrial system may explain differences in the structure of networks of symbiotic exchanges that develop in different places of the world. A simple answer to this question is that structural differences may be explained by the extent that institutional capacity building actually takes place. In this regard Hall and Soskice suggest that collaborative approaches to economic coordination depend on the presence of institutions of deliberation, which they define as '. . . institutions that encourage the relevant actors to engage in collaborative discussion and to reach agreements which each other' (2001: 11). In the Netherlands, self-regulation is rather common and business is relatively well organised through business associations. Heeres et al. (2004) suggest that these serve as platforms to educate and inform firms of the potential benefits of symbiotic exchanges and as much needed communication platforms. Because of these factors it is also relatively easy for firms and other relevant actors in the Netherlands to find platforms for collaboration on environmental issues. In China, the presence of organised business is more limited and the repeated interactions of the kind we observe in the Netherlands are far less common. Historically, there has been a stronger role for regulatory approaches to environmental issues in China, although things may be gradually changing in that regard (Shi and Zhang, 2006).

Another explanation points to the role that strategic visions may play in the development of networks of symbiotic exchanges. For example, in the Canal Zone of the Netherlands (a regional industrial system in the province of Zeeland), firms, governments and knowledge institutes are developing Biopark Terneuzen, which is based on a vision of a bio based cluster that links the chemical process industry to the agricultural industry. The types of exchanges that actors develop throughout the development of this cluster are strongly related to this shared vision. Indeed, such visions also depend on the opportunities generated by situational factors such as the type of industries present in the system and the geographical features of the system.

Influencing the Institutional Context

Actors may also attempt to influence their institutional context. Boons (2009) suggests that firms may engage in marketing, public relations and public affairs activities to influence the institutional pressures that they face. These activities can be directed at governmental agencies, politicians, NGOs and the general public. Through these activities firms aim to align institutional pressures with their own motivations. Innes and Booher (1999) suggest that when actors have developed sufficient institutional capacity they may also work together to influence public action in ways they were unable to do before. In the regional industrial system of the Canal Zone actors involved in the development of symbiotic exchanges have occasionally made attempts to influence public opinion and national policies and regulations with regard to the stimulation of bio-based industry.

INVESTIGATING MECHANISMS

In this chapter I have introduced a conceptual framework that is grounded in an understanding of industrial symbiosis as a process, and building on this framework I introduced several mechanisms that may explain how different types of symbiotic exchanges may emerge throughout the process.

I propose that a fruitful way to investigate these mechanisms is to undertake a longitudinal research approach in which multiple cases of industrial symbiosis are compared. For this purpose, Event Sequence Analysis (ESA) was developed by researchers of the Erasmus University Rotterdam (Boons et al., 2014). ESA is a longitudinal research approach that is inspired by methods developed in the Minnesota Innovation Research Program (MIRP) (Van de Ven and Poole, 1990; Poole et al., 2000; Van de Ven et al., 2000) and by theory and methods developed by Abbott (1988, 1990, 2001) and Abell (1987, 1993). Using this approach the actions and interactions of the actors involved in the development of industrial symbiosis are recorded and entered into event sequence datasets as incidents. These incidents are empirical descriptions that include (at the least) a description of the action or interaction, the actor(s) involved, the date on which the action or interaction occurred, and the data source. Researchers can code these incidents using a coding scheme that is derived from the conceptual or theoretical perspective of the researcher. The coded incidents serve as indicators for theoretical events (Poole et al., 2000). For example, based on the conceptual framework introduced in this chapter one would develop a coding scheme that identifies events related to (changes in) opportunities, motivations, institutional capacity, the institutional context, etc. From the stream of coded incidents one or more sequences of events may be derived that can be analysed for temporal patterns using a variety of methods, such as phasic analysis, stochastic modelling, event time series analysis (Poole et al., 2000), narrative analysis (Abell, 1987), template matching (Langley, 1999) and optimal matching (Abbott and Tsay, 2000). The investigation of whole event sequences is a relatively straightforward way to study concatenations of mechanisms. The sequence effects associated with such concatenations can be investigated by comparing sequences across multiple cases. Such investigations should also include an analysis of the conditions under which alternative mechanisms are triggered.

Industrial symbiosis can be viewed as a process through which actors increase their connectedness in terms of material, energy and information flows (Boons et al., 2014). From this perspective, industrial symbiosis revolves around change rather than a certain state affairs. A mechanism-based approach, accompanied with ESA, ties in well with a view of industrial symbiosis as a process and is therefore a promising way forward for research on industrial symbiosis.

NOTE

1. A regional industrial system is 'a more or less stable collection of firms located in proximity to one another, where firms in principle can develop social and material/energy connections as a result of that proximity' (Boons et al., 2011: 907).

REFERENCES

Abbott, A. (1988), 'Transcending General Linear Reality', *Sociological Theory*, **6** (2), 169–186.
Abbott, A. (1990), 'A Primer on Sequence Methods', *Organization Science*, **1** (4), 375–392.
Abbott. A. (2001), *Time Matters: On Theory and Method*, Chicago: University of Chicago Press.

Abbott, A. and A. Tsay (2000), 'Sequence Analysis and Optimal Matching Methods in Sociology', *Sociological Methods & Research*, **29** (1), 3–33.

Abell, P. (1987), *The Syntax of Social Life: the Theory and Method of Comparative Narratives*, Oxford, UK: Clarendon Press.

Abell, P. (1993), 'Some Aspects of Narrative Method', *Journal of Mathematical Sociology*, **18** (2–3), 93–134.

Andrews, C.J. (2000), 'Building a Micro Foundation for Industrial Ecology', *Journal of Industrial Ecology*, **4** (3), 35–52.

Ashton, W.S. (2010), 'Managing Performance Expectations of Industrial Symbiosis', *Business Strategy and the Environment*, **20** (5), 297–309.

Baas, L.W. and F.A.A. Boons (2007), 'The Introduction and Dissemination of the Industrial Symbiosis Projects in the Rotterdam Harbour and Industry Complex', *International Journal of Environmental Technology and Management*, **7** (5), 551–577.

Boons, F.A.A. (2009), *Creating Ecological Value: An Evolutionary Approach to Business Strategies and the Natural Environment*, Cheltenham, UK and Northampton, MA, USA: Edward Elgar.

Boons, F.A.A. and M.A. Janssen (2004), 'The Myth of Kalundborg: Social Dilemmas in Stimulating Eco-Industrial Parks', in J. C.J.M. Van den Bergh and M.A. Janssen (eds), Cambridge, MA: MIT Press, pp. 337–355.

Boons, F.A.A. and W.A.H. Spekkink (2012), 'Levels of Institutional Capacity and Actor Expectations about Industrial Symbiosis: Evidence from the Dutch Stimulation Program 1999–2004', *Journal of Industrial Ecology*, **16** (1), 61–69.

Boons, F.A.A., W.A.H. Spekkink and Y. Mouzakitis (2011), 'The Dynamics of Industrial Symbiosis: A Proposal for a Conceptual Framework Based Upon a Comprehensive Literature Review', *Journal of Cleaner Production*, **19** (9–10), 905–911.

Boons, F.A.A., W.A.H. Spekkink and W. Jiao (2014), 'A Process Perspective on Industrial Symbiosis', *Journal of Industrial Ecology*, **18** (3), 341–355.

Chertow, M.R. (2007), '"Uncovering" Industrial Symbiosis', *Journal of Industrial Ecology*, **11** (1), 11–30.

Deutz, P. and D. Gibbs (2008), 'Industrial Ecologyand Regional Development: Eco-Industrial Development aCluster Policy', *Regional Studies*, **42** (10), 1313–1328.

Ehrenfeld, J.R. and N. Gertler (1997), 'Industrial Ecology in Practice: The Evolution of Interdependence at Kalundborg', *Journal of Industrial Ecology*, **1** (1), 67–79.

Eilering, J.A.M. and W.J.V. Vermeulen (2004), 'Eco-industrial Parks: Toward Industrial Symbiosis and Utility Sharing in Practice', *Progress in Industrial Ecology*, **1** (1–2), 245–270.

Elster, J. (2007), *Explaining Social Behaviour: More Nuts and Bolts for the Social Sciences*, Cambridge, UK: Cambridge University Press.

Geng, Y. and B. Doberstein (2008), 'Developing the Circular Economy in China: Challenges and Opportunities for Achieving "Leapfrog Development"', *International Journal of Sustainable Development and World Ecology*, **15** (3), 231–239.

Gertler, M. (2010), 'Rules of the Game: The Place of Institutions in Regional Economic Change', *Regional Studies*, **44** (1), 1–15.

Gibbs, D. and P. Deutz (2007), 'Reflections on Implementing Industrial Ecology Through Eco-Industrial Park Development', *Journal of Cleaner Production*, **15** (17), 1683–1695.

Gross, N. (2009), 'A Pragmatist Theory of Social Mechanisms', *American Sociological Review*, **74** (3), 358–379.

Hall, P.A. and D. Soskice (2001), 'An Introduction to Varieties of Capitalism', in P.A. Hall and D. Soskice (eds), *Varieties of Capitalism: The Institutional Foundations of Comparative Advantage*, Oxford: Oxford University Press, pp. 1–68.

Healey, P. (1998), 'Building Institutional Capacity through Collaborative Approaches to Urban Planning', *Environment and Planning A*, **30** (9), 1531–1546.

Healey, P., C. de Magalhaes, A. Madanipour and John Pendlebury (2003), 'Place, Identity and Local Politics: Analysing Initiatives in Deliberative Governance', in M.A. Hajer and H. Wagenaar (eds), *Deliberative Policy Analysis: Understanding Governance in the Network Society*, Theories of Institutional Design, Cambridge, UK: Cambridge University Press, pp. 60–87.

Hedström, P. and R. Swedberg (eds) (1998), *Social Mechanisms: An Analytical Approach to Social Theory*, Cambridge and New York: Cambridge University Press.

Heeres, R.R., W.J.V. Vermeulen and F.B. de Walle (2004), 'Eco-industrial Park Initiatives in the USA and the Netherlands: First Lessons', *Journal of Cleaner Production*, **12** (8–10), 985–995.

Innes, J.E. and D.E. Booher (1999), 'Consensus Building and Complex Adaptive Systems: A Framework for Evaluating Collaborative Planning', *Journal of the American Planning Association*, **65** (4), 412–423.

Langley, A. (1999), 'Strategies for Theorizing from Process Data', *The Academy of Management Review*, **24** (4), 691–710.

Lowe, E.A. and L.K. Evans (1995), 'Industrial Ecology and Industrial Ecosystems', *Journal of Cleaner Production*, **3** (1–2), 47–53.

Mayntz, R. (2004), 'Mechanisms in the Analysis of Social Macro-Phenomena', *Philosophy of the Social Sciences*, **34** (2), 237–259.

North, D.C. (1990), *Institutions, Institutional Change, and Economic Performance*, Cambridge, UK: Cambridge University Press.

Oliver, C. (1991), 'Strategic Responses to Institutional Processes', *The Academy of Management Review*, **16** (1), 145–179.

Paquin, R.L. and J. Howard-Grenville (2012), 'The Evolution of Facilitated Industrial Symbiosis', *Journal of Industrial Ecology*, **16** (1), 83–93.

Peck, J. and N. Theodore (2007), 'Variegated Capitalism', *Progress in Human Geography*, **31** (6), 731–772.

Poole, M.S., A.H. Van de Ven, K. Dooley and M.E. Holmes (2000), *Organizational Change and Innovation Processes: Theory and Methods for Research*, New York: Oxford University Press.

Posch, A. (2010), 'Industrial Recycling Networks as Starting Points for Broader Sustainability-Oriented Cooperation?', *Journal of Industrial Ecology*, **14** (2), 242–257.

Scott, W.R. (1987), 'The Adolescence of Institutional Theory', *Administrative Science Quarterly*, **32** (4), 493–511.

Shi, H. (2011), *Industrial Symbiosis from the Perspectives of Transaction Cost Economics and Institutional Theory*, Charleston: UMI Dissertation Publisher.

Shi, H. and L. Zhang (2006), 'China's Environmental Governance of Rapid Industrialization', *Environmental Politics*, **15** (2), 271–292.

Stinchcombe, A.L. (1991), 'The Conditions of Fruitfulness of Theorizing About

Mechanisms in Social Science', *Philosophy of the Social Sciences*, **21** (3), 367–388.

Van Berkel, R., J. Majer and D. Stehlik (2007), *Regional Resource Synergies for Sustainable Development in Heavy Industrial Areas: An Overview of Opportunities and Experiences*, Perth: Curtin University of Technology – Centre of Excellence in Cleaner Production.

Van de Ven, A.H. and M.S. Poole (1990), 'Methods for Studying Innovation Development in the Minnesota Innovation Research Program', *Organization Science*, **1** (3), pp. 313–335.

Van de Ven, A.H., H.L. Angle and M.S. Poole (eds) (2000), *Research on the Management of Innovation: The Minnesota Studies*, Oxford, UK: Oxford University Press.

Williamson, O.E. (1975), *Markets and Hierarchies, Analysis and Antitrust Implications: A Study in the Economics of Internal Organization*, New York: Free Press.

Williamson, O.E. (1985), *The Economic Institutions of Capitalism : Firms, Markets, Relational Contracting*, New York: Free Press.

Williamson, O.E. (1996), *The Mechanisms of Governance*, New York: Oxford University Press.

Yuan, Z., J. Bi and Y. Moriguichi (2006), 'The Circular Economy: A New Development Strategy in China', *Journal of Industrial Ecology*, **10** (1–2), 4–8.

Zhu, Q. and R.P. Côté (2004), 'Integrating Green Supply Chain Management into an Embryonic Eco-Industrial Development: A Case Study of the Guitang Group', *Journal of Cleaner Production*, **12** (8–10), 1025–1035.

Zhu, Q., E.A. Lowe, Y.-A. Wei and D. Barnes (2007), 'Industrial Symbiosis in China: A Case Study of the Guitang Group', *Journal of Industrial Ecology*, **11** (1), 31–42.

10. Institutional context of eco-industrial park development in China: environmental governance in industrial parks and zones

Lingxuan Liu, Bing Zhang and Jun Bi

INTRODUCTION

Industrial parks and zones (IPZs) have been playing an essential economic role in China's rapid development during the past three decades since the Reform and Opening-up. Over the same period, China's industrialisation has engendered serious problems with the degradation of ecosystems and pollution of the environment. According to life cycle analysis (LCA), comprising detailed calculations of direct and indirect carbon emissions from production, construction, use, maintenance, the energy consumption (H. Wang et al. 2013), carbon footprint (Dong et al. 2013) and water consumption (Liang et al. 2011) of IPZs are becoming leading challenges to the country's limited resources.

Western observers have expressed concerns that IPZs are pollution havens (Eskeland and Harrison 2003; Cole 2004), but the pollution haven hypothesis is not merely a reference to geographical or spatial relocation of investment, industries or pollutions, avoiding regulations from the developed world. The phenomenon and its consequences cannot be explained without consideration of the institutional context (Cole and Fredriksson 2009) of specific countries and specific industries. In addition, current literature also shows that there is a need to explore the links between institutional arrangements and environmental policies. This is especially true for developing countries experiencing rapid economy growth and social change (Liu et al. 2012).

The high densities of industry and population among IPZs have greatly influenced not only regional economic growth, but also technological innovation and approaches to environmental quality (Yuan et al. 2010). It is also argued that industrial ecosystems, in addition to promoting resource efficiencies, can be seen as influential institutional spaces (or 'niches') for the development of new technology (Adamides and Mouzakitis 2009; Gibbs 2009) and regional economy (Deutz and Gibbs 2008). Such institutional niches are particularly interesting to China, not only because of the rapid growing material flows, land-use changes and financial powers, but also because of the multi-level governance regimes that allow IPZs to interact with China's national environmental programmes. China's decade-long exploration with Eco-Industrial Park (EIP) development as a means of environmental management offers an opportunity to study the practical implementation of EIPs in a unique institutional set-up (Shi et al. 2012a). Thus, this chapter develops an institutional perspective at the level of local industrial ecosystems.

In this chapter we will review the history, patterns and governance of China's industrial parks and zones. We examine the role of industrial parks that has facilitated, if not led, local environmental regulation and enforcement within China, and thus provided a solid institutional background of EIPs. The realities and characteristics of local environmental governance and institutions in IPZs are discussed. The content is based on a range of policy documents, industrial planning programmes, reports and collaboration projects. In a decade of various projects among regions of Yangtze River Delta and Pearl River Delta, we have also conducted semi-structured interviews with local decision-makers, officers from relevant agencies, industry representatives and experts. All the interview data were then transcribed, categorised, condensed and paraphrased for this chapter.

History and Concepts: China's Development Zones and Industrial Parks

An industrial park or zone can be defined as a land area developed and subdivided into plots according to an integrated plan with provision for roads, transport and public utilities for the use of a group of industrialists, and perhaps local authorities (UNIDO 1997). The birth of IPZs was a direct result of China's Reform and Opening-up strategies, which resulted in the coastal special economic zones (Bao et al. 2002). Following their excellent economic performance in the 1980s, the central government initiated a programme to facilitate economic growth by attracting foreign direct investment (FDI) to coastal areas (Jones et al. 2003; Ng and Tuan 2006). During the years 1984–1988, the Chinese government approved the first group of National Economic and Technology Development Zones (NETDZ) in 14 coastal cities, and provided preferential policies for foreign investors who inject capital into these areas (Table 10.1).

Since the 1990s, the scale of IPZs has increased tremendously, in tandem with the great economic success of Reform and Opening-up and a high

Table 10.1   The first group of National Economic and Technology Development Zones

Location of NETDZ	City name where NETDZ located
Liaoning Province, northeast coast	Dalian
Hebei Province, near Beijing	Qinhuangdao
	Tianjin
Shandong Province, eastern coast	Yantai
	Qingdao
Jiangsu Province, eastern coast	Lianyungang
	Nantong
Shanghai, eastern coast	Minhang
	Hongqiao
	Caohejing
Fujian Province, southeast coast	Fuzhou
Zhejiang Province, southeast coast	Ningbo
Guangdong Province, southern coast	Guangzhou
	Zhanjiang

Source: Ministry of Commerce, China (2009).

growth of FDI in China. At the end of 2005, the number of NETDZs increased to 54 over the country, including five industrial parks which share the same preferential national policies and regulations as NETDZs. In addition, other types of IPZs have also emerged (Table 10.2) and developed with their own paradigms. The national or provincial governments have provided special policies for foreign investment and taxes within such IPZs. For example, according to incomplete statistics from the Ministry of Land and Resources, there are 6866 industrial parks in China, of which 113 were government-approved national and provincial parks (Geng and Doberstein 2008).

Not only inspired by the Reform and Opening-up policy, the development of IPZs was also regulated by the environmental mechanism of 'concentrated pollution control' in China (SEPA 2002). In order to develop local industry without too much degradation of local environmental quality, it was required that the location of certain sectors of manufacturing industry should be in a well-planned industrial park or zone, in which pollution control and energy saving facilities were planned, designed and constructed in advance with adequate capacity (Shi et al. 2012b).

Despite the various synonyms of development zones in China, they have played the similar role of 'national factory' during China's industrialisation. With less than 0.5% of the country's construction land area,

Table 10.2   Synonym and characteristics of China's industrial parks and zones[1]

Title	Characteristics and functions
Economic and technology development zones	Government approved, national or provincial districts, with comprehensive manufacturing industries and social functions
Bonded zones	Similar to free trade zone, but focus on international export and logistics
New and hi-tech industrial development zones	Part of the National Torch Program, focus on a variety of new and hi-tech industries, like IT, biotech, renewable energy, and so on
Border economic cooperation zones	Mainly in middle and west regions for international trade with Middle Asian countries and nations
Export processing zones	Export processing business working with customs
Investment zones	Usually at provincial or local level, cooperating with a major investor region from certain countries or areas, including Hong Kong and Taiwan
Industrial parks	Could be either one part of or independent to the industrial zones mentioned above. Classified into the following three categories:
	Comprehensive — diversified manufacture industries Sector integrated — focus on a few sectors of industries Vein — recycling industry

Source: Chinese Association of Development Zones (2010).

NETDZs contributed 10%–30% of GDP of their corresponding cities, 5.15% of China's GDP, and attracted 23.2% of total foreign investment in China (MC and MLR 2006).

Urbanisation During and After Industrialisation

The initiation of IPZs in southern and eastern China was also coupled with rural industrialisation (Christerson and Lever-Tracy 1997). After 1995, the development of NETDZs spread into middle and west regions of China (Figure 10.1), which was also greatly facilitated by the national strategy of West Development after the year 2000. More than 30 of the current 54 NETDZs are located near the capital cities of China's provinces or municipal areas, including Tibet (i.e., the capital city of any province usually has a national industrial zone nearby). Investments and

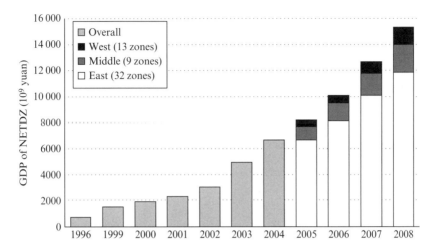

Source: Calculated by author from information from Invest in China (2009–2010).

Figure 10.1   Economic growth of NETDZs in east, middle and west areas of China, 1996–2008

enterprises are attracted into IPZs, as well as the increasing immigrants including labourers and their dependents, which leads to increased population density. Erstwhile, previous landowners and farmers have had to change their residential places and style of life from those of rural villages to suburban communities, or, in many cases, to become migrant workers of other regions if they are willing to (Akay et al. 2012). Thus, most of the IPZs are developing into urban areas within the corresponding cities.

Nowadays when local people talk about a variety of industrial parks/ zones of their cities, one simple phrase is used: the new district. During or since the industrialisation of IPZs, the functions of IPZs are changing from manufacture and export to a more integrated community. Take the top three industrial zones[2] in China for example (Table 10.3). Combined with corresponding cities, those industrial zones have been assigned to a new administrative level as a county or suburban area.

Table 10.3   Land area used and new zone development in three typical industrial parks and zones of China

	Tianjin Economy Development Area	Guangzhou Economy-Technology Development District	Suzhou Industrial Park
Area	33 km^2 planned in 1984	Approximately 30 km^2 planned in 1984	260 km^2 planned in 1994
First phase as initiation	Approximately 5 km^2	4.6 km^2	70 km^2
Area as a developed industrial zone	42 km^2 until 2006	61.3 km^2 until 2002	
Area of new zone combined with corresponding cities	2270 km^2 in 2008, the coastal new zone	390 km^2 after 2005, the Luogang county area	288 km^2
Urban area of corresponding cities	City of Tianjin 4335 km^2	City of Guangzhou 3843 km^2	City of Suzhou 1650 km^2

Sources: Websites of Guangzhou Economy-Technology Development District (2009); Suzhou Industrial Park (2009); Tianjin Economy Development Zone (2009).

ENVIRONMENTAL PROGRAMMES IMPLEMENTED IN IPZS

The industrialisation and urbanisation of China's IPZs have made a great contribution not only to China's economic growth and social development, but also to its energy and resource consumption. During the past two decades and likely even in the coming decade, many of the IPZs in China remain as the destination of national and global industry transfer. However, we argue that in contemporary China, IPZs increasingly defy the concept of a pollution haven (Cole and Fredriksson 2009; Matus et al. 2012). This is a result of endogenous environmental policies and institutional context given that: 1) although the high intensity of industry in IPZs brings high intensity of energy consumption, it also allows a scale effect enabling energy efficiency and applications of renewable energy by inter-firm collaboration; and 2) with a tradition of long-term planning and a background of technology innovation, IPZs are usually able to plan their infrastructure during the phase of urbanisation, rather than after it.

During the last decade, the environmental performance and resource efficiency of IPZs in China have been improved. National environmental regulation makes an industrial agglomeration and pollution control mechanisms more effective by offering a potential mechanism of cost-effective pollution treatment. For example, a water and wastewater plant of large capacity with a pre-planned sewage network, or a power plant and steam heating provider of large capacity, which could thereby afford high technology to improve efficiency, and desulphurisation facilities. Meanwhile, with extremely limited land and resources ('one inch of land, one inch of gold'), local governments of IPZs would now consider the features (capital, category, technology, etc.) of the new-coming investment much more carefully than they did in 1980s. New IPZs are changing the investment conducting strategy from 'looking for investment by all means' to 'choose better investment'. Conversely, old IPZs are trying to 'empty the cage and replace the bird', which means replace old or traditional industries of heavy pollution with new and cleaner ones.

Figure 10.2 shows the energy intensity improvement of China's leading IPZs, which is just a simple example of the good environmental performance of IPZs. Well-enforced environmental management and regulation are encouraged among IPZs, not only because of national pollution

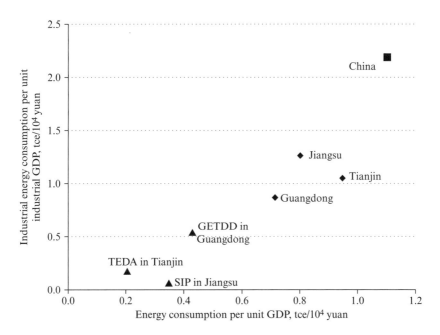

Figure 10.2   Energy intensity of developed IPZs compared with their provinces and with China, 2008

control policy, but also with the various environmental programmes for IPZs. The following two policies of environmental performance and regulations are well known: EIPs and the Circular Economy (Peters et al. 2007; Geng et al. 2010).

Eco-industrial Parks

The development of EIPs in China is closely interwoven with efforts to improve the environmental performance of IPZs. While the development of IPZs was initially under the regulation of the Ministry of Commerce alone, two agencies were involved in the supervision of sustainable industrial strategies: the Ministry of Environmental Protection (MEP) and the National Development and Reform Commission (NDRC). In the late 1990s, EID (Eco-Industrial Development) in China was introduced during the development of IPZs (Zhang et al. 2010) to improve the environmental performance of IPZs through pilot projects and demonstrations. According to the national standard for EIPs of China (HJ/T274-2006), an EIP should retain a high industrial economic growth rate of at least 25% per annum, while maintaining high environmental performance, such as in energy efficiency etc. For example, a national EIP should keep its energy intensity below 0.5 Tce/104yuan (standard coal equivalent, which means twice China's current average energy efficiency). EIPs are also required to achieve 75% industrial wastewater reuse, 85% industrial solid waste reuse and 40% reclaimed water use. These targets have led to the exchange of unwanted materials between firms (industrial symbiosis) and material flow efficiency, and could also lead to greenhouse gas (GHG) emission reduction. Most of the national EIPs come from the reconstruction or development of important national IPZs. At the end of 2009, immediately after COP15, China's MEP announced a notice of requirement (Ministry of Environmental Protection, 2009) to encourage low-carbon economy development among national EID demonstration parks/zones. The notice required not only industry structure adjustment and new energy designing and application, but also institutional innovation at IPZ level.

Circular Economy Pilot Areas

The Circular Economy (CE) was a concept introduced to China from the environmental protection movements and laws of German, Swedish, Japan and other industrialised countries (Mathews et al. 2011). It was formally accepted in 2002 by the central government as a new development strategy to cope with the conflicts between rapid economic growth and the shortage of raw materials and energy (Yuan et al. 2006). The core of CE is the

Table 10.4   National CE pilot projects of China

	Number in 2005	Number increase in 2008
Provinces, municipals and cities	10	17
IPZs	13	20
Key sectors and enterprises	56	59

Source: Ministry of Environmental Protection, China. (2010).

circular flow of materials and the multi-use of raw materials and energy, which is concluded as the '3R' principles – reduction, reuse and recycling.

At the local level the CE was initiated predominantly by IPZs. The latter had both high intensity industry clusters to be regulated and optimised and offered potential to address resource shortages by forming industrial symbiosis networks (Geng et al. 2012). After more than five years of volunteer local pilot practices, the central government initiated the CE pilot projects in 2005, offering certain funds to encourage cities, IPZs and enterprises from different industrial sectors to design their proper strategies (Mathews and Tan 2011). Such a high tide of pilot programmes finally led to a national law of Promoting Circular Economy in 2009. The number of pilots doubled by the end of 2008 (Table 10.4). In addition, key local IPZs which had not been nominated at the national level could also be included as an essential part of a provincial CE pilot project.

More than 100 industrial parks all over China have claimed that they are developing themselves as EIPs and/or CE zones, in which chemical engineering, management science and engineering, and sociology experts are involved (Yuan et al. 2006). IPZs in China are continuing their role as not only initiators but also implementation agents to improve regional environmental performance, as long as they can fit in China's institutional background (e.g., legal and regulatory framework) and the changing economic patterns of the rest of the world (e.g., the economic crisis of 2008). A good example can be found in another chapter of this book, which introduces the low carbon development strategies since 2008 among Chinese IPZs (H. Wang et al., Chapter 13, this volume).

FROM POLICIES TO GOVERNANCE

Organisational Structure of IPZ Management

Many western authors (White 1991; Shirk 1993) have examined the role of China's local government as an investment inviter, or even as an entrepreneurial government (Hubbard 1995). Such a role may lead to rent-seeking problems, corruption (Caulfield 2006) and environmental problems, for GDP was still the major political achievement of a local governor. In order to make a change, the central government has tried to redesign the GDP-based evaluation system. Local governments of China are emerging as major players in translating environmental protection policies into local patterns of social and environmental regulation (Skinner et al. 2003). They also have increasing freedom to specify their environmental policies and regulations to cope with the realities of local conditions (Geng et al. 2007). The 11th environmental five-year plan (FYP) of China established a top-down allocation system of pollution control targets, in which every local authority has an allocated goal of pollution reduction. A local leader would consider the environmental performance of IPZs as an attractive political achievement. Meanwhile, the environmental management of IPZs also relies on specific governance components from administrative levels that are usually lower than city governments. This section examines how such governance components can be helpful to the environmental performance of IPZs.

A typical title of the local government branch of IPZs is the Administrative Committee (AC). The governance level of ACs varies, depending on the scale and title (national, provincial or municipal development zones) of a given IPZ. Mostly, ACs focus on the management of IPZ itself, which makes them administratively independent from their parent cities (to a certain degree, of course) and equipped with necessary supporting agencies and infrastructure. The main function of an AC is to attract, plan for and manage the industries and community within its IPZ. Unlike the traditional municipal level of local government in China, the administrative mechanism and structure of ACs has been generally endogenous to IPZs during the past twenty-five years, rather than a branch of China's hierarchical system.

The institutional arrangement of ACs was born among the first group of NETDZs. During the late 1980s and early 1990s, the early period of Reform and Opening-up, international capital was uncertain about the future of investing in China, and IPZs were facing a lack of investment. ACs at that time acted as a business development agency, trying to make their parks attractive to investment. Since then, a service-oriented management style and administrative structure has been developing. Thirty years after the Reform and Opening-up, compared with traditional local governments, ACs have shown a number of traits which are conducive to institutional innovation.

Active engagement

As the pilot areas of Reform and Opening-up, IPZs' economic performance of IPZs greatly influenced the reputation of corresponding areas, the potential for investment, and the personnel evaluation toward AC officers (since they are reporting to local leaders of corresponding cities or even provinces). Because of the great opportunity cost of having land authorised for use as an IPZ vacant, ACs were active, even aggressive, in attracting and facilitating foreign investment. After the initial phase, some ACs reassigned the task of investment consulting to consultancies, which still maintain a close relationship with the AC, or were directly established by the AC. Such unusual organisational efficiency and motivation compared to the norm for local government in China was later developed into a leading attitude at different aspects, including both economic and environmental activities.

Flexibility

The development and reform of IPZs were rapid, continuous and extensive. Every year or even every quarter, new issues and new challenges about economic growth, social development or environment protection could emerge for ACs to deal with, and there was no time to wait for traditional top-down reporting and assignment, or the establishment of new agencies. To cope with such challenges in a relatively small area, the administrative structure of ACs was kept flexible, which led to advantages in institutional arrangement. A new duty would go directly to an old agency which would be appropriately renamed. For example, in Luogang District of Guangzhou city, there has been an endogenous mechanism named 'One AC, four zones', because four economic zones came up in succession over ten years, and the responsibility of the original AC kept growing, with a limited growth of additional vacancies, facilities and buildings. Finally, in 2005, the area developed into one county area of Guangzhou city, and the original AC simply upgraded into a county-level government.

Innovativeness

For both central governmental decision-makers and academic observers, IPZs are considered experimental plots of economic, institutional and technological reform and innovation in China. They are usually the first teams to implement market-based policies, so that they keep learning and adapting. For example, some ACs have their own 'policy research office' in the agency, which is usually an office in provincial or municipal government. Many ACs are not only active as business administrators, but also in developing their own organisational culture as well, such as what is known in China as the 'TEDA spirit' of creativity, responsibility and 'never-give-up' in Tianjin Economic Development Area (Shi et al. 2010) as an endogenous example, or the concepts of the plan-oriented, brand-marketing sustainable park of Suzhou Industrial Park, as an external example introduced from Singapore (Wong and Goldblum 2000).

Symbiosis: A Governance Context

Policy programmes from local governments are usually referred to as a major conditioning factor in industrial symbiosis, while in China such influence of policies is probably most evident as a coercive mechanism (Boons et al. 2011), e.g., the Chinese policy on CE is one of the central factors of influence on Chinese industrial symbiosis development. Being active, flexible and innovative, over the past ten years ACs were sensitive enough to notice how important the environment protection issues were, and were highly motivated to get involved in environmental innovations such as EIPs and CE. Moreover, the mechanism and scale of ACs determined that it is better to guide and serve, not to blindly command and control, the development of their IPZs, so that the companies and communities are involved in the strategy of industrial symbiosis.

To improve the performance of local leaders, the mechanism of a veto system based on environmental performance has been conducted during the implementation of the 11th FYP. If a leader could not fulfil regional environmental goals on pollution control and energy efficiency, s/he would receive a negative assessment whatever the regional economic performance. Meanwhile, those who failed to achieve the local tasks/targets of resource efficiency and environmental quality would also probably receive more local environmental complaints, which means the local governor would lose support from both the central/provincial level and the local/community level. As a result, from the end of the 1990s, the 'investment inviter' has not been the only role of a local government, nor of the AC in IPZs. Due to continuously emerging new pressures (both social and environmental), the role of ACs has had to change into the agents of sustainable development, i.e., combining economic, environmental and social aspirations.

Technology Innovation and Encouragement of IPZs

In general, the approaches to improve environment-related performance of industries are limited by the technological possibilities and affordability of new techniques (Lehtoranta et al. 2011). On one hand, the industrial development of China's IPZs and the urbanisation of those areas facilitated each other; on the other hand, the technological innovation brought dynamism to IPZs, which further enabled industrialisation and urbanisation.

In 1998, the government of China initiated the 'National Torch Programme' to facilitate the industrialised and commercial production of new and hi-tech achievements. An essential part of the programme is to build up new and hi-tech industrial development zones. Fifty-three zones have been set up since 1991, most of which are located near China's industrialised cities. In 2005, the new and hi-tech industrial development zones of China contributed 20% of industrial sector growth in their corresponding cities, 9% of national industrial sector growth, and 14.7% of national gross export. The R&D investment in new and hi-tech industrial development zones has achieved 30.7% of national R&D investment. If there are going to be more new energy/clean production technologies available for a wider application and marketing in China, IPZs would be expected to be at the forefront of them. The China Power Valley is a good example of such innovation. In 2008, the economic performance of 'low-carbon industry' in the city of Baoding increased by 40%, mostly because of Baoding's China Power Valley, which is the only national high-tech industry park that focuses on new energy facilities and technology, providing 500 MW of solar products and 5089 MW of wind power products to China and the world. The core strategy of Baoding is to devote itself to becoming a new energy city of facility and equipment manufacture.

While green innovation of institutions or technology is encouraged in IPZs, it is also initiated in enterprises themselves. FDI has great influence in China's IPZs, and they introduced not only capital, but also concepts and management, into the local level of China (Cheung and Lin 2004; Tang and Hussler 2011; D.T. Wang et al. 2013). It has been acknowledged that a niche market and polices could facilitate the growth of new technologies into increasing returns-driven expansion (Unruh 2002); the innovation platforms lie in most NETDZs, and national new and hi-tech industrial development zones would be great niches for the investment and marketing of new technologies.

TOWARDS ECO-DEVELOPMENT

Since the 11th FYP, China has implemented more stringent environmental regulation and delivered top-down allocated environmental protection goals to provincial and local levels (Liu and Diamond 2008). As clusters of local industries, IPZs are thus facing great pressure to reduce environmental pollution and energy consumption, while keeping relatively high economic growth to ensure local development. Despite the technological advantages in IPZs and the flexibility of ACs, there are still institutional barriers to overcome on the way to eco-development (Liu et al. 2013): willingness; budget and capacity; balancing regulatory enforcement and consensual negotiation (Sakr et al. 2011); and localising strategies.

Willingness is important in that the greening of industrial zones towards EIPs must be stimulated by the combination of economic and environmental initiative rather than pure environmental concerns (Shi et al. 2012a). Officers in ACs act as a participator in both economic and policy affairs, so they would seek both economic benefit and career promotion. Thus, they are usually motivated to make decisions that lead to short-term achievement rather than long-term sustainability.

Each AC has its own budget or environmental investment fund, depending on the revenue of the park, local policy, and whether it is a national/provincial pilot area (so that they could receive financial support from the upper level). The investment in energy auditing, online monitoring, sustainable planning or R&D for new energy technologies could lead to a higher cost than developing areas can afford.

The balancing of regulatory enforcement and consensual negotiation is not easily achieved (Sakr et al. 2011). There has been a consensual legal culture with a practical approach of policy implementation at local level, which prefers informal regulation, negotiation and mediation towards enterprises and private business, rather than formal regulation. Such negotiation may lead to everyday trade-offs that weaken the local enforcement of environmental laws.

It was popular for developing IPZs to reproduce the patterns of successful, leading IPZs, while sustainable strategies are usually difficult to be rationalised and localised, to fit the reality of local industries and communities. The failure of such reproduction was not infrequent during previous environmental programmes.

The central government played a major steering role in environmental policies, while the local ACs mainly played a rowing role. We argue that a polycentric planning and decision mechanism would help. With a 'locality knows best' premise, we recommend the central government to provide only guidelines and incentives to ACs. To avoid or at least reduce the nonfeasance of local governments on environmental protection, participatory approaches need to be conducted and improved at local level. This could help break institutional gridlock, reducing the misinformation that weakens the relationship between planners and citizens during the implementation of local plans.

CONCLUSIONS

Against a changing economic and institutional background, industrial parks and zones are ideal for the 'natural experiments' of China's social and environmental policies with a rapid development history, a significant trend of urbanisation, and a strong background of environmental campaigns. The organisational structure of ACs in IPZs is more active, flexible and innovative than China's traditional local governments, which helps them to achieve balance among the triple roles of investor, server and protector. In the future, energy consumption and GHG emission could also be a crucial bottleneck for the development of China's manufacturing industry; thus the current EIPs should engage in energy efficiency and GHG control practices, as the national factory of China.

We predict that local low-carbon strategies would follow the same life cycle as EID or the CE, which means combining bottom-up innovation and top-down encouragement and enforcement. There is also a need for future research on case studies of certain EIPs, in order to explore and develop some patterns of low-carbon strategies and GHG control at a local level, and a comparison with developed countries or areas. We assert that IPZs in China are no longer ideal pollution havens for western companies. The converse possibility – that they are at the forefront of progress in environmental protection, and provide potential lessons for industrial parks in the rest of the developing world – needs further investigation.

NOTES

1. The reason why we put industrial parks *and* zones together in discussion is the policy of central government towards those IPZs. Regardless of the location, area, or main industry sectors of the park/zone, the importance of a certain industrial park/zone can be distinguished by its administrative level and economy scale. For example, Suzhou Industrial Park lies in a sub-area of Suzhou city, south of Jiangsu Province, but it is a state-level industrial park which is considered to be the same as a NETDZ while under any policy or regulation.
2. Ranking for IPZs is difficult, and there is no perfect index to satisfy everyone. However, the Tianjin Economy Development Area, Guangzhou Economy and Technology Development District and Suzhou Industrial Park here mentioned are usually referred

to as 'images' among China's IPZs. In a comprehensive comparison of local GDP, total investment, resource efficiency and environmental management, they are the best of all of China's IPZs.

REFERENCES

Adamides, E.D. and Y. Mouzakitis (2009), 'Industrial ecosystems as technological niches', *Journal of Cleaner Production*, **17** (2), 172–180.
Akay, A., O. Bargain and K.F. Zimmermann (2012), 'Relative concerns of rural-to-urban migrants in China', *Journal of Economic Behavior & Organization*, **81** (2), 421–441.
Bao, S., G.H. Chang, J.D. Sachs and W.T. Woo (2002), 'Geographic factors and China's regional development under market reforms, 1978–1998', *China Economic Review*, **13** (1), 89–111.
Boons, F., W. Spekkink and Y. Mouzakitis (2011), 'The dynamics of industrial symbiosis: a proposal for a conceptual framework based upon a comprehensive literature review', *Journal of Cleaner Production*, **19** (9), 905–911.
Caulfield, J.L. (2006), 'Local government reform in China: a rational actor perspective', *International Review of Administrative Sciences*, **72** (2), 253–267.
Cheung, K.-Y. and P. Lin (2004), 'Spillover effects of FDI on innovation in China: evidence from the provincial data', *China Economic Review*, **15** (1), 25–44.
Chinese Association of Development Zones (2010), accessed January to March 2010 at http://www.cadz.org.cn/.
Christerson, B. and C. Lever-Tracy (1997), 'The third China? Emerging industrial districts in rural China', *International Journal of Urban and Regional Research*, **21** (4), 569–588.
Cole, M.A. (2004), 'Trade, the pollution haven hypothesis and the environmental Kuznets curve: examining the linkages', *Ecological Economics*, **48** (1), 71–81.
Cole, MA. and P.G. Fredriksson (2009), 'Institutionalized pollution havens', *Ecological Economics*, **68** (4), 1239–1256.
Deutz, P. and D. Gibbs (2008), 'Industrial ecology and regional development: eco-industrial development as cluster policy', *Regional Studies*, **42** (10), 1313–1328.
Dong, H., Y. Geng, F. Xi and T. Fujita (2013), 'Carbon footprint evaluation at industrial park level: a hybrid life cycle assessment approach', *Energy Policy*, **57**, 352–361.
Eskeland, G.S. and A.E. Harrison (2003), 'Moving to greener pastures? Multinationals and the pollution haven hypothesis', *Journal of Development Economics*, **70** (1), 1–23.
Geng, Y. and B. Doberstein (2008), 'Developing the circular economy in China: challenges and opportunities for achieving "leapfrog development"', *International Journal of Sustainable Development and World Ecology*, **15** (3), 231–239.
Geng, Y., M. Haight and Q. Zhu (2007), 'Empirical analysis of eco-industrial development in China', *Sustainable Development*, **15** (2), 121–133.
Geng, Y., P. Zhang, S. Ulgiati and J. Sarkis (2010), 'Emergy analysis of an industrial park: the case of Dalian, China', *Science of the Total Environment*, **408** (22), 5273–5283.
Geng, Y., J. Fu, J. Sarkis and B. Xue (2012), 'Towards a national circular economy

indicator system in China: an evaluation and critical analysis', *Journal of Cleaner Production*, **23** (1), 216–224.

Gibbs, D. (2009), 'Eco-industrial parks and industrial ecology: strategic niche or mainstream development', in F. Boons and J. Howard-Grenville (eds), *The Social Embeddedness of Industrial Ecology*, Cheltenham, UK and Northampton, MA, USA: Edward Elgar, pp. 73–102.

Guangzhou Economy-Technology Development District (2009), accessed December 2009 at http://www.getdd.gov.cn/.

Hubbard, M. (1995), 'Bureaucrats and markets in China – the rise and fall of entrepreneurial local government', *Governance: An International Journal of Policy and Administration*, **8** (3), 335–353.

Invest in China (2009–2010), accessed 2009–2010 at http://www.fdi.gov.cn/pub/FDI/wztj/kfqtj/default.jsp.

Jones, D.C., C. Li and A.L. Owen (2003), 'Growth and regional inequality in China during the reform era', *China Economic Review*, **14** (2), 186–200.

Lehtoranta, S., A. Nissinen, T. Mattila and M. Melanen (2011), 'Industrial symbiosis and the policy instruments of sustainable consumption and production', *Journal of Cleaner Production*, **19** (16), 1865–1875.

Liang, S., L. Shi and T. Zhang (2011), 'Achieving dewaterization in industrial parks', *Journal of Industrial Ecology*, **15** (4), 597–613.

Liu, J. and J. Diamond (2008), 'Revolutionizing China's environmental protection', *Science*, **319**, 37–38.

Liu, L., B. Zhang and J. Bi (2012), 'Reforming China's multi-level environmental governance: lessons from the 11th Five-Year Plan', *Environmental Science & Policy*, **21** (0), 106–111.

Liu, L., S. Matsuno, B. Zhang, B. Liu and O. Young (2013), 'Local governance on climate mitigation: a comparative study of China and Japan', *Environment and Planning C: Government and Policy*, **31** (3), 475–489.

Mathews, J.A. and H. Tan (2011), 'Progress toward a Circular Economy in China: the drivers (and inhibitors) of eco-industrial initiative', *Journal of Industrial Ecology*, **15** (3), 435–457.

Mathews, J.A., Y. Tang and H. Tan (2011), 'China's move to a Circular Economy as a development strategy', *Asian Business & Management*, **10** (4), 463–484.

Matus, K.J.M., X. Xiao and J.B. Zimmerman. (2012), 'Green chemistry and green engineering in China: drivers, policies and barriers to innovation', *Journal of Cleaner Production*, **32** (0), 193–203.

MC and MLR (2006), *The 11th Five Year Plan of Economic and Social Development in NETDZ*, Beijing: Ministry of Commence and Ministry of Land Resource.

Ministry of Commerce, China (2009), accessed October to December 2009 at http://wzs.mofcom.gov.cn/.

Ministry of Environmental Protection (MEP), China (2009), accessed January 2010 at http://www.mep.gov.cn/gkml/hbb/bgth/200912/t20091229_183603.htm.

Ministry of Environmental Protection (MEP), China (2010), accessed January 2010 at http://www.zhb.gov.cn/.

Ng, L.F.-Y. and C. Tuan (2006), 'Spatial agglomeration, FDI, and regional growth in China: locality of local and foreign manufacturing investments', *Journal of Asian Economics*, **17** (4), 691–713.

Peters, G.P., C.L. Weber, D. Guan and K. Hubacek (2007), 'China's growing CO_2 emissions – a race between increasing consumption and efficiency gains', *Environmental Science & Technology*, **41** (17), 5939–5944.

Sakr, D., L. Baas, S. El-Haggar and D. Huising (2011), 'Critical success and limiting factors for eco-industrial parks: global trends and Egyptian context', *Journal of Cleaner Production*, **19** (11), 1158–1169.

SEPA (2002), *The 10th Five-Year Plan of National Ecological Environmental Protection*, Beijing: SEPA.

Shi, H., M. Chertow and Y. Song (2010), 'Developing country experience with eco-industrial parks: a case study of the Tianjin Economic-Technological Development Area in China', *Journal of Cleaner Production*, **18** (3), 191–199.

Shi, H., J. Tian et al. (2012a), 'China's quest for eco-industrial parks, Part I', *Journal of Industrial Ecology*, **16** (1), 8–10.

Shi, H., J. Tian et al. (2012b), 'China's quest for eco-industrial Parks, Part II', *Journal of Industrial Ecology*, **16** (3), 290–292.

Shirk, S. (1993), *The Political Logic of Economic Reform in China*, Berkeley and Los Angeles: University of California Press.

Skinner, M.W., A.E. Joseph and R.G. Kuhn (2003), 'Social and environmental regulation in rural China: bringing the changing role of local government into focus', *Geoforum*, **34** (2), 267–281.

Suzhou Industrial Park (2009), accessed December 2009 at http://www.sipac.gov.cn/.

Tang, M. and C. Hussler (2011), 'Betting on indigenous innovation or relying on FDI: the Chinese strategy for catching-up', *Technology in Society*, **33** (1–2), 23–35.

Tianjin Economy Development Zone (2009), accessed December 2009 at http://www.teda.gov.cn/.

UNIDO (1997), *Industrial Estates: Principles and Practices*, Vienna: United Nations Industrial Development Organization.

Unruh, G.C. (2002), 'Escaping carbon lock-in', *Energy Policy*, **30** (4), 317–325.

Wang, D.T., F.F. Gu, D.K. Tsu and C.K. Yim (2013), 'When does FDI matter? The roles of local institutions and ethnic origins of FDI', *International Business Review*, **22** (2), 450–465.

Wang, H., Y, Lei and J. Bi (2015), 'Greenhouse gases reduction strategies for eco-industrial parks in China', in P. Deutz, D.I. Lyons and J. Bi (eds), *International Perspectives on Industrial Ecology*, Cheltenham, UK and Northampton, MA, USA: Edward Elgar, pp. 209–227.

Wang, H., Y. Lei, H. Wang, M. Liu, J. Yang and J. Bi (2013), 'Carbon reduction potentials of China's industrial parks: a case study of Suzhou Industry Park', *Energy*, **55**, 668–675.

White, G. (1991), 'Urban government and market reforms in China', *Public Administration and Development*, **11**, 149–170.

Wong, T.C. and C. Goldblum (2000), 'The China-Singapore Suzhou Industrial Park: a turnkey product of Singapore?', *Geographical Review*, **90** (1), 112–122.

Yuan, Z.W., J. Bi and Y. Moriguichi (2006), 'The circular economy – a new development strategy in China', *Journal of Industrial Ecology*, **10** (1–2), 4–8.

Yuan, Z., L. Zhang, B. Zhang, I. Huang, J. Bi and B. Liu (2010), 'Improving competitive advantage with environmental infrastructure sharing: a case study of China-Singapore Suzhou Industrial Park', *International Journal of Environmental Research*, **4** (4), 751–758.

Zhang, L., Z. Yuan, J. Bi, B. Zhang and B. Liu (2010), 'Eco-industrial parks: national pilot practices in China', *Journal of Cleaner Production*, **18** (5), 504–509.

11. Intersection of industrial symbiosis and product-based industrial ecologies: considerations from the Japanese home appliance industry

Jerry Patchell

INTRODUCTION

Korhonen (2002) described industrial symbiosis (IS) and product-based (PB) approaches as the two paths of industrial ecology (IE). As these approaches have been investigated distinctly, this chapter explores the linkages. Investigations of IS have examined enhanced material and energy, and information, flows afforded by colocation or some degree of geographical proximity of diverse industrial activities. Understanding IS began with Kalundborg (Ehrenfeld and Chertow, 2002; Symbiosis Institute, 2007), and advanced with investigation of other unplanned sites and eco-industrial parks (Chertow, 1999; Van Leeuwen et al., 2003; Gibbs et al., 2005; Hewes and Lyons, 2008; Shi et al., 2010). Although a generalised understanding is established (Deutz and Gibbs, 2008), considerable debate focuses on geographical boundaries and how connectivity and transactions evolve.

IS has been extended from local to regional to deal with mismatches between quality and quantities of material and energy flows (Sterr and Ott, 2004; Lyons, 2007; Deutz and Gibbs, 2008), and others have broadened the analysis to agglomeration economies with their diversity of industries, firms, infrastructure and other external economies (Ashton, 2008; Chertow et al., 2008; Deutz and Gibbs, 2008). On the other hand, the diffusion of the IS model has been vexed by the difficulties of initiating inter-firm exchanges. Understanding has changed with the realisation that Kalundborg's evolution depended on serendipitous relationships nurtured by a particular local culture (Boons and Janssen, 2004); that planning similar connectivity in an eco-industrial park (EIP) is difficult (Chertow, 2007; Gibbs and Deutz, 2007); and acceptance that IS is an institutional process that evolves over time (Chertow and Ehrenfeld, 2012).

One way to address these issues is to integrate PB IE into the IS discussion. PB IE recognises that most products are integrated into global economic flows, passing through environments along a spatially extended value chain. The literature on sustainable supply chains, green distribution, reverse logistics, operations management and related issues (Srivastava, 2007; Seuring and Müller, 2008) testifies to spatially expansive approaches to IE. IE enters PB systems with the coordination of lifecycle analysis and design for environment (DfE), and the regulatory, market and social pressures needed to compel use of these tools. The PB approach is incorporated in extended producer responsibility and the combination of DfE at the beginning of product life with recycling at end-of-life (Lindhqvist and Lifset, 2003; Van Rossem et al., 2006; Lifset and Lindhqvist, 2008).

Japan offers an opportunity to investigate linkages between IS and PB approaches. First, Japan has attempted to establish a large number of eco-towns for localised exchange of industrial outputs and inputs typical of IS. Although local companies exchange recycled products and other residuals, Van Berkel et al. (2009) describe eco-towns as urban systems that draw on recyclable resources from an urban area to support industrial systems, that is including the product cycles of other firms. Second, Japan established a closed-loop system for products that provide constant and ubiquitously produced residuals that can supply local IS situations. This chapter focuses on the Home Appliance Recycling Law (HARL) which compels companies to recycle their products via a country-wide network. Third, HARL forces companies to practise individual producer responsibility, making lead companies improve the network's organisational and geographical efficiency. A company's search for network efficiency could cause it to seek cooperation with the eco-towns. The aim of this chapter, therefore, is to examine whether PB recycling centres engage eco-towns. Following a description of methods, the following section outlines the two systems. Subsequent sections analyse inter-linkages between the systems, and consider how the producers have met their responsibilities, before offering some reflections.

METHODS

The analysis triangulates information from three areas. Eco-town information is derived from the Ministry of Economy, Trade and Industry's (METI's) ten-year review of the eco-town project (Fujita, 2006), the Ministry of the Environment (MOE) and METI websites, and websites of the eco-towns occupying companies. HARL information is drawn from

MOE, METI and the Association for Electric Home Appliances (AEHA) publications and websites, interviews with government representatives, and company websites. The organisational information emphasises Panasonic's network, drawing on published and website materials; and three interviews with representatives from its environmental division headquarters, recycling facilities, network recyclers, and distributors. Information and interviews with the competing networks are also utilised.

OVERVIEW OF THE ECO-TOWN AND HARL SYSTEMS

As part of a comprehensive set of resource savings regulations, HARL was developed by government and industry stakeholders in the late 1990s, enacted in 1998 and enforced in 2001 (Tasaki et al., 2005; DTI, 2006). Developed contemporaneously, the eco-town programme was intended to reinforce general and sector waste management laws by providing localised recycling. Initiated by the Ministry of Health, Labor and Welfare, MOE and METI, the latter two ministries assumed responsibility for its implementation and governance (Van Berkel, 2009). The programme coupled reducing pressure on landfills with revitalising local industry.

The HARL is an extended producer responsibility law emphasising the user-pays principle and individual producer responsibility for the four main home appliances (refrigerator [freezer], washing machine [dryer], air-conditioner, and television [TV]). A post-consumption recycling fee paid by consumers achieves the former and requiring major manufacturers to take back and recycle their own products achieves the latter. AEHA coordinates the HARL with performance guidelines and a recycling ticket [*ken*] centre (RKC) that manages custody and payments from consumers to distributors to manufacturers. The Japan Refrigeration and Air Conditioning Industry Association (JRAIA) helps coordinate by providing technical support for refrigerants recovery and by labelling their global warming potential.

Distributors are crucial because they dominate product recovery from consumers, ensure the safe removal of refrigerants from air conditioners, send appliances to collection centres, and monitor product flow. Consumers can buy tickets from the post office and take appliances to municipalities or collectors. All manufacturers and importers must participate in the system either directly or indirectly to facilitate collection and recycling of their products. Manufacturers and importers determine the fee to be paid by consumers and provide standardised labelling of plastics, metals, disassembly marks on appliances and by following DfE guidelines.

The HARL system has two distinct networks of recovery and recycling facilities distributed throughout Japan, and evocatively named the A and B groups. Japan's largest original equipment manufacturers (OEMs) manage the groups and directly run several recycling facilities, but a total of 41 manufacturing firms support the networks through investment, financing, and managerial and technological expertise. Firm participation is proportional to market shares, and hence recycling responsibilities. Two special designated corporations deal with the products of 66 SMEs, small-scale importers or defunct companies. The A and B groups consist of 31 and 16 recycling facilities respectively and share 379 collection facilities (AEHA, 2011a).

In 2001, product and recycling targets were set at: refrigerators 50 per cent, cathode ray TVs 55 per cent, washing machines 50 per cent, and air conditioners 60 per cent. These targets were soon surpassed. Products and targets were increased in 2009 to refrigerators and freezers 60 per cent, cathode ray TVs 55 per cent, washing machines and clothes dryers 65 per cent, air conditioners 70 per cent, and panel TVs 50 per cent. Actual recycling rates were 76 per cent, 85 per cent, 86 per cent, 88 per cent and 79 per cent respectively (AEHA, 2011a), and represent the proportion of products received at recycling facilities converted into products used in original product types, other products or thermal recycling.[1] The remainder is disposed of by landfill or incineration. Although these recycling rates are high, a large proportion of appliances go overseas for reuse or for recycling and a very small proportion is illegally disposed of. The exports have been estimated at 45 per cent (Terazono et al., 2004) and 38 per cent (DTI, 2006), while others reported 43 per cent domestic retrieval and unidentified destination for 22 per cent (Tasaki et al. 2005). These estimates were made shortly after the inception of HARL, but a more recent estimate based on METI's presumed 5–10-year lag between purchases in 2001 and recycling figures from 2010 (AEHA, 2011b) gives a sales to recycling rate for refrigerators and freezers of 77 per cent, cathode ray TVs of 194 per cent, washing machines and clothes dryers of 70 per cent, air conditioners of 42 per cent, and panel TVs of 73 per cent. The spike in cathode TV recycling reflects the hurried disposal of analogue TVs before full digitalisation of TV signals. Although air-conditioner recycling remains low, domestic recycling of refrigerators and washing machines improved significantly.

The MOE and METI established the eco-town programme, its purposes and guidelines and provided financing for local governments, firms and non-profit organisations (NPOs), academia and other research institutions to establish innovative waste recovery systems. By the financings' expiry in 2005, 26 municipalities or prefectures received modest planning funding, but 61 firms received US$1.65 billion to subsidise innovative recycling facilities (Van Berkel, 2009). Although the eco-towns depend on resources from the surrounding area, co-location of the recycling facilities and the potential for IS are their conceptual and practical foundation.

Eco-towns differ in geographic scope and by functions. Six encompass metropolitan areas and provide infrastructure for household, commercial, and construction and demolition waste streams; another six coordinate regional waste streams among towns and villages; two cover the islands of Hokkaido and Naoshima; ten are a diverse set of city or sub-city configurations; and two focus on an industrial or port area (Van Berkel et al., 2009a). Only a few centres such as Kyoto do not encompass an eco-town. Sato et al. (2004) categorised 14 eco-towns as focused on the promotion of environmental industries; seven on treatment of wastes; and five on community development. Van Berkel (2009) characterised them into four groups: 12 emphasising eco-efficiency; two corporate social responsibility (with two sharing those emphases); seven environmental restoration; and two environmental technology innovation.

METI (2006) estimated that the eco-towns were responsible for about 20 per cent of the yearly increase in national recycling capacity, or additional capacity of 5.89 million tons (Hotta, 2011). A later evaluation of 90 recycling facilities in 26 eco-towns found that virgin material use was reduced by 900 000 tons/yr and CO_2 emissions by 480 000 t-CO_2/yr (Fujita, 2006). Moreover, the programme promoted investment, business start-ups and attracted several hundred thousand visitors. However, employment gains were a modest 1000, and Hotta (2011, paragraph 19) concluded that the policy 'was not very successful as a response to a decline in the base materials industry and a revitalization of the local economy, but was very successful in developing a nation-wide role sharing for wide area recycling to respond to the waste management and recycling policy reform'. Norton (2007) also sees mixed results because, while local systems of innovation developed, they did not generate substantial material or energy exchanges even with local environmental clusters.

ECO-TOWN AND HARL INTERACTIONS

Only six eco-towns include HARL recycling facilities in their regional framework or on IS sites, and the level of recycled HARL materials utilised varies. The eco-towns, their HARL group, plant ownership, and characteristics of material or energy outputs are described in Table 11.1. Most of the six plants belong to the B group, and three established by the B group

Table 11.1   Eco-towns with HARL recycling plants

Eco-town/Firm	Group	Ownership	Co-location market
Hokkaido: Eco-Recycling Systems	B	Mitsubishi Materials 43.75%; Hitachi Plant Technologies 41.25%; 6 appliance cos 15%	Dismantling, crushing, separation of home and office appliances for primary and secondary markets; some plastic and so on fuels nearby paper mill
Aomori: Tokyo Tekko	A	Tokyotekko 100%	Pre-existing scrap steel furnace; separation of metals, plastics, and so on for local and non-local metal production, thermal recycling
Akita: Eco-Recycle (Dowa)	B	Dowa 100%	Pre-existing smelting plant; separation of (rare) metals, plastics; plastics and so on for thermal recycling
Miyagi: East Japan Recycling Systems	B	Mitsubishi Materials 78.6%; 6 appliance cos 24.4%	Pre-existing smelting facilities (defunct); home and office appliance recycling
Kawasaki: JFE Urban Recycle Corporation	B	Sanyo 45% JFE 45%	Dismantling, crushing, separation of home and office appliances for primary and secondary markets; metals to JFE collocated plant, some plastic and so on for thermal recycling
Kitakyushu: West Japan Home Appliance Recycle	A and B	Toshiba lead; 8 other appliance cos	Dismantling, crushing, separation of home appliances for primary and secondary markets; plans for thermal recycling

Sources: Fujita (2006); company websites (accessed December 2011–January 2012): http://www.go-hers.co.jp; http://www.tokyotekko.co.jp; http://www.dowa-eco.co.jp/business/ recycle/home_ele_recycle/; http://www.ejrs.co.jp/index.html; http://www.urrec.co.jp; http:// www.nkrc.co.jp.

consortium were greenfield, confirming that this group preferred new facilities (Tojo, 2004). Mitsubishi materials, a metals company linked to the Mitsubishi keiretsu and its Home Electric company, set up two plants. Independent metal firms established two facilities. In Aomori, Tokyo

Tekko recycles steel into rebar products, while, in Akita, Dowa transfers expertise in refining metals to extracting rare metals from disposed appliances. Transfer of materials for production purposes occurs through internal integration within the metal firms Tokyo Tekko and JFE. Both firms also thermally recycle plastics from appliances, as does the Akita metal firm. Only the Hokkaido firm supplies another firm with plastics for thermal recycling. These practices indicate that internal integration and high-value materials are prerequisites for maintaining material quality in IS recycling.

The super eco-town of Tokyo conceptually encompasses the largest urban area. Future Ecology recycles electronics for A and B groups and considers itself part of the super eco-town framework, however, the super eco-town collocates a small number of specialised recycling facilities that are not part of HARL. In actual resource flows and diversity of activities, Kawasaki and Kitakyushu are the largest eco-towns. Kawasaki's recycling facilities collocate with the metal processing plant of the parent firm in an old industrial area. Kitakyushu's HARL centre collocates several firms recycling cars, office automation, fluorescent tubes, PET bottles, and so on, on an ocean landfill. Collocation of HARL recycling facilities without IS suggests difficulty in melding PB and IS industrial ecologies, at least in EIPs. That likelihood is reinforced by the characteristics of the eco-towns without HARL facilities. Most are small and focus on local industries and/or deal with ubiquitous urban residue such as packaging.

INDIVIDUAL PRODUCER RESPONSIBILITY THROUGH RECYCLER INTEGRATION

The majority of eco-towns were established to generate symbiosis with local industries rather than serve the HARL system. Moreover, the integration of the two systems was limited by the coordination parameters of the HARL system that we now turn to.

The AEHA coordinates appliance recovery and recycling with a ticketing system that ensures consumers pay and collectors, retailers, recyclers and manufacturers get paid. The government stipulates that manufacturers record recycling rates and empowered the AEHA to collect the records. The AEHA surveys the practices and problems of half the recyclers yearly and reports this information through its website and consultations; an effort appreciated by recyclers (AEHA, 2010). With this feedback, government and manufacturers revise policies, enforcement practices, facilities management and marketing programmes.

Alongside sector-wide coordination, the HARL system is characterised by internal integration of recycling. That is, OEMs exert a high degree of control over recycling. Manufacturers and importers are responsible for recovering products and ensuring substantial recycling rates. The government allows them to charge consumers actual recycling costs, but such costs should not impede consumers' willingness to recycle. The costs are implemented on a flat national rate. Thus, producers had to establish an efficient national system. They achieved economies of scope in logistics and facilities by combining recovery and recycling of the product groups and the range of products in each group. Economies of scale were achieved in facilities, but as indicated by differences in the numbers of recycling facilities (see below), what is considered a minimally efficient scale differs between the two networks. To gain these efficiencies, the firms in the two networks pooled products and cooperatively invested in facilities. They also integrated system management under a few lead firms.

The networks differ primarily in spatial coverage and proprietary control over recyclers. The A group's more numerous facilities provide a denser distribution, while the B group's cover wider areas with larger facilities. After a few years of complete separation, the government decided to let the two groups share two facilities owned by advanced independent recyclers and establish joint ownership of two recyclers. Additionally, each originally had to establish 190 collection centres distributed according to demand and convenience of retailers. Although each group is responsible for a network, independent firms run most facilities. Further consultation between government and industry resulted in all collection centres converted to common use in 2010. The switch to common use readjusted the markets for some collection depots and required investment for equipment necessary to deal with the products of both groups.

The A group selected pre-existing and independent firms experienced in recycling items such as packaging, automobiles, or scrap metal, but few had experience in home appliances. These firms employ about 100–200 people, often claim innovations in recycling technologies, have environmental and quality performance accreditation, and make appropriate statements about the environment and building a circular society. Several A group firms had pre-established networks of collection centres and regional recycling facilities that they expanded after taking on HARL activities. These independent networks provide the A group with proximate and distributed service provision in some areas (e.g., Hirakin in Shikoku and Chugoku). Nine B group facilities are owned jointly by seven of the larger firms in the consortium, but in several cases one firm with dominant ownership leads. The B group relies on strong independent companies to a lesser extent (e.g., Nakadaya's four facilities in the Kanto and Chubu; Dowa's expertise in rare metal recovery).

Panasonic and Toshiba lead the A Group (23 members), while Hitachi and Mitsubishi lead the B Group (18 members) (AEHA, 2011a). The larger firms have the resources and geographical presence to organise a network of collection and recycling centres, yet depend on others to achieve economies of scale and compensate for a small presence in some areas. Panasonic dominates in western Japan and Mitsubishi and Hitachi dominate in the east, and need balancing partners in their group. Thus, in the A group, Panasonic leads in the west, while Toshiba takes care of east Japan. (This west–east divide is a historical transmission reflected in everything from choice of noodles to a split into an eastern 50 hz voltage zone and a western 60 hz zone). Osaka-based Sharp is the predominant western presence for the B group, but still relies on support from independents.

Panasonic began negotiating with the government in 1992–1993 and in 1996 was subsidised for five years of research on collection, recycling and facilities operation. Together, they decided that a network under the leadership of OEMs had to be established because, in comparison with the long evolution of automobile recyclers, few recyclers could deal with the HARL requirements (Panasonic interview). Mirroring relations with upstream subcontractors in forming a cooperative firm association, Panasonic established Ecology Net Ltd to organise A Group recyclers. Ecology Net firms receive technological and managerial guidance, employee visits and training, and share safety information. However, each firm is expected to stand on its own, develop its own recycling system and training manual, and contribute to the system. The recycler Toei's engineers and workers reduced costs and developed products and patents. Some methods are passed on to Ecology Net firms, occasionally resulting in a prize from Panasonic. On the other hand, recyclers must deal with Panasonic's cost reduction demands; limited income from recycling fees; the transaction costs of the ticketing system; large and disorderly shipments and paperwork from volume retailers; seasonality; and so on. On the bright side, amortisation of equipment with significant economies of scale provides some security against volatile markets (Toei interview).

The B group is more vertically integrated because more major OEMs operate recycling facilities. Hitachi operates three plants directly and provided processes for two others (DTI, 2006). Hitachi also enjoyed government support in the years before HARL was formally legislated and implemented. Sharp and Sanyo operate two plants and Mitsubishi, Sony and Fujitsu operate one as well. Moreover, Mitsubishi Materials dominates ownership in one site and has major shares in three others. The group is horizontally integrated through shared ownership in most facilities, enhancing commitment and information sharing. Hitachi hosts several meetings a year and personnel from group members visit each other. Visiting and information sharing between the A and B groups is possible since only old appliances are being recycled and few technological secrets can be lost (Sharp interview).

The OEM operated recycling plants reinforce network integration from the perspectives of individual producers and the system as a whole. Enhancing DfE is considered the most important role of the plants. Hundreds of engineers and designers visit yearly to see how difficult it is to disassemble, crush, separate material, determine which materials should be substituted, and so forth. Parent firms use the information to redesign products and processes, to educate affected suppliers, and to collaborate with material recyclers (Panasonic and Sharp interviews). Metals companies, such as Dowa and Mitsubishi, have been drawn into ownership and operation within the HARL system to collaborate on material recovery (Dowa interview). Significant research goes into the development of the equipment and processes, and most plants have onsite engineers working on improvements. At Panasonic and Sharp's plants, substantial refits have taken place in ten years of operation (Panasonic and Sharp interviews).

Recycling materials into the appliance manufacturing process is another motivation for integration by individual firms. However, this is limited. Metals predominate by mass, yet must return to smelters for further processing. Much is also sold overseas (Murakami et al., 2006). Where reprocessing of metals is fairly straightforward, plastics tend to degrade in quality and their value is inherently lower. Moreover, Panasonic found plastics firms indifferent to such problems. Yet as plastic recycling symbolises the Circular Economy, the government encourages OEMs to pursue it (Panasonic and Sharp interviews). Recycling plastic is also a benchmark for DfE programmes, and OEMs use it as a tool to build their green credentials with customers and environmental stakeholders. Thus OEMs invest into improving plastics and incorporating them in an appliance-to-appliance loop, although often changing appliance and/or application (Aizawa et al., 2008). Still, plastic recycling remains minor, with most sold on secondary markets (Panasonic and Sharp interviews). Significant amounts are used for fuel, but are only considered recycled if they have been sold rather than given away. Cathode ray tubes lead glass cullets have been exported for reuse in TVs, but the number of tubes in Japan is dwindling due to replacement by flat-screen displays. Refrigerants are sent to specialists for reuse or destruction. Polychlorinated biphenyls (PCBs) and other components are sent to firms such Sumitomo Metals, Nippon Mining and Metals and other metal specialists for rare metals extraction. Only Dowa extracts at its HARL site (Dowa interview). After separation and pulverisation at the A and B group facilities, most materials are sent to secondary processing and secondary markets in national and international contexts.

All OEM operated facilities have dedicated touring facilities, exhibits and routes for consumers, students and professionals to fulfill HARL's educational mandate. Thousands have visited, reinforcing the value of recycling and environmental protection, and also have been educated in how they can clean refrigerators and so on to make the recycling easier. Many professionals come from overseas and the facilities are used to promote Japan's environmental programmes and products. In A group, only Panasonic has built a facility to accommodate these tours (although others offer lesser opportunities). All B group's OEM plants offer tours, but vary in commitment to tour facilities.

Plant location requires convenient access from collection depots (access to main highways) and acceptance within communities, the latter difficult because of the perception of recycling facilities. Panasonic built its facility in the countryside adjacent to an existing Panasonic plant after extensive discussions with the community on plant design, hiding appliances, jobs and protection for a rice crop prized for premium sake (Panasonic PETEC interview). Sharp located in the urban congestion of Osaka's Hirakata City because Mitsubishi Materials owned land there (Sharp interview), welcomed by a municipality interested in environmental industries. Toei's TV recycling for A group outgrew its parent firm's location, but was rebuffed by communities until Tokoname, in need of jobs, encouraged it to locate in an industrial park (Toei interview). EIPs offer the potential to minimise conflict with communities because in such sites difficulties have been overcome. However, such advantages seem outweighed by organisational priorities.

DISCUSSION: CONSULTATION AND LOCALISATION VERSUS EXIGENCIES OF NATIONAL INTEGRATION

Japan envisions a 'sound material recycling society' with both PB (sector-based) and geographical approaches to recycling, represented by the HARL and eco-town initiatives. While the two approaches are expected to interact, the mechanisms encouraging interaction have not been explicitly designed. Interactions have evolved when local industry characteristics serendipitously meet efficiency requirements of an integrated national system for home appliance firms, but there is not a spatial distribution rationale whereby recycling home appliances provides inputs into eco-towns. Organisational efficiencies direct the location of recycling, rather than facilities evolving in concert with locations where recyclate could become input to other processes (i.e., IS). Organisational efficiencies include recovery and recycling costs, and transaction costs involved with establishment and operation networks and R&D considerations.

Gestation of the systems, in government–industry negotiations, concurrent around the mid-1990s, allowed for coordination – the first eco-town established in 1997, while promulgation of the HARL occurred in 1998 (Hotta, 2011). However, the trajectories of development hindered symbiosis. The eco-towns evolved disparately over a ten-year programme, while HARL's national network had to be planned and implemented by 2001. The government sponsored the eco-towns, but local governments and stakeholders had to be protagonists. Discussions were complex and long, and most eco-towns focused on the residuals of local enterprises. In four cases where home appliance residuals achieved IS, pre-existing local industries used scrap metal. In the other two cases, OEM home appliance recycling facilities helped anchor EIPs, but are not intermeshed in IS. Locating recycling by the OEMS also faced negotiation challenges, but not as complex, and benefited existing facilities or company land (Panasonic and Sharp interviews).

The two greatest reasons for limited eco-town–HARL interactions appear to be the exigencies of integrating a national network and the need to access geographically disparate secondary markets for recycled materials. On the one hand, collection and recycling facilities, at an efficient scale and logistics, had to be distributed throughout the country, but these rarely produce residuals fitting the eco-towns or regional industry. On the other hand, the majority of recycled materials require further processing to re-enter the industrial system; simple reprocessing such as the smelting of metals or further extraction of rare metals from circuit boards and so on are not performed at the recycling centres. Secondary markets are necessary despite OEM efforts to internally close the loop with recycling. Moreover, closed-loop recycling, for plastics or other materials, requires returning materials to specific suppliers or the OEM. Such recycling materials will be shipped to those one or two factories necessary to provide the intermediate input or the finished product, even when production scales serve national (and international) production. Thus, uptake of residuals into localised production is precluded. Terazono et al. (2004) describe these secondary markets as existing in both Japan and overseas, but this information was drawn from the early days of HARL and needs updating. That said, all the stakeholders interviewed, while acutely aware of secondary market instability (and the limited value potential for recycled plastics), were not worried about the long-term system viability. Consumer responsibility to pay for recycling and the research drawn from the OEMs' recycling centres provided the value basis for the system's stability.

Beyond the production efficiencies of the recycling network and secondary markets, other issues inhibit strong interdependencies between the eco-towns IS and the HARL PB systems. The A and B group consortiums are complex in terms of ownership structure, management, information and cost sharing. Transaction costs are high in establishing and operating the consortiums and would be exacerbated by the negotiations initiating and sustaining eco-towns. Efforts to minimise location-based transaction costs can be seen in: the search for local independent collectors and recyclers; OEMs establishing R&D recycling centres proximate to their headquarters, primary production locations and markets; and leadership of the A and B groups by dominant firms in the eastern and western halves of the country. Although OEMs committed to extended producer responsibility and claim to support material and energy recovery, few consumers see recycled content and recyclability as value-adding attributes. The OEMs find it easier to rationalise energy saving as a saleable characteristic. Moreover, according to Panasonic, profit margins in the appliance sector are so low they could be erased by the costs of recycling (Panasonic interview).

CONCLUSIONS

The Japanese eco-town–HARL experience reveals limitations on IS not considered in existing explanations. The geographical scope and integration of IS does not readily expand beyond the catchment of the original co-location site even if a stable supply of materials and energy becomes available. This may be simply a function of the fact that recycling and production facilities specialise in particular inputs and cannot utilise the HARL waste streams. On the other hand, the evolution of connectivity, the initiation of exchanges among firms that may expand the geographical scope, seems to be stymied by the priority given to organisation-based efficiency and thereby a disinclination to connect with local or agglomeration IS. This disconnect is occurring despite Japan's vision of a sound material recycling society that encompasses geographic spheres of material flows expanding from the local to the regional, national and continental realms, and despite a vision that allows for an evolution of flows according to policy initiatives and economic and environmental efficiencies. The profile presented here provides a glimpse of how the evolution of the system has been shaped by constraints of both eco-town developments and the integration required for individual producer responsibility. The constraints and possibilities for IS–PB interactions could be further detailed by examining secondary markets or by comparison with other major products.

NOTE

1. In Japan, energy recovery from waste via incineration, pyrolysis or gasification is termed recycling. This contrasts with EU terminology, in which recycling refers to material recovery.

REFERENCES

AEHA (2010), 'Home Appliance Design for Environment and Recycling Survey Report' (電器製品の環境配慮設計及びルサイクル処理に関する調査研究報告書), accessed December 2011–January 2012 at http://www.aeha.or.jp/02/a.html.

AEHA (2011a), 'Electronic product's environmentally conscious design: focusing on the 3Rs' (電器製品の環境配慮設計3Rを中心として), accessed December 2011–January 2012 at http://www.aeha.or.jp/02/pdf/a/assessment/AEHA-ECD.pdf.

AEHA (2011b), 'Home Appliance Recycling Yearly Report 2010 No. 10' (家電リサイクル 年次報告書 平成 **22** 年度版(第 **10** 期), accessed December 2011–January 2012 at http://www.aeha.or.jp/recycling_report/pdf/kadennenji22.pdf.

Aizawa Hirofumi, Yoshida Hideto and Sakai Shin-ichi (2008), 'Current results and future perspectives for Japanese recycling of home electrical appliances', *Resources, Conservation and Recycling*, **52**, 1399–1410.

Ashton, W.S. (2008), 'The structure, function and evolution of a regional industrial ecosystem', *Journal of Industrial Ecology*, **13** (2), 228–246.

Boons, F. and M.A. Janssen (2004), 'The myth of Kalundborg: social dilemmas in stimulating eco-industrial parks', in J. van den Bergh and M. Janssen (eds), *Economics of Industrial Ecology: Materials, Structural Change, and Spatial Scales*, Cambridge, MA: MIT Press, pp. 337–356.

Chertow, M.R. (1999), 'The eco-industrial park model reconsidered', *Journal of Industrial Ecology*, **2**, 8–10.

Chertow, M.R. (2007), '"Uncovering" industrial symbiosis', *Journal of Industrial Ecology*, **11**, 1, 11–30.

Chertow, M. and J. Ehrenfeld (2012), 'Organizing self-organizing systems: toward a theory of industrial symbiosis', *Journal of Industrial Ecology*, **16** (1), 13–27.

Chertow, M.R., W.S. Ashton and J.C. Espinosa (2008), 'Industrial symbiosis in Puerto Rico: environmentally related agglomeration economies', *Regional Studies*, **42**, 1299–1312.

Deutz, P. and D. Gibbs (2008), 'Industrial ecology and regional development: eco-industrial development as cluster policy', *Regional Studies*, **42**, 1313–1328.

DTI (UK Department of Trade and Industry) (2006), *Waste Electrical and Electronic Equipment (WEEE): Innovating Novel Recovery and Recycling Technologies in Japan*, UK Department of Trade and Industry.

Ehrenfeld, J. and M.R. Chertow (2002), 'Industrial symbiosis: the legacy of

Kalundborg', in R. Ayres and L. Ayres (eds), *Handbook of Industrial Ecology*, Cheltenham, UK and Northampton, MA, USA: Edward Elgar, pp. 334–350.

Fujita, T. (2006), *Eco-town Projects/Environmental Industries in Progress*, Japan Ministry of Economy, Trade and Industry, accessed December 2011–January 2012 at http://www.meti.go.jp/policy/recycle/main/3r_policy/policy/pdf/eco town/ecotown_casebook/english.pdf.

Gibbs, D. and P. Deutz (2007), 'Reflections on implementing industrial ecology through eco-industrial park development', *Journal of Cleaner Production*, **15**, 1683–1695.

Gibbs, D., P. Deutz and A. Proctor (2005), 'Industrial ecology and eco-industrial development: a new paradigm for local and regional development?', *Regional Studies*, **39**, 171–183.

Hewes, A.K. and D.I. Lyons (2008), 'The humanistic side of eco-industrial parks: champions and the role of trust', *Regional Studies*, **42** (10), 1329–1342.

Hotta, Y. (2011), 'Is resource efficiency a solution for sustainability challenges?', *S.A.P.I.EN.S* [online], 4.2 | 2011, Online since 9 September 2011, accessed 14 December 2011 at http://sapiens.revues.org/1161.

Korhonen, J. (2002), 'Two paths to industrial ecology: applying the product-based and geographical approaches', *Journal of Environmental Planning and Management*, **45** (1), 39–57.

Lifset, R. and T. Lindhqvist (2008), 'Producer responsibility at a turning point?', *Journal of Industrial Ecology*, **12**, 144–147.

Lindhqvist, T. and R. Lifset (2003), 'Can we take the concept of individual producer responsibility from theory to practice?', *Journal of Industrial Ecology*, **7** (2), 3–6.

Lyons, D.I. (2007), 'A spatial analysis of loop closing among recycling, remanufacturing, and waste treatment firms in Texas', *Journal of Industrial Ecology*, **11** (1), 43–54.

METI (Ministry of Economy, Trade and Industry) (2006), 'Case studies of eco-town development and industry progress' (エコタウン・環境産業進行形 環境調和型まちづくり事例集), accessed December 2011–January 2012 at http://www.meti.go.jp/policy/recycle/main/3r_policy/policy/ecotown_casebook.html.

Murakami, S., A. Terazono, N. Abe, Y. Moriguchi and H. Miyakawa (2006), 'Material flows of end-of-life home appliances in Japan', *Journal of Material Cycles and Waste Management*, **8**, 46–55.

Norton, M. (2007), 'Japan's eco-towns – industrial clusters of local innovation systems', *Proceedings of the 51st Annual Meeting of the ISSS*, **17**.

OECD (2010), *OECD Environmental Performance Reviews: Japan*, OECD.

Sato, M., Y. Ushiro and H. Matsunga (2004), 'Categorisation of eco-town projects in Japan', International Symposium on Green Technology for Resources and Materials Recycling, Seoul, Korea.

Seuring, S. and M. Müller (2008), 'From a literature review to a conceptual framework for sustainable supply chain management', *Journal of Cleaner Production*, **16**, 1699–1710.

Shi, H., M. Chertow and Y. Song (2010), 'Developing country experience with eco-industrial parks: a case study of the Tianjin Economic-Technological Development Area in China', *Journal of Cleaner Production*, **18**, 191–199.

Srivastava, S.K. (2007), 'Green supply-chain management: a state-of-the-art literature review', *International Journal of Management Reviews*, **9** (1), 53–80.

Sterr, T. and T. Ott (2004), 'The industrial region as a promising unit for eco-industrial development – reflections, practical experience and establishment of innovative instruments to support industrial ecology', *Journal of Cleaner Production*, **12**, 947–965.

Symbiosis Institute (2007), *Industrial Symbiosis – Exchange of Resources – Kalundborg, Denmark*, Kalundborg Industrial Symbiosis Institute, Kalundborg, accessed at http://www.symbiosis.dk.

Tasaki, T., A. Terazono and Y. Moriguchi (2005), 'Effective assessment of Japanese recycling law for electrical home appliances – four years after the full enforcement of the law', *Proceedings of the IEEE International Symposium on Electronics and the Environment 2005*, pp. 243–248.

Terazono A., A. Yoshida, J. Yang, Y. Moriguchi and S. Sakai (2004), 'Material cycles in Asia: especially the recycling loop between Japan and China', *Journal of Material Cycles and Waste Management*, **6**, 82–96.

Tojo, N. (2004), 'Extended producer responsibility as a driver for design change – utopia or reality?', Doctoral Dissertation, Lund: IIEE Lund University.

Van Berkel, R., T. Fujita, S. Hashimoto and Y. Geng (2009), 'Industrial and urban symbiosis in Japan: analysis of the Eco-Town program 1997–2006', *Journal of Environmental Management*, **90**, 1544–1556.

Van Leeuwen, M.G., W.J.V. Vermeulen and P. Glasberg (2003), 'Planning eco-industrial parks: an analysis of Dutch methods', *Business Strategy and the Environment*, **12**, 147–162.

Van Rossem, C., T. Naoko and T. Lindhqvist (2006), *Lost in Transposition? A Study of the Implementation of Individual Producer Responsibility in the WEEE Directive*, Greenpeace, Friends of the Earth, European Environmental Bureau.

12. Institutional capacity for sustainable industrial systems in Caldas, Colombia

Bart van Hoof

INTRODUCTION

Markets and regulatory pressures have been recognised as significant drivers for diffusing concepts related to sustainability (Boons et al., 2011), in addition to coercion, imitation, training and professionalisation (DiMaggio and Powell, 1983). Governments and other stakeholders have used these mechanisms to induce sustainability-related actions among firms (Darnall, 2003).

In emerging markets, societal forces promoting sustainability in industrial systems are often weak (Blackman, 2006). Enforcement of environmental regulation, a traditional driver for environmental improvement (Boons and Baas, 1997), is generally limited: overseeing large numbers of small firms is burdensome for underfinanced and understaffed environmental agencies (Blackman, 2006). Moreover, most firms in these economies serve local markets where environmental advocacy or pressure from local customers is lacking (Dasgupta et al., 1997). Also, non-governmental organisations (NGOs) and communities have little capacity and power to impose meaningful pressure on small firms (Maranto-Vargas and Gomez-Tagle, 2007). Compounding matters, transparency and availability of environmental information is often scarce (Velázquez et al., 2008).

Related concepts such as Industrial Ecology (IE) (Baas, 2006; Deutz and Gibbs, 2008) and Cleaner Production (CP), a strategy for industrial process resource reduction (Hirschhorn, 1997), have been employed in cooperative approaches that build on inter-organisational relationships as resources for collective action (Puppim de Oliveira, 2006). Essentially, these approaches rely on agglomeration economies emerging from geographically connected stakeholders, including customers, governmental agencies, service providers and universities (Baas, 2006). Synergistic possibilities between these actors can influence the learning process among actors in industrial systems and improve regional efficiency, organisational learning and sustainability (Boons et al., 2011). Moreover, Puppim de Oliveira (2006) shows how collective and multi-stakeholder approaches are especially important in overcoming obstacles to environmental engagement faced by small, isolated firms.

Interaction among stakeholders in a given geographic region is also recognised as an element of regional institutional capacity (Healey, 2003). Recent studies have examined the institutional capacity of industrial systems in relation to the adoption and diffusion of environmental management in firms based in industrialised countries (Deutz and Gibbs, 2008; Hekkert and Ossebaard, 2010; Boons et al., 2011). These studies provide frameworks for the analysis of regional institutional capacity, offer guidelines on how to build such capacity, and describe experiences of industrial symbiosis, eco-industrial parks, and eco-efficiency clusters. On the other hand, little is known about institutional capacity building in emerging economies (Montiel and Husted, 2009); additional research is urged to deepen understanding of how regional industrial systems change their connectivity, and consequently their environmental impact (Boons et al., 2011).

This chapter aims to understand the dynamics involved in sustainable industrial systems in emerging markets by reviewing the experience of a regional CP project in Caldas, Colombia, in 2000–2010. The Caldas experience offers an appropriate opportunity for the study of how the process of institutional capacity evolved in the field of IE, given that longitudinal information concerning CP initiatives is available for a significant span of time. Two research questions guide the research described in this chapter: 1) what triggers institutional capacity building for sustainable industrial systems?, and 2) how can interconnectivity among stakeholders as part of institutional capacity building be achieved?

The following sections offer a conceptual framework based on Boons et al. (2011) for understanding how institutional capacity in CP evolves, and what its outcomes are; present the research methods used to gather and analyse empirical data; provide background information on the institutional capacity building process under review; present the CP initiatives in Caldas during the ten-year period as mechanisms for institutional capacity building; and review environmental and institutional outcomes. The final section responds to the research questions, presents conclusions, and proposes recommendations for further research.

INSTITUTIONAL CAPACITY FOR SUSTAINABLE INDUSTRIAL SYSTEMS

Institutional theorists recognise institutions as structures that provide stability and legitimacy to social behaviour (Scott, 2001). Over time, the role of social structures among economic actors, such as relationships, culture and social values, as well as regulative, normative and cognitive systems, became known as 'neo' institutionalism (Scott, 2008). From an organisational perspective, these structures are viewed as adaptive and responsive to influence (Scott, 2008). Within this context, the process of institutionalisation describes how structural components of organisational arrangements evolve (Selznick, 1996; Scott, 2008) and new concepts are disseminated in society.

In recent years a growing number of environmental researchers have examined the role of institutions in environmental improvement (e.g., Hoffman, 2003; Boons et al., 2011). Their interest stems from limitations observed in traditional, technical, and often fragmented approaches employed to promote a more sustainable society. Both intra- and interorganisational awareness of the need for reducing environmental load emerges once institutions and factors that promote institutionalisation are taken into account, accelerating a systemic view of the dissemination process of new ecological paradigms (Baas, 2006).

Advances in exploring institutional thinking have also been made in IE (Boons, 2009). In an effort to combine institutional analysis with IE, Boons et al. (2011) propose a conceptual framework for understanding the industrial diffusion of IE practice by focusing on the dynamics of industrial systems in terms of connectivity and environmental impact reduction. Considered first are pre-existing organisational conditions, such as firm location, sector, and size, together with specific triggers that affect diffusion such as enforcement of regulation and market demand. Second, institutional pressures at a societal level, and institutional capacity building at the industrial system level, are identified as mechanisms influencing IE diffusion. Third, outcomes of the IE diffusion process become evident in social and environmental indicators once knowledge flows and concepts are applied, and social and professional networks evolve.

The framework presented in Figure 12.1 identifies links between the development of IE practices in a given region and the pre-existing industrial geography. Institutional capacity building lies at the heart of this approach (Boon et al., 2011).

Boons et al. (2011: 907) define institutional capacity building as 'the qualities of social relations (the nature of bonds of trust and norms in networks which link people together), and the knowledge resources which

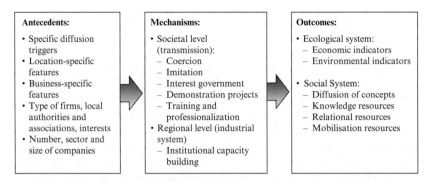

Source: Adapted from Boons et al., 2011.

Figure 12.1 Conceptual framework employed to view Caldas' industrial system dynamics

flow and emerge from these relations'. Furthermore, Healey (2003: 61) identifies three forms of capital that can be used to analyse the process of institutional capacity building:

- Knowledge resources: the availability and structural sharing of explicit and tacit knowledge; i.e., frames of reference, formal education, guidelines, and learning.
- Relational resources: networks or webs of relations within which actors play a given role; i.e., number of organisations involved, inter-organisational collaborations, degree of actor involvement.
- Mobilisation capacity: the structure and means by which knowledge resources and relational resources are formed and mobilised; i.e., change agents, core arena, momentum.

The aforementioned elements describe the movements and evolution over time of a given concept among different institutions in a geographic region, from one situation to another. Hence the framework highlights the complex and ongoing process of capacity building, rather than spotlighting a stock of assets as proposed by Healey et al. (2003). Studies of institutional capacity building follow the tradition of interpretive policy analysis, used in the early 1990s to study the process of rural development deregulation policies in the UK. Deregulation was seen as a planning practice of continual interaction and mutual constitution of structure and agency, comparable to the Caldas environmental management experience.

Accordingly, the framework as described is useful for studying the

Caldas experience, where an IE-related concept, such as CP, is examined over a period of time. CP has been used by several countries and international organisations as a strategy to complement environmental regulatory instruments and to reduce industry's environmental load (UNEP, 2004). Examples include the adoption of CP policies by numerous national and regional authorities (Leal, 2006), and the establishment of a global network of CP centres by multilateral organisations and development banks in more than 100 countries (Ehrenfeld et al., 2002). These national and international initiatives seek to persuade firms to adopt CP strategies on a voluntary basis. The Caldas experience describes how CP was disseminated in the region by a process of institutional capacity building from 2000 to 2010.

METHODS

The methods employed to address the aforementioned research questions include documenting the experience of CP development in Caldas. For reasons that follow, this kind of experience was identified as a 'critical case' (Flyvbjerg, 2006), useful to provide logical deductions for institutional capacity building in industrial systems in emerging markets.

The Caldas experience involves several collective CP efforts developed by diverse stakeholders in the regional industrial system. Most of the organisations involved confined their operations to the region, and shared similar social and cultural characteristics. Also, as noted earlier, longitudinal information concerning varied CP initiatives is available for ten years. Accordingly, analysis of the Caldas experience offers a worthy opportunity to study the process of institutional capacity building in emerging markets, a relatively untapped research area (Puppim de Oliveira, 2006).

Evidence from several sources allowed for triangulating data (Rowley, 2002). Detailed reports of CP initiatives were reviewed, and a variety of stakeholder representatives were interviewed by means of a semi-structured research protocol. An independent consultant, who participated actively in several CP initiatives in Caldas, identified key stakeholders to be interviewed. Interviews were recorded and transcribed for follow-up review by interviewees. Additional follow-up telephone calls were made to verify or supplement information. Interview reports were included in a case study database. Table 12.1 presents the profiles of stakeholders interviewed.

Empirical information drawn from Caldas is analysed in light of the framework discussed earlier. The following sections describe the antecedents, mechanisms and outcomes of CP dissemination in Caldas in 2000–2010.

Table 12.1   Key stakeholders interviewed for the Caldas study

Stakeholder	Organisational profile	Representatives interviewed
Corpocaldas	Public environmental agency for Caldas. Responsible for enforcing environmental regulations and environmental management	Deputy director of the Natural Resource department Technical operator of the industry programme
ODES Foundation	Colombian foundation promoting cleaner production and sustainable development	Former project coordinator of the Caldas CP programme Former ODES director and CP specialist
ANDI Caldas	Regional chapter of the national business association. ANDI-Caldas features 35 affiliated companies	Environmental manager
Manizales Chamber of Commerce	Private, not-for-profit organisation that promotes business growth and entrepreneurship	Coordinator of regional business development projects
University of Manizales	A leading public university in Caldas	Director of research centre in environment and development Director of Master's programme in sustainable development
Caldas coffee growers' unit	Part of the National Coffee Growers' Federation, representing over 500 000 small growers	Coordinator of environmental affairs
Super de Alimentos	Leading local privately owned food processor	Environment, health, and safety manager
Caldas Distillery	Leading state-owned local firm	Environment, health, and safety manager

ANTECEDENTS OF CP DEVELOPMENT IN CALDAS

CP dissemination in Caldas was an outgrowth of the national CP policy, Caldas' social, economic and geographic features, and actions by local authorities.

Diffusion Trigger: Promulgation of National CP Policy

CP efforts in Caldas stem from Colombia's National Cleaner Production policy, announced by the Ministry of Environment in 1997. The policy introduced a voluntary perspective for environmental management aimed at strengthening the national environmental system (SINA), launched in 1993. The policy responded to international efforts supported by international organisations such as the United Nations Environmental Programme (UNEP); consultants from the Netherlands provided support to Colombia's CP programme (Blackman et al., 2013).

Colombia's CP policy was implemented by regional agencies including Corpocaldas, the local environmental authority under SINA. Moreover, the National Association of Industry (ANDI), which operates a regional chapter in Caldas, was a key stakeholder promoting the adoption of a voluntary CP approach by private companies.

Location-specific Features

Caldas is one of Colombia's 32 departments, with an area of 7888 km², representing 0.69 per cent of the country's surface (DNP, 2012). Manizales, the capital city, with a population of 1 million, is one of Caldas' 27 municipalities (DNP, 2012).

Caldas' economy centres on agriculture (coffee, sugarcane), light manufacturing (food processing, metalworking, apparel), and tourism (Secretaria de Planeación, 2008). About one-half of the tightly knit region's GDP is generated largely by subsistence agriculture and cattle growing, which occupies about four-fifths of land use. Caldas' financial and business sector trails the national average, and is considered a development challenge.

Manizales is home to five universities, drawn from throughout the country. The comparatively high educational level of local professionals should serve to influence the acceptance of new paradigms such as CP.

Caldas' location-specific characteristics, featuring steep hills with risk of landslides during the rainy season, influence local environmental problems. Also, the region is crossed by the Cauca and Magdalena rivers, thus increasing sensitivity to water overuse and contamination from waste disposal of local farms and food processors, as well as hazardous materials such as burnt acids and chemicals used in coal and gold mining.

Role of Local Authorities

Environmental management in Caldas relied largely on Corpocaldas, the local authority representing SINA. Prior to the new CP policy, Corpocaldas had been primarily concerned with law enforcement and imposing sanctions stemming from soil erosion. Dominated by local political interests, the agency had given little attention to CP (personal interview, Deputy Director of the Natural Resource department, March 2011).

Following promulgation of the CP policy a new, non-political director was designated to head Corpocaldas. Soon, the agency's 'three-year plan 2004–2007' shifted its focus to what became known as 'shared environmental management' (Cruz, 2004). The plan sought to actively involve the region's stakeholders in environmental management practices. Subsequent Corpocaldas directors continued a largely preventive environmental management approach, together with regulation enforcement (personal interview, Deputy Director of the Natural Resource department, March 2011). From 2006 onwards, Corpocaldas' organisational structure featured a formal CP unit.

MECHANISMS FOR CP DEVELOPMENT IN CALDAS

Mechanisms influencing CP dissemination in Caldas spanned both societal and regional levels.

Societal-level Transmission

Colombia's National Cleaner Production policy sparked the negotiation of voluntary environmental agreements with leading industrial sectors throughout the country. These agreements sought to generate the exchange of information and capacity building among industries and environmental authorities, thus fostering participation of industrial representatives in strengthening the country's environmental regulations; from 1997 to 2006, some 65 agreements were signed between representatives of industrial sectors and national and regional environmental authorities (Blackman et al., 2013). Notwithstanding initial enthusiasm, regional authorities apparently failed to provide the needed follow-up.

In 2000, Corpocaldas launched its first voluntary agreements with local poultry and pork growers to improve the environmental impact of their production units (Quinaxi, 2004). Unfortunately, no follow-up was made to commitments signed, and no tangible results reported. Corpocaldas' deputy director of natural resources termed the voluntary agreements a kind of 'political intention for improvement' in Caldas.

Regional-level Dissemination

Caldas' CP dissemination mechanisms included the three central elements of the institutional capacity building process: knowledge resources, relational resources, and mobilisation capacity.

Actors involved in the Caldas experience deployed a broad range of knowledge and information resources. Interview responses record the formal 'train-the-trainers' programme offered by the ODES Foundation as a key resource steering the region's knowledge resources. From 2005 onwards, both the University of Manizales and the local Catholic University built on experience with the training programme to develop CP content for their academic and executive education offerings in environmental engineering, mechanical engineering, and accounting; a Master's programme in sustainable development was also launched (personal communication, Director of Master's Programme in Sustainable Development, University of Manizales, March 2011). CP concepts were disseminated to large numbers of students, many of whom were employed by firms and other local organisations. The clearinghouse led by the Manizales Chamber of Commerce (CCM) was also recognised by those interviewed as a significant knowledge resource. Building on CCM credibility and prestige among region firms, the clearinghouse distributed information about preventive options in sectors such as sugarcane processing, petrol stations, hotels, coffee farms, and other industries.

Over time, CP knowledge resources were observed to gain ground in wider organisational structures. Examples include the appointment of permanent staff assigned to CP dissemination and implementation among key stakeholder organisations. These specialised knowledge resources became a source for developing further CP strategies by additional firms.

Strengthening of relational resources was evidenced by the evolution of existing networks, such as the ANDI business association; for example, the Caldas ANDI office became closely involved in CP activities by participating in the CREAS programme[1] with Corpocaldas, the Manizales mayor's office, and certain larger companies that were not necessarily ANDI members. This kind of CP initiative improves trust between privately owned firms and public agencies such as Corpocaldas. Other examples of trust among stakeholders included a growing number of joint initiatives financed by Corpocaldas and CCM, including the CP clearinghouse and a joint technological mission.[2]

Examples of lack of interest from potential participants may also be cited. ACOPI, an association of small and medium-sized firms, showed little interest in participating in any activity. Other organisations, such as the regional units of the National University and the National Technical Training Centre (SENA), took part in early initiatives but appeared to have lost interest once key staff left. Reasons given for lack of participation, according to interviews, include lack of financial resources, lack of priority, competing issues, lack of capacity, or simply lack of interest. Other reasons mentioned for not becoming involved in CP initiatives were the occurrence of natural disasters and changes in political priorities.

A barrier of long standing that appears to have hampered participation in CP networks was Corpocaldas' reputation as an aggressive regulator. The agency's deputy director, in her interview, stated: 'in the beginning, the community and private sector viewed Corpocaldas as the "enemy", only there to pressure them; fortunately this perception changed once CP initiatives led by Corpocaldas advanced' (personal communication, Deputy Director, March 2011).

Stakeholders interviewed recognised Corpocaldas as the main change agent for CP dissemination in the Caldas industrial region. As an environmental agency, Corpocaldas launched the first CP efforts, financed ongoing initiatives, brokered participation by a variety of actors and led strategic moves such as shaping a CP regional policy. Moreover, Corpocaldas maintained its momentum as a CP promoter by means of key staff appointments. Other organisations that assumed a leadership role as interest in CP grew include the Manizales CCM and the University of Manizales, as illustrated by the CP clearinghouse and academic programmes.

Corpocaldas, the CCM and the University of Manizales all viewed CP as an important means for innovation, and as a motive to undertake initiatives (personal communication, former project coordinator, Corpocaldas-ODES regional CP programme, March 2011). For companies, CP sparked opportunities for both product and process innovation. For the University of Manizales, CP offered a pass key to academic programme innovation and research. Organisations such as CCM found CP a valuable addition to technical assistance services offered to region companies. For the local ANDI and Fendipetroleo chapters, collaboration in CP initiatives contributed to their mission of promoting innovation among member firms, and strengthened their reputation and negotiating power with regional authorities. For public institutions such as Corpocaldas and the Manizales municipality, CP also represented an alternative to costly law enforcement procedures and a means for legitimising operations.

Mobilisation capacity also contributed to brokering. From 2004, Corpocaldas and the ODES Foundation linked a number of organisations, thus spawning networks. In turn, these networks became vehicles for a range of opportunities. The CCM was at the centre of a primary network thanks to the CP clearinghouse. This illustrates an increase in stakeholder mobilisation over time, whereby a growing number of actors gain access to technical assistance and other benefits. Also, the ANDI-Caldas environmental committee became a significant political force in promoting CP initiatives. Lastly, the University of Manizales, through its academic programmes and research initiatives, enrolled about 50 students per semester in programmes featuring CP content.

In summary, a wide range of CP mechanisms and instruments show evidence of CP institutional capacity building in Caldas' industrial system. Figure 12.2 shows the timeline of Caldas' CP initiatives from 2000 to 2010. Some efforts are ongoing (shown in bold), where others have occurred only once (shown in italics).

OUTCOMES OF CP IMPLEMENTATION IN CALDAS

Environmental and social indicators reveal considerable CP dissemination progress in Caldas' regional industrial system, as first outlined in Figure 12.1.

Environmental Indicators

Environmental indicators resulting from CP initiatives undertaken by different stakeholders can be determined partially, as not all initiatives reported estimates. In 2005, CP interventions under the Corpocaldas-ODES 'Regional CP programme' estimated the environmental impacts as follows (ODES, 2005): water savings, 103 516 m^3/year; reduction of affluent discharge, 60 000 m^3/year; prevention of mercury dumping, 12 kg/year; prevention of waste disposal, 385 tonnes/year; energy savings, 200 000 kWh/year; prevention of CO_2 emissions, 675 tonnes/year.

Additionally, ANDI assessed the environmental impact of the 'learning-by-doing' training programme promoted in 2005 (Van Hoof, 2006): water savings, 106 000 m^3/year; prevention of waste disposal, 51 tonnes/year; energy savings, 206 000 kWh/year; prevention of emissions, 630 tonnes/ CO_2/year. The CCM estimated environmental impacts resulting from the clearinghouse initiative (CCM, 2011): water savings, 224 000 m^3/year; prevention of waste disposal, 766 tonnes/year; energy saved, 461 000 kWh/year. No indicators are available for other CP initiatives shown in Figure 12.2.

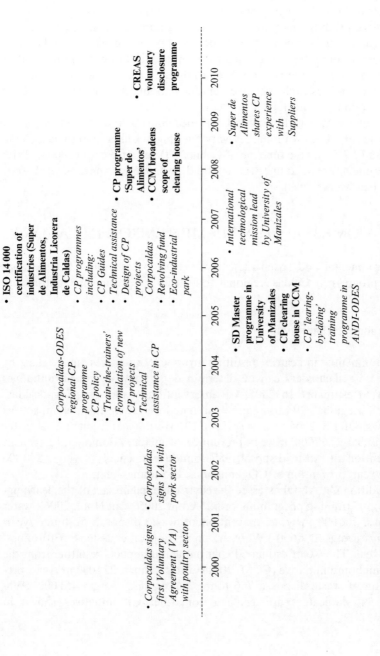

Note: Ongoing efforts are identified in bold, whereas those occurring only once are identified in italics.

Figure 12.2 Disseminating CP in Caldas, 2000–2010

Social Indicators

Social indicators showing the extent of CP development reflect diffusion of the CP concept and strengthened institutional capacity across Caldas' industrial system. Prior to 2000 there is no evidence of CP activity. As shown in Figure 12.2, the number of CP initiatives in Caldas has grown, together with the number of institutions recognising CP as a strategy for environmental management. At least 14 CP initiatives are noted, of which six are ongoing. Active CP participation was reported for at least 183 firms and eight regional institutions (ODES, 2005, Van Hoof, 2006; CCM, 2011). This evidence shows how CP became diffused in Caldas as a legitimate approach to manage environmental impacts within industrial systems.

The Caldas experience also shows how institutional capacity in CP was strengthened over the years. Knowledge resources included both formal and informal training offered by the ODES Foundation, and later by region-based universities. Professionals and employed students applied CP concepts in their respective companies. Technical assistance programmes offered by CCM mobilised firms and contributed to spreading CP benefits among business firms. Other initiatives, such as academic seminars and the CREAS disclosure programme, disseminated information in the wider community.

Strengthened relational resources are evidenced by substantial growth in Caldas' inter-organisational connectivity focused on CP. Most initiatives involved collaborative efforts between participating public and private organisations. Collaboration is evidenced by the wide range of regional programmes, together with the participative nature of efforts undertaken and projects financed.

Mobilisation was pursued at different levels. At a strategic level, the regional CP policy, and subsequently the 2007–2019 Regional Environmental Management Plan, added political legitimacy to mobilisation efforts. On an operational level, permanent offices and programmes under way by Corpocaldas, the CCM and the University of Manizales were locally recognised as significant sources of support for CP development in Caldas.

In sum, environmental and social indicators provide evidence of environmental improvement, institutional capacity building and CP diffusion as outcomes of efforts undertaken by a variety of public and private agencies, as well as large and small firms in the Caldas industrial system.

CONCLUSIONS

This chapter reviewed antecedents, process and outcomes of CP dissemination undertaken in a regional industrial system in the context of an emerging market. The analysis uncovered triggers for institutional capacity building for sustainable industrial systems in a particular region.

Key triggers for regional institutional capacity building include, first, promulgation of national policy addressed to CP, followed by a 'train-the-trainers' programme jointly developed by the regional environmental agency together with a local foundation. The latter initiative may be credited with promoting an ongoing knowledge resource and innovation programme that clearly impacted the regional industrial system. Leadership and mobilisation capacity by these organisations, buttressed by support from the local chamber of commerce and the University of Manizales, ensured continuity in mobilisation capacity. The brokering role played by the ODES Foundation, an 'outside' organisation, drew on existing social ties in building a CP-related network fostering interactions among regional actors.

The fortuitous appointment of a politically independent director spearheaded CP dissemination in Caldas just as a voluntary environmental management approach was launched to complement command and control regulation. Also, existing social ties in a comparatively small, tightly-knit region facilitated network interactions and helped shape collaborative initiatives. Moreover, the existence of leading universities contributed to developing knowledge resources in CP.

Remarkably, regional institutional capacity building in Caldas took hold despite decreasing interest elsewhere in Colombia. This finding confirms that if a critical mass of institutional capacity can be built on a regional scale, reduction of environmental pollution might compensate for the common volatility in implementing national environmental policies in emerging markets (Puppim de Oliveira, 2006). IE is thus a viable approach to promoting engagement with environmental policies and self-organisation in emerging markets, where capacity for enforcement of environmental regulation can be weak (Blackman, 2006).

Outcomes of the Caldas experience provide ready answers to the second research question: of how actions by stakeholders can be induced to build institutional capacity. In Caldas, a region based in an emerging market, industrial flows and transformation became more sustainable by crafting mechanisms that stimulated a critical mass and diverse group of stakeholders to undertake collaborative and ongoing actions aimed at institutional capacity building.

Additionally, this chapter highlights institutional capacity as part of CP and IE. This consideration implies taking into account the dynamics and processes of institutional capacity building as part of intentional actions towards preventive environmental measurement at a regional scale. It supports the complementary analysis of cluster approaches in regional industrial systems as antecedents of IE (Puppim de Oliveira, 2006; Deutz and Gibbs, 2008). Accordingly, fostering the process of institutional capacity building provides an alternative to firm-focused performance improvement in emerging markets such as Colombia, where resources to enforce environmental regulation are limited.

The framework provided by Boons et al. (2011) proved appropriate for understanding the dynamics occurring in CP dissemination in a regional industrial system in an emerging economy. This comprehensive framework brings out the dynamics among stakeholders entailed in institutional capacity building. By connecting antecedents, mechanisms and outcomes, the framework highlights lessons drawn from the Caldas experience that may help motivate similar efforts elsewhere for environmental improvement of industrial systems. The framework highlights inter-organisational dynamics, but appears to fall short in considering intra-organisational features.

Measurements of environmental indicators resulting from institutional capacity building remain challenging. Hence, further research focused on ways to measure environmental impacts of preventive voluntary actions in regional industrial systems is required, as already noted by Van Berkel (2006) and Lyon and Maxwell (2007). Such efforts should make use of control groups to test the outcomes of voluntary environmental improvement programmes in emerging markets, where public databases are generally scant. Additionally, using network analysis (Ashton, 2008) in the study of the Caldas experience could provide complementary insights into how relationships emerge among actors as part of institutional capacity building.

NOTES

1. CREAS (Corpocaldas Recognizes Excellence in Environmental Sustainability) is a voluntary disclosure programme promoted by Corpocaldas, ANDI-Manizales and the regional CP centre to engage companies in an environmental audit (Corpocaldas, 2010).
2. The technological mission involved capacity building in new cleaner technologies. In 2007, the University of Manizales, together with Corpocaldas and the Manizales CCM, organised a technological mission to Spain, financed by the national research development agency, Colciencias.

REFERENCES

Ashton, W. (2008), 'Understanding the organization of industrial ecosystems: a social network approach', *Journal of Industrial Ecology*, 12, 34–51.

Baas, L. (2006), 'To make zero emissions technologies and strategies become a reality, the lessons learned of cleaner production dissemination have to be known', *Journal of Cleaner Production*, 15, 1205–1216.

Blackman, A. (ed.) (2006), *Small Firms and the Environment in Developing Countries: Collective Impacts, Collective Action*, Washington, DC: Resources for the Future Press.

Blackman, A., E. Uribe, B. Van Hoof and T.P. Lyon (2013), 'Voluntary environmental agreements in developing countries: the Colombian experience', *Policy Sciences*, 46, 1–51. DOI: 10.1007/s11077-013-9176-z.

Boons, F. (2009), *Creating Ecological Value: An Evolutionary Approach to Business Strategies and the Natural Environment*, Cheltenham, UK and Northampton, MA, USA: Edward Elgar.

Boons, F. and L. Baas (1997), 'Types of industrial ecology: the problem of coordination', *Journal of Cleaner Production*, 5, 79–86.

Boons, F., W. Spekking and Y. Mouzakitis (2011), 'The dynamics of industrial symbiosis: a proposal for a conceptual framework based upon a comprehensive literature review', *Journal of Cleaner Production*, 19, 1773–1776.

CCM (2011), *Resultados de la ventanilla ambiental y los proyectos pilotos de PML [Results of the Clearing House and of Demonstration Projects in Cleaner Production]*, internal document, Chamber of Commerce of Manizales, Manizales, Colombia.

Corpocaldas (2010), *Programa Corpocaldas reconoce la excelencia ambiental sostenible – CREAS [Corpocaldas Recognizes Excellent Performance Towards Sustainability]*, document published by the University of Manizales, Manizales, Colombia.

Cruz, F. (2004), *Informe de Gestión, vigencia 2004* [report of management advances], Corpocaldas, Manizales, Colombia, accessed 15 December 2011 at http://www.corpocaldas.gov.co/publicaciones/401/Arc2004/1-Informe%20 de%20Gestion%202004.pdf.

Darnall, N. (2003), 'Motivations for participating in a US voluntary environmental initiative: the multi-state working group and EPA's EMS pilot program', in S. Sharma and M. Starik (eds), *Research in Corporate Sustainability: The Evolving Theory and Practice of Organizations and the Natural Environment*, Cheltenham, UK and Northampton, MA, USA: Edward Elgar, pp. 123–154.

Dasgupta, S., H. Hettige and D. Wheeler (1997), *What Improves Environmental Performance? Evidence from the Mexican Industry*, Washington, DC: World Bank Development Research Group.

Deutz, P. and D. Gibbs (2008), 'Industrial ecology and regional development: eco-industrial developments as cluster policy', *Regional Studies*, 42, 1313–1328.

DiMaggio, P.J. and W.W. Powell, (1983), 'The Iron Cage revisited: institutional isomorphism and collective rationality in organizational fields', *American Sociological Review*, 48, 147–160.

DNP (2012), Información básica departamental: Caldas, Departamento Nacional de Planeación (DNP), [Basic information about the Caldas region; National Planning Department], Bogota, Colombia.

Ehrenfeld, J.R., W. Ashton and A. Luqu (2002), *Mejoras practicas para la producción más limpia, su fomento e implementación en la pequeña empresas [Best Practices for the Promotion and Implementation of Cleaner Production in Small Enterprises]*, Washington, DC: Inter-American Development Bank (IADB), Multilateral Investment Fund.

Flyvbjerg, B. (2006), 'Five misunderstandings about case-study research', *Qualitative Inquiry*, **12**, 219–245.

Haeley P., C. De Magalheas, A. Madanipour and J. Pendlebury (2003), 'Place, identity and local politics: analysing initiatives in deliberative governance', in M. Hajer and H. Wagenaar (eds), *Deliberative Policy Analysis: Understanding Governance in the Network Society*, Cambridge, UK: Cambridge University Press, pp. 60–87.

Healey, P. (2003), 'Collaborative planning in perspective', *Planning Theory*, **2**, 101–123.

Hekkert, M. and M. Ossebaard (2010), *De innovatiemoter, het versnellen van baanbrekende innovaties [The Motor of Innovation; Spurring Structural Innovations]*, Assen, Holland: Koninklijke Van Gorcum.

Hirschhorn, J.S. (1997), 'Why the pollution prevention revolution failed – and why it ultimately will succeed', *Pollution Prevention Review*, **7**, 11–31.

Hoffman, A. (2003), 'Linking social systems analysis to the industrial ecology framework', *Organization & Environment*, **16**, 66–86.

Leal, J. (2006), *Eco-eficiencia: marco de análisis, indicadores y experiencias [Eco-efficiency: Framework, Indicators and Experience]*, Economic Commission for Latin America and the Caribbean (ELAC), Series Environmental and Development No. 105, Santiago de Chile, Chile.

Lyon, T.P. and J.W. Maxwell (2007), 'Environmental public voluntary programs reconsidered', *Policy Studies Journal*, **35**, 723–750.

Maranto-Vargas, D. and R. Gomez-Tagle (2007), 'Development of internal resources and capabilities as resources of differentiation of SME under increased global competition: a field study in Mexico', *Technological Forecasting and Social Change*, **74**, 90–99.

Montiel, I. and B. Husted (2009), 'The adoption of voluntary environmental management programs in Mexico: first movers as institutional entrepreneurs', *Journal of Business Ethics*, **88**, 349–363.

ODES (2005), *Avances regionals en Producción más Limpia en Caldas [Advance in Cleaner Production in Caldas; Report of Advances]*, internal document ODES Foundation, Bogota, Colombia.

Puppim de Oliveira, J.A. (2006), *Upgrading Clusters and Small Enterprises in Developing Countries: Environmental, Labor, Innovation and Social Issues*, Farnham, UK: Ashgate Publishing Limited.

Quinaxi (2004), *Construccion participative de los escenarios prospectivos del plan de ordanamiento ambiental de la Cuenca hidrografica del rio de la Miel [Participative Construction of Land Use Planning of the Area around the River Miel]*, Cooperative Agreement, Manizales, Caldas, Colombia.

Rowley, J. (2002), 'Using case studies in research', *Management Research News*, **25**, 16–27.

Scott, W.R. (2001), *Institutions and Organizations*, Thousand Oaks, CA: Sage.

Scott, W.R. (2008), 'Approaching adulthood: the maturing of institutional theory', *Theory and Society*, **37**, 427–442.

Secretaría De Planeación (2008), Plan de desarrollo 2008–2011; para hacer de Caldas nuestra major empresa, Departamental Grupo Proyectos Estratégicos Despacho del Gobernador, Manizales, Colombia [Secretary of Planning of the Governor's Office, Departamental Development Plan 2008–2011; making Caldas our best enterprise], accessed 15 December 2011 at http://www.gobe rnaciondecaldas.gov.co/index.php?option=com_content&view=article&id=21 8&Itemid=181.

Selznick, P. (1996), 'Institutionalism "old" and "new"', *Administrative Science Quarterly*, **41**, 270–277.

UNEP (2004), 'Guidance manual: how to establish and operate Cleaner Production Centre', United Nations Environmental Programme, accessed 15 December 2011 at http://www.unep.fr/shared/publications/pdf/WEBx0072xPA-CPcentre.pdf.

Van Berkel, R. (2006), 'Cleaner production and eco-efficiency initiatives in Western Australia 1996–2004', *Journal of Cleaner Production*, **20**, 1–15.

Van Hoof, B. (2006), *Liderazgo ambiental y valor agregado en empresas del sector de alimentos en Caldas [Environmental Leadership in Food Processing Firms in Caldas]*, Bogota, Colombia: National Association of Industry.

Velázquez, L., N. Munguía, A. Zavala and M. d. l. Á. Navarrete (2008), 'Challenges in operating sustainability initiatives in Northwest Mexico', *Sustainable Development*, **16**, 401–409.

13. Greenhouse gases reduction strategies for eco-industrial parks in China

Haikun Wang, Yue Lei and Jun Bi

INTRODUCTION

As global climate change becomes more apparent, efforts to control and reduce greenhouse gas (GHG) emissions have become a focus of attention worldwide. Currently, in China 157 national economic and technological development zones have been approved by the State Council (Ministry of Commerce [MOC], 2013); there are also over 1200 provincial-level industrial parks, which account for an increasing proportion of China's gross industrial output (Liang et al., 2011; Shi et al., 2012), and thus increasing proportional energy consumptions and GHG emissions (Zhang et al., 2010).

An eco-industrial park (EIP) is usually regarded as an example of green and low carbon community (Lowe et al., 1997), which seeks enhanced environmental and economic performance through collaboration in the management of the environment and resources. It is a tenet of industrial ecology that such organisational developments, in conjunction with technological advances, can promote both environmental and economic efficiencies (Jacobsen, 2006; Geng et al., 2007) and mitigate local carbon emissions (Jung et al., 2012). Experiences gained from EIPs in carbon emission control and mitigation strategies are of critical importance for sustainable industrial development, as well as the vigorous expansion of industrial parks and economic development zones in China (Shi et al., 2010), particularly in the context of national targets and local mitigation objectives (Qiu, 2009).

However, there have been very few empirical studies that examine carbon accounting, climate mitigation activities and strategies in industrial parks (Liu et al., 2012; Wang et al., 2013). Wang et al. (2013) selected Suzhou Industrial Park for a case study to depict its GHG emission trajectories under three different pathways with the scenario analysis method.

Liu et al. (2012) analysed energy related carbon emissions of Suzhou Industrial Park using emission factors from the Intergovernmental Panel on Climate Change (IPCC), followed by some policy suggestions related to industrial symbiosis (exchange of unwanted materials/energy). Jung et al. (2012) analysed regional energy-related CO_2 emission characteristics and potential mitigation of South Korean EIPs, and Block et al. (2011) studied the way to achieve the CO_2 neutrality of Herdersbrug Industrial Park by evaluating renewable electricity and heat generation as well as energy-saving measures. These existing studies could provide valuable experience for GHG management of Chinese industrial parks. However, quantifying GHG emissions of China's EIPs is difficult as they usually include communities as well as industries, which make the GHG emission boundary complex. Therefore, it is important to present a methodology and example of analysing reduction potentials of energy consumption and carbon emissions in China's EIPs.

In this chapter, a methodology which incorporates consumption and production perspectives is recommended to account for GHG emissions for China's EIPs. This method has been adopted in other carbon emissions inventory studies for Chinese cities (Bi et al., 2011; Wang et al., 2012) and complements GHG emissions methodologies for industrial parks. It will be applied to calculate GHG emissions of a pilot EIP in China from 2005–2010. The scenario analysis approach is applied to predict emissions of given strategies and regulations, and calculate mitigation potential by 2020. Policy recommendations are also provided to improve energy and environmental performance of Chinese EIPs. The remaining sections are as follows: introduction to EIPs in the Chinese context; review of the various carbon accounting systems that are available, and an appropriate methodology for industrial parks, which incorporates hybrid life-cycle perspectives, is recommended; report of the GHG emissions result; prediction of GHG emissions and mitigation potentials up to 2020; and policy recommendations for Chinese EIPs.

ECO-INDUSTRIAL PARKS IN CHINA

An EIP is a good example of an organised form of the industrial eco-system. At a workshop hosted by the United States President's Council on Sustainable Development in October 1996, participants considered an EIP as 'a community of businesses cooperating with each other and with the local community to efficiently share resources (information, materials, water, energy, infrastructure and natural habitat). This leads to economic gains, improves environmental quality, and enhances human resources for the business and local community' (PCSD, 1996, unpaginated).

EIPs were initially promoted in China at the end of the 1990s by the State Environmental Protection Administration (the predecessor of the Ministry of Environmental Protection [MEP]), as an effective strategy for governments at all levels to implement the Circular Economy (CE) strategy (Geng et al., 2010), namely to cope with the conflicts between rapid economic growth and the shortage of raw materials and energy. In recent years, China has rapidly developed a number of EIPs. The impetus for developing EIPs reflects severe conflict between economic growth and natural resources, energy shortage and heavy pollution (Shi et al., 2002).

EIPs could play a significant role in local carbon mitigation and low-carbon development (Jung et al., 2012). However, the effectiveness of EIPs in promoting environmental efficiencies such as emissions control has rarely been analysed. In the context of a rapidly developing country like China, it is extremely important that efficiencies are introduced into production, in order to prevent the emissions from increasing to absolute levels. It is therefore necessary to analyse carbon emissions and the low-carbon strategies at industrial park level. In China, many industrial parks have a dual function as production and residential areas, in contrast to the North American model wherein parks are predominantly manufacturing based (Geng and Côté, 2001, 2003). Consequently, a typical Chinese industrial park has an industrial production area, a scientific research area, a residential area, a recreational area, and a business and service area (Geng and Zhao, 2009). From this perspective, an industrial park in China is similar to a mini-city elsewhere.

We use Suzhou Industrial Park (SIP) as a case to illustrate GHG emissions modelling and reduction strategies for EIPs in China. SIP lies east of the old Suzhou city, with a total planned area of 288 km^2 of which 80 km^2 is co-developed by both the Chinese and Singaporean governments, and was officially launched in May 1994. It has established a management committee,[1] which has a sound institutional framework and is directly authorised by the central government. Following eighteen years' development, SIP has a population of 0.7 million, its Integrated Development Index (IDI) ranks second among all national development zones, and ranks first in terms of environmental protection, energy conservation and emission reduction in China (SIPAC, 2010). SIP was approved as a national EIP, national CE pilot, and is also one of the 24 low-carbon pilots in Jiangsu Province, China. Now, SIP is striving for a new positioning of an internationally competitive high-tech industrial park and an internationalised, innovation-oriented, new ecological township. It is seen as a good example for Chinese EIPs in coordinating social, economic and environmental development (Zhang et al., 2010).

CARBON ACCOUNTING METHOD FOR INDUSTRIAL PARKS

IPCC provided a general and widely used model for accounting national GHG emissions (IPCC, 2006). Further, the methodology developed by the International Council for Local Environmental Initiatives (ICLEI) has also been applied in many cities to estimate their GHG emissions at local level. However, GHGs accounting for individual cities (communities) typically have been confounded by spatial scale and boundary issues, which impact on the allocation of regional responsibilities for carbon mitigation. Life-cycle assessment methodologies have therefore been started to apply for accounting local GHG emissions from the consumption perspective in recent years. The Economic Input–Output Life-Cycle Assessment (EIO-LCA) is a useful tool at the national scale to account for upstream GHG emissions from all consumer behaviors (Hendrickson and Horvath, 1998). The well-developed LCA tools and regional material flow accounts (MFAs) can be used together to allocate the indirect emissions associated with key materials used in cities. This approach is consistent with World Resources Institute scope 3 GHGs accounting protocol (WRI, 2004), which could provide a more holistic picture of a city's GHG impacts. There is, however, a paucity of published data on comprehensive energy use at the city scale, and even less data from cities in developing countries (Hillman and Ramaswami, 2010), which hinders the application of LCA methodologies. To compensate for deficiencies in each method, the hybrid methodology, which combines LCA, MFA, IPCC and ICLEI, has been applied to measure the carbon emissions from some local areas (Ramaswami et al., 2008; Kennedy et al., 2009, 2010).

In this chapter, the methodology of calculating GHG emissions from EIPs is similar to that applied in our previous research on Chinese cities and industrial parks (Bi et al., 2011; Wang et al., 2012, 2013). We focus on the scope 1 and scope 2 GHG emissions defined by ICLEI, and include emissions of energy consumption, landfill and industrial process. We included GHGs of CO_2, CH_4, N_2O, CF_4 and C_2F_6, and transferred them into carbon dioxide equivalents (CO_{2e}) emissions by multiplying global warming potential (GWP) parameters, which are respectively 1, 21, 310, 6500 and 9200 as recommended by the IPCC (IPCC, 2006). CO_{2e} emissions from energy consumption (industry energy, transportation, commerce and residence) were calculated using following equation:

$$E = \Sigma_i\Sigma_j A_{i,j} \times NCV \times C_{i,j} \times CO_{2\text{eff}} \times 10^6 \qquad (13.1)$$

Where, E is the total CO_{2e} emissions from energy consumption, tonne; $A_{i,j}$ is the total consumption of fuel type j in sector i, tonne; NCV is the net calorific value, TJ/Gg and $C_{i,j}$ is the carbon oxidation rate of fuel type j in sector i, %; $CO_{2\text{eff}}$ is the Effective CO_2 emission factor, Kg/TJ. The fuel types considered in this study cover all the fuel categories used in SIP.

The industrial, commercial and residential energy consumption data were collected from the official statistics of SIP. Due to lack of vehicle data, traffic energy consumption (mainly gasoline and diesel) data were obtained from local fuel sales at gas stations. It should be noted that power production related energy consumption was excluded from the total emissions calculation. Detailed discussion (Bi et al., 2011) has explained that electricity consumption-related carbon emissions were calculated for all sectors from the consumption perspective, so emissions from power plants were excluded when counting the total emissions, in order to avoid double counting.

CO_{2e} emission factors for primary energy sources were calculated using the IPCC recommended method (Table 13.1) and the default value for oxidation rate (100%) was applied. Emission factors for secondary energy (e.g., power and heat) were calculated using local power plants' energy input, output data and the Jiangsu-specific electricity emission factors (part of electricity was purchased from Jiangsu Province), which were calculated based on data from the East China Power Grid (ECPG) (Bi et al., 2011). SIP specific electricity emission factors and heat emission factors are shown in Table 13.2.

We applied IPCC First Order Decay Model to calculate carbon emissions generated by solid waste landfill, shown as Equation (13.2):

$$E_w = \{[\Sigma_i CH_{4x,\,T} - R_T](1 - OX_T)\} \times GWP \qquad (13.2)$$

Where, E_w is CO_{2e} emissions generated by solid waste landfill (tonne); $CH_{4x,\,T}$ is the CH_4 outputs for inventory year T and waste type x; R_T is CH_4 recovery for inventory year T (tonne) and OX_T is oxidation factor for inventory year T (%). GWP is global warming potential of CH_4, which is referred to IPCC recommended value.

GHG emissions from industrial processes mainly refer to the emissions released due to the chemical or physical transformation of materials during the industrial production processes, such as cement processing, steel production, advanced electronic manufacturing, etc. Some electronic companies, which emit GHG emissions during the production process, were

Table 13.1   GHG emission factors for various energy types

Fuel types	Default carbon content kg/GJ	Default carbon oxidation rate %	Effective CO_2 emission factor kg/TJ	Net calorific value TJ/Gg	Emission factor tonne CO_2/tonne (except a)
Crude Coal	25.8	100	87 300	20.9	1.83
Washed Coal	25.8	100	87 300	26.3	2.30
Other Washed Coal	25.8	100	87 300	8.4	0.73
Briquette	26.6	100	87 300	20.9	1.83
Coke	29.2	100	95 700	28.4	2.72
Coke Oven Gas	12.1	100	37 300	16 726	6.23 a
Natural Gas	15.3	100	54 300	38 931	21.14 a
LNG	17.5	100	58 300	44.2	2.58
Crude Oil	20	100	71 100	41.8	2.97
Gasoline	20.2	100	67 500	43.1	2.91
Kerosene	19.5	100	69 700	43.1	3.00
Diesel	20.2	100	72 600	42.7	3.10
Fuel Oil	21.1	100	75 500	41.8	3.16
LPG	17.2	100	61 600	50.2	3.10
Other petroleum products	20	100	75 500	41.8	3.16

Note: a = tonne $CO_2/10000m^3$.

Table 13.2   GHG emission factors for heat and electricity in Suzhou Industrial Park between 2005 and 2010

Year	EF_e	EF_h
2005	8.61	0.08
2006	8.94	0.10
2007	6.91	0.11
2008	6.87	0.10
2009	7.10	0.10
2010	7.21	0.11

Notes:
EF_e represents emission factor for electricity.
EF_h represents emission factor for heat.

included in our calculation. Equation (13.3) shows the accounting method for carbon emissions from these industrial processes:

$$E_e = \sum_i [C_d \times EF_i \times GWP_i] \times 10^{-6} \qquad (13.3)$$

Where, E_e is CO_{2e} emissions generated from process i, tonne; C_d is the annual product output (e.g., m^2 or tonne); EF_i is the emission factor of product i (e.g. g/m^2- or g/tonne); i is the type of process (such as cement production, steel production); GWP_i is global warming potential of GHGs released from process i, which are referred to as IPCC recommended value.

CARBON EMISSION CHARACTERISTICS OF EIPS

Total Emissions

Using the methodology above, carbon emissions for the industrial, commercial and residential sectors were calculated, and aggregated to get the total carbon emissions for SIP between 2005 and 2010 (Figure 13.1). Along with an annual GDP growth rate of 15.3% (based on the 2005 constant price) and an annual residential population growth rate of 10% during the 11th Five Year Plan (FYP)[2] (2006–2010), SIP has shown a large increase in energy demand and carbon emissions. The total emissions of CO_{2e} from SIP have increased from 5.58 million tonnes in 2005 to 9.45 million

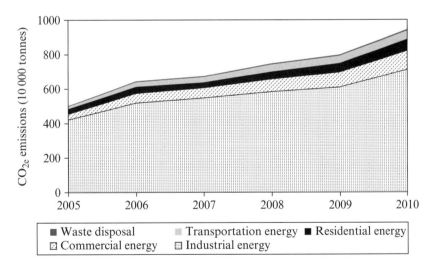

Figure 13.1　GHG emissions from Suzhou Industrial Park, 2005–2010

tonnes in 2010, with an average annual growth rate of 13.11%, which is 2% lower than annual GDP growth rate in this period. This partly reflects the sustainable development strategies implemented in SIP in recent years, including the CE Plan, the Ecological Civilization Plan, and the Ecological Optimisation Plan[3] supported by various programmes and projects by local governments. Significant increases of 27% and 18% in carbon emissions occurred in 2006 and 2010, respectively. This was mainly caused by increases in energy consumption from the industrial sector, which contributed 70% and 73% to total emission increment in 2006 and 2010, respectively. For the industrial energy sector, an increase of electricity consumption explains 64% of the total emission increment. Paper manufacturing, electronic equipment manufacturing and the construction industry are the three major industries, which contributed over 50% to the total emission increment. Emissions from industrial processes, mainly semiconductor and crystal silicon cell production processes, were very small and negligible compared to energy consumption related emissions, and are not included in Figure 13.1.

Sectoral Emissions

The emission inventory comprised several sectors and each sector's carbon emissions showed a rapid growth trend between 2005 and 2010. The industrial, commercial, residential, transportation and solid waste disposal sectors showed an annual growth rate of 10.94%, 26.57%, 19.54%, 14.39% and 43.76%, respectively. The carbon emissions from the solid waste disposal sector, the commercial energy sector and the residential energy sector increased relatively faster than the other sectors due to the rapid development of tertiary industry, a high population growth rate and an improvement in people's living standards in SIP during the 11th FYP.

Each sector's contribution to the total carbon emissions varied (Figure 13.2). Clearly, industrial energy consumption was the largest contributor accounting for 74.00–81.97% of the total carbon emissions in SIP. Commercial energy consumption contributed 7.59–12.51%, and ranks second. Residential energy consumption contributed 5.94–7.25%. Thus, emissions related to building operations (including commercial and residential) contributed 13.63–19.40% to the total emissions. Transportation contributed 4.04–5.62% to the total emissions, which is far less than in developed municipalities (Kennedy et al., 2009, 2010).

Transportation-related emissions, including both public traffic and private cars, were calculated from local fuel sales, which assume that the amount of fuel purchased locally but used elsewhere is balanced by the

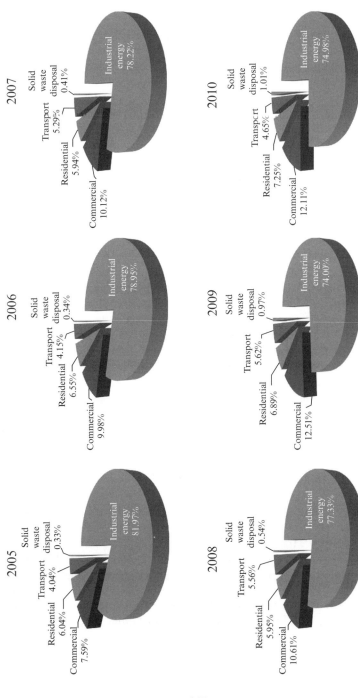

Figure 13.2   Sectoral contributions to the total carbon emissions of Suzhou Industrial Park, 2005–2010

local use of fuel purchased elsewhere. This assumption may cause a lower estimation of SIP's traffic related emissions than the situation in reality.

Although the industrial energy sector contributed the most to total emissions, the share decreased from 81.97% in 2005 to 74.98% in 2010. In contrast, the commercial energy sector's share increased from 7.59% in 2005 to 12.11% in 2010. This may reflect both industrial structure optimisation and technical progress within SIP in recent years. As a consequence of the development of the tertiary sector, the economic importance of industry decreased from 75.05% in 2005 to 66.05% in 2010. Moving from a simple industrial manufacturing zone to a future urban area with balanced industrial, commercial and residential function will help China's industrial parks become more eco-friendly, and control carbon emissions while maintaining economic development.

Emissions from Industrial Energy Consumption

As mentioned above, industrial energy consumption was the main contributor to carbon emissions from SIP. SIP has 34 industries in total (including the construction industry). According to data from the local statistical office, the most important industries to the local economy include electronics and the information industry, machinery manufacturing and the chemical materials and products manufacturing industry. The economic output of the former two industries made up 79.79% of the total industrial output by value in 2010.

The paper manufacturing industry was the largest contributor to industrial energy related carbon emissions (Figure 13.3), followed by the electronic manufacturing industry, the power, heat production and supply industry and the construction industry. The four main contributors produced 77.71% of the total industrial energy related emissions. When comparing the shares of carbon emissions with economic output for the same industry, it can be seen that although the electronic manufacturing industry contributed 24.34% of the total emissions, its share of economic output reached 47.89%, and the emission per output was half the average level. In contrast, the power production industry and paper manufacturing industry produced a large proportion of the emissions but made only a low economic contribution. Thus, developing less energy-intensive industries with high added value instead of traditional energy-intensive manufacturing industries with low added value could help Chinese EIPs to realise carbon mitigation while maintaining aggregate economic growth.

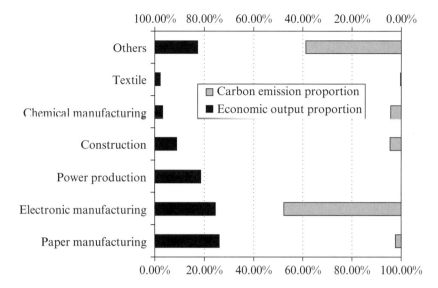

Note: 'Others' refers to the other 28 industries not listed.

Figure 13.3 Carbon emissions and economic outputs for key industries of Suzhou Industrial Park in 2010

Carbon Emission Levels

Measuring carbon emissions intensity, namely the amount of carbon emitted per unit of production over time, could quantitatively reflect the emission efficiency of industrial parks. Overall, the carbon intensity of SIP shows a decreasing trend except for 2006 (Figure 13.4). It decreased 9.03% during the 11th FYP, with an annual rate of decrease of 1.9%. Carbon emission intensities of industry declined continuously, as SIP successively fulfilled the 'Four Plans' goals of ecological optimisation, manufacturing industry upgrading, service industry multiplying, and sci-tech leap-frogging, to reduce the proportion of the carbon-intensive manufacturing industries since 2005 (SIPAC, 2010). Although CO_{2e} emissions per commercial added value remained virtually constant up to 2010, it is only 30% of the industrial carbon intensity in SIP. This means that SIP should encourage the development of commercial industry and improve its economic proportion in the gross output.

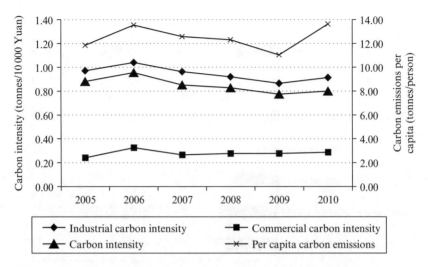

Figure 13.4   Carbon intensities and per capita emission of Suzhou Industrial Park, 2005–2010

EIP CARBON REDUCTION POTENTIALS

In order to demonstrate future CO_{2e} emissions potential, and to recommend and evaluate the pathway to slow down the growth rate of carbon emissions in SIP, this section applies scenario analysis to predict the carbon emissions up to 2020, by considering the policies and measures that have influenced the main driving factors for SIP's development, such as economic development, industrial structural adjustment, technical innovation, etc. Three scenarios are projected: 1) assume rates of change of socio-economic and technological development remain at 2010 levels; 2) and 3) assume respectively moderate and large carbon mitigation efforts are deployed.

Scenario 1), business as usual (BAU), is a conservative projection of socio-economic and technological development (using energy efficiency as an indicator), which assumes that rates of change will remain at the 2010 level. According to the 12th FYP on economic and social development of SIP, this projection is estimated that: 1) GDP will maintain an annual growth rate of 15% during the 12th FYP, and 12% during the 13th FYP; 2) primary and secondary industries will gradually decline and eventually account for 46% of the total GDP in SIP, while the tertiary industry will account for the remaining 54%; 3) the population growth rate will be 6%.

To indicate alternatives to the rapid growth of carbon emissions, two more

Table 13.3   Scenario definitions of low carbon development for Suzhou Industrial Park

	ILS-L	ILS-H
Economy	15% annual GDP growth in 12th FYP, 13% in 13th FYP	
Population	6% annual growth in 12th FYP, 4% in 13th FYP	
Industrial	Tertiary industry accounts for 59% by 2020	
structure	Chemical industrial ratio reduces 2% in 2013 from 2010	Chemical industrial ratio reduces 4% in 2013 from 2010
	Paper manufacturing ratio reduces 0.5% in 2013	Paper manufacturing ratio reduces 1% in 2013
	Textile and dyeing industries are shut down	Textile and dyeing industries are shut down
Technology innovation	Energy efficiency improves by 16%[a] during 12th FYP, 8% during 13th FYP	Energy efficiency improves by 16%[a] during 12th FYP, 10% during 13th FYP
	Textile and dyeing, and paper manufacturing energy efficiency improves 20% and 12% respectively	Textile and dyeing, and paper manufacturing energy efficiency improves 23% and 13% respectively

Notes:
Scenarios are Integrated Low-carbon Scenario-Low (ILS-L) and Integrated Low-carbon Scenario-High (ILS-H).
a This is the energy conservation target of SIP according to its 12th FYP, in accordance with Jiangsu Province.

scenarios of Integrated Low-carbon Scenario-Low (ILS-L) and Integrated Low-carbon Scenario-High (ILS-H) were developed, which considered medium and large efforts to control SIP's carbon emissions (Table 13.3).

Generally speaking, as the economy and infrastructure develop continuously, carbon emissions of SIP will keep increasing until 2020 even under the ILS scenario. However, after the implementation of the mitigation strategies in Table 13.3, the carbon emissions reduction is obvious compared to the BAU scenario (Figure 13.5). Under the BAU scenario, where few considerations had been given to environmental protection and climate change issues, the carbon emissions in 2020 would reach 22.25 million tonnes, five times higher than in 2005. Yet, under the ILS, where measurements such as improving energy efficiency by conducting an ecological optimisation plan, and upgrading industry structure by developing an advanced manufacturing industry in tandem with a modern service industry, were introduced, the carbon emissions in 2020 would be 18.29 and 16.15 million tonnes respectively under the low and high low-carbon development scenarios, achieving a carbon reduction of 3.96 and 6.09 million

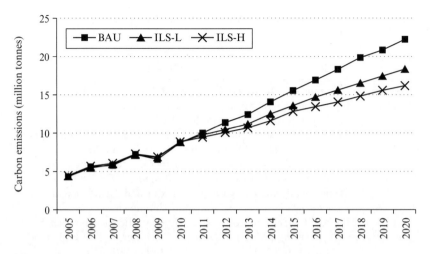

Notes:
BAU: Business as usual.
ILS-L and ILS-H: Integrated Low-carbon Scenario-Low and Integrated Low-carbon
Scenario-High, respectively.

*Figure 13.5   Scenario analysis of carbon emissions in Suzhou Industrial
                Park up to 2020*

tonnes respectively. Energy-intensive enterprises, such as textile and paper
mills, were suggested to be controlled (e.g., to reduce production, move
out and even close these kinds of plants) to mitigate the carbon emission
in SIP.

Emission intensity will continue to decrease up to 2020 (Figure 13.6).
Under the BAU scenario, SIP would fail to achieve China's mitigation
target, indicating that it is impossible to achieve the mitigation goals
without fuel economy improvement and industrial structural adjustment.
The projected emissions of ILS-L and ILS-H in 2015 and 2020 are below
the target line. Thus, with proper control of industrial structure and technical innovation to become more eco-friendly, SIP could achieve its local
carbon intensity mitigation target to reduce by 19% in 2015 from 2010, as
well as the national target of 40–45% in 2020 from 2005 levels.

CARBON MANAGEMENT INITIATIVES

During the 11th FYP, SIP has achieved great progress in eco-development
and carbon mitigation, especially due to industrial structural adjustment

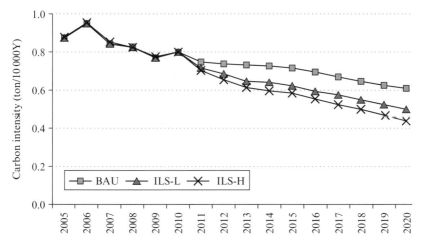

Notes:
The dashed line represents the emission intensity target in 2015, which means carbon
intensity should decrease by 20% compared to 2010 (SIP's mitigation target).
The dotted line represents the emission intensity target in 2020, a decrease of 40% compared
with 2005 (Chinese national mitigation target).

*Figure 13.6   Scenario analysis of carbon intensity in Suzhou Industrial
            Park until 2020*

and the regulation of key industries. This section outlines the policy initiatives employed by SIP that have contributed to the reductions in emissions and emissions intensity. Some of these initiatives could be shared with, and transferred to, other EIPs in China.

First: transforming and upgrading industrial structure (Zhang and Huang, 2012) and energy structure, and optimising economic growth pattern. SIP has sought to eliminate or upgrade backward industries (including the power supply industry, the steel industry, the cement industry, the building materials industry, the textile industry and the chemical industry) and laggard equipment (JSPG, 2010). This has been done by projects such as energy audit, clean production audit and energy-saving retrofit, and tertiary industries upgrading, thereby SIP has built a modern industrial system featuring high added value, high efficiency and low pollution outputs. In the tertiary sector, upgrading and promoting the development of modern services have helped SIP to maintain a steady, rapid economic growth and have improved the quality of the developments that are taking place.

Second: emphasising technological innovation. SIP intends to launch a 'double-hundred' project[4] covering the fields of biomedicine, converged communications, software and animation, and ecological protection, which will further promote development of the higher value-added industries.

Third: promoting energy-saving measures in key industrial sectors. In order to coordinate the developments of environmental protection, ecology and the socio-economy, many policies and measures, such as piloting the CE, clean production, energy auditing, the reinforcement of energy management and the implementation of energy-saving technological renovation projects, were applied in the industrial sectors. These policies and measures could produce significant mitigations of carbon emissions (Jung et al., 2012).

Last but not least: saving energy consumptions in non-industrial sectors. Other measures – (e.g. promoting the concept of green building (Newsham et al., 2009), popularising the use of renewable energy technologies (e.g., ground- and water-source heat pumps (Yang et al., 2010)) and solar power (Liu et al., 2010), central air-conditioning and heating systems for the local area, clean-energy bus services and starting a campaign to promote green travel and public awareness of green consumption and the low-carbon lifestyle (Heiskanen et al., 2010)) could also be beneficial to eco- and low-carbon consumption.

All these measures and strategies set a good example for other Chinese EIPs. As the above scenario analysis suggests, measures aimed at industrial structural adjustment and technical innovation are still the most important policies available to enforce the low carbon development of EIPs. However, other joint strategies, such as promoting energy-saving measures in key industrial sectors, buildings and transportations should also be involved.

The high economic growth rate and associated industrial and urban activity are the main drivers behind the tremendous rise in energy consumption and GHG emissions in Chinese cities and EIPs (Li et al., 2010). However, it is exactly the high economic growth rate that has enabled the economic transitions and environmental measures outlined above. Thus, in many other geographic contexts the energy efficiency measures would be the only tools that EIPs could use to reduce emissions. Attempting to control the type of industry locating in an EIP did not, for example, work well in the US context (Deutz and Gibbs, 2008).

In-depth studies of how the policies outlined above have been implemented would be helpful for reference elsewhere. As a cautionary note, however, one of the key strategies in promoting industrial ecology practices at SIP has been to eliminate more polluted and energy-intensive industries, which clearly has request for developing lower carbon-intensive industries and relocating (or eliminating) backward industries to other regions. However, this kind of relocation could be the efficient specialisation of industrial production aligned with China's economic geography rather than an efficiency loss (Qi et al., 2013).

CONCLUSIONS

A methodology which incorporates consumption and production perspectives was proposed and applied to calculate GHG emissions of a pilot EIP in China. SIP is moving from a manufacturing industrial park to a future urban area; the carbon emissions continue to grow, but slower than the growth rate of economic development. The turning point of carbon emission seems not to appear before 2020 even under the most optimistic scenario of our projections, indicating strong obstacles to curb the total emissions without fundamental changes of development (e.g., energy structure, economic development and structure, etc.) in SIP. The carbon accounting methods and carbon management initiatives discussed in this study could be applied to other industrial parks in China to facilitate a low carbon development scenario. Of course, the method and results of this research are also valuable to the communities beyond China after suitable adaptation.

NOTES

1. Generally, a Chinese industrial park is land reserved by its municipal authority for industrial development. It usually includes an administrative authority, making provisions for continuing management, enforcing restrictions on tenants and detailed planning with respect to lot sizes, access and facilities.
2. The FYPs of the People's Republic of China are a series of economic development initiatives since 1953, shaped by the Communist Party of China (CPC) through the plenary sessions of the Central Committee and national congresses. The central government will make the plan in the first year of a five-year period, under which the local government will make its own plan partially in accordance with the local development situation. Thus, SIP has its own FYP, made by the park management, while the content of the plan was partially self-making, and partially referred to a higher authority direction.
3. Sorted according to the local government website accessed 13 January 2014 at http://www.sipac.gov.cn/.
4. Website accessed 13 January 2014 at http://tech.sipac.gov.cn/.

REFERENCES

Bi, J., R. Zhang, H. Wang, M. Liu and Y. Wu (2011), 'The benchmarks of carbon emissions and policy implications for China's cities: case of Nanjing', *Energy Policy*, **39** (9), 4785–4794.

Block, C., B. Van Praet, T. Windels, I. Vermeulen, G. Dangreau, A. Overmeire, E. D'Hooge, T.M. Ugent, G. van Eetvelde and C. Vandecasteele (2011), 'Toward a carbon dioxide neutral industrial park: a case study', *Journal of Industrial Ecology*, **15** (4), 584–596.

Deutz, P. and D. Gibbs (2008), 'Industrial ecology and regional development: eco-industrial development as cluster policy', *Regional Studies*, **42** (10), 1313–1328.

Geng, Y. and R. Côté (2001), 'EMS as an opportunity for enhancing China's economic development zones: the case of Dalian', in *Environmental Management for Industrial Estates – A Resource and Training Kit*, Paris: UNEP Division of Technology, Industry and Economics, Production and Consumption Branch.

Geng, Y. and R. Côté (2003), 'Environmental management systems at the industrial park level in China', *Environmental Management*, **31**, 784–794.

Geng, Y. and H. Zhao (2009), 'Industrial park management in the Chinese environment', *Journal of Cleaner Production*, **17** (14), 1289–1294.

Geng, Y., M. Haight and Q. Zhu (2007), 'Empirical analysis of eco-industrial development in China', *Sustainable Development*, **15**, 121–133.

Geng, Y., P. Zhang, S. Ulgiati and J. Sarkis (2010), 'Emergy analysis of an industrial park: the case of Dalian, China', *Science of The Total Environment*, **408** (22), 5273–5283.

Heiskanen, E., M. Johnson, S. Robinson, E. Vadovics and M. Saastamoinen (2010), 'Low-carbon communities as a context for individual behavioural change', *Energy Policy*, **38** (12), 7586–7595.

Hendrickson, C. and A. Horvath (1998), 'Economic input–output models for environmental life-cycle assessment', *Environmental Science & Technology*, **32** (7), 184A–191A.

Hillman, T. and A. Ramaswami (2010), 'Greenhouse gas emission footprints and energy use benchmarks for eight U.S. cities', *Environmental Science & Technology*, **44**, 1902–1910.

IPCC (2006), in H.S. Eggleston, L. Buendia, K. Miwa, T. Ngara and K. Tanabe (eds), *IPCC Guidelines for National Greenhouse Gas Inventories*, Japan: Prepared by the National Greenhouse Gas Inventories Programme, IGES.

Jacobsen, N.B. (2006), 'Industrial symbiosis in Kalundborg, Denmark: a quantitative assessment of economic and environmental aspects', *Journal of Industrial Ecology*, **10**, 239–255.

JSPG (Jiangsu Provincial Government) (2010, 29 July), 'Implementing opinions of speeding up the backward production capacity elimination by Jiangsu Provincial Government', accessed 13 January 2014 at http://www.jiangsu.gov.cn/.

Jung, S., K.-J. An, G. Dodbiba and T. Fujita (2012), 'Regional energy-related carbon emission characteristics and potential mitigation in eco-industrial parks in South Korea: logarithmic mean Divisia index analysis based on the Kaya identity', *Energy*, **46** (1), 231–241.

Kennedy, C., J. Steinberger, B. Gasson, T. Hillman, M. Havranek, D. Pataki, A. Phdungsilp, A. Ramaswami and G. Villalba Mendez, (2009), 'Greenhouse gas emissions from global cities', *Environmental Science & Technology*, **42**, 7297–7302.

Kennedy, C., J. Steinberger, B. Gasson, Y. Hansen, T. Hillman, M. Havránek, D. Pataki, A. Phdungsilp, A. Ramaswami and G. Villalba Mendez (2010), 'Methodology for inventorying greenhouse gas emissions from global cities', *Energy Policy*, **38** (9), 4828–4837.

Li, L., C. Chen, S. Xie, C. Huang, Z. Cheng, H. Wang, Y. Wang, H. Huang, J. Lu and S. Dhakal (2010), 'Energy demand and carbon emissions under different development scenarios for Shanghai, China', *Energy Policy*, **38** (9), 4797–4807.

Liang, S., L. Shi and T. Zhang (2011), 'Achieving dewaterization in industrial parks', *Journal of Industrial Ecology*, **15** (4), 597–613.

Liu, L., Z. Wang, H. Zhang et al. (2010), 'Solar energy development in China – a review', *Renewable and Sustainable Energy Reviews*, **14** (1), 301–311.

Liu, L., B. Zhang, J. Bi, Q. Wei and P. He (2012), 'The greenhouse gas mitigation of industrial parks in China: a case study of Suzhou Industrial Park', *Energy Policy*, **46**, 301–307.

Lowe, E., S. Moran and J. Warren (1997), *Discovering Industrial Ecology: An Executive Briefing and Source Book*, Columbus, OH: Battelle Press.

Ministry of Commerce of the People's Republic of China (MOC) (2013), 'National economic and technological development areas (NETDAs) in China', accessed 13 January 2014 at http://www.mofcom.gov.cn/xglj/kaifaqu.shtml.

Newsham, G.R., S. Mancini and B.J. Birt (2009), 'Do LEED-certified buildings save energy? Yes, but . . .', *Energy and Buildings*, **41** (8), 897–905.

PCSD (1996), *Proceedings for the Eco-industrial Park Workshop*, 17–18 October 1996, 77pp, accessed 13 January 2014 at http://clinton2.nara.gov/PCSD/Publications/Eco_Workshop.html.

Qi, Y., H. Li and T. Wu (2013), 'Interpreting China's carbon flows', *PNAS*, **110** (28), 11221–11222.

Qiu, J. (2009), 'China's climate target: is it achievable?', *Nature*, **462**, 550–551.

Ramaswami, A., T. Hillman, B. Janson et al. (2008), 'A demand-centered, hybrid life-cycle methodology for city-scale greenhouse gas inventories', *Environmental Science & Technology*, **42**, 6455–6461.

Shi, H., Y. Moriguichi and J. Yang (2002), 'Industrial ecology in China, Part I: research', *Journal of Industrial Ecology*, **6**, 7–11.

Shi, H., M. Chertow and Y. Song (2010), 'Developing country experience with eco-industrial parks: a case study of the Tianjin Economic-Technological Development Area in China', *Journal of Cleaner Production*, **18** (3), 191–199.

Shi, H., J. Tian and L. Chen (2012), 'China's quest for eco-industrial parks, Part I', *Journal of Industrial Ecology*, **16** (1), 8–10.

SIPAC (2010, 24 November), 'SIP eco-environment ranks no.1 among national-level development parks', accessed 13 January 2014 at http://www.sipac.gov.cn/english/2010y/201011/t20101126_78548.htm.

Wang, H., R. Zhang, M. Liu and J. Bi (2012), 'The carbon emissions of Chinese cities', *Atmospheric Chemistry and Physics*, **12** (14), 6197–6206.

Wang, H., Y. Lei, H. Wang, M. Liu, J. Yang and J. Bi (2013), 'Carbon reduction potentials of China's industrial parks: a case study of Suzhou Industry Park', *Energy*, **55**, 668–675.

WRI (2004), *The Greenhouse Gas Protocol: A Corporate Accounting And Reporting Standard* (revised edition), Geneva, Switzerland: World Business Council For Sustainable Development and World Resource Institute.

Yang, W., J. Zhou, W. Xu and G. Zhang (2010), 'Current status of ground-source heat pumps in China', *Energy Policy*, **38** (1), 323–332.

Zhang, L., Z. Yuan, J. Bi, B. Zhang and B. Liu (2010), 'Eco-industrial parks: national pilot practices in China', *Journal of Cleaner Production*, **18** (5), 504–509.

Zhang, M. and X.-J. Huang (2012), 'Effects of industrial restructuring on carbon reduction: an analysis of Jiangsu Province, China', *Energy*, **44** (1), 515–526.

14. Embedding an international perspective in industrial ecology

Donald I. Lyons, Pauline Deutz and Jun Bi

This book has presented surveys and case studies of industrial ecology (IE) practices and theories (especially industrial symbiosis [IS]-related) from across the world. There have been chapters from developing, developed and emerging economic contexts written by authors with first-hand experience in those settings, drawing on a wide range of primary and secondary data, sometimes including active personal involvement in IE projects. We hope that these contributions will be useful to both academics and practitioners in alerting them to relevant considerations in framing their work. In this brief final chapter, we consider the themes that emerge from the contributions to this book, incorporating thoughts on future directions.

It is clear from the chapters herein that IE practices are taking hold across the world and that the geographic spread of IE is mirrored by the variability of form. From the continent wide bilateral exchanges reported in Australia, or the regional networks more common in the EU, the Japanese eco-town approach to the integrated farm practices of the Songhai Farms in Republic of Benin, West Africa, the specific details vary widely around the central concept of resource efficiency and material flows (Olayide, Chapter 3, this volume; Boons et al., Chapter 5, this volume; Patchell, Chapter 11, this volume). As Boons et al. found in Europe, so also there are variations in terminology elsewhere (e.g., compare the scale and style of US and Chinese EIPs [Lowitt, Chapter 4, this volume; Wang, H. et al., Chapter 13, this volume]), and IE activity can be found well divorced from any use of the term (e.g., in India, Ashton and Shenoy, Chapter 2, this volume). Also noticeable is the variability of forms that can be found within a given national context, as demonstrated by the chapters on Australia, India, Europe, Japan and the US. Patchell (Chapter 11) was exploring the co-ordination of two different forms of IE (place and product oriented), though more typically different forms are considered separately. The inter-relationships between different types of IS (and IE) in different contexts need further consideration in terms of policy drivers, company engagement and public perspectives. For example, whilst the resilience of the EIP concept in the US is sadly yet to be matched by success in generating IS, bilateral IS is taking an increasing proportion of non-hazardous industrial waste in Pennsylvania (Lyons et al., Chapter 7, this volume).

Fundamental geographical properties such as the spatial distribution and sectoral composition of industry within a region or country are confirmed as important underlying factors in IE development across a wide range of contexts (see Jensen et al., 2011). This is illustrated by Branson and McManus' analysis of long-distance IS in the context of sparsely populated Australia (Chapter 8, this volume). However, the industrial mix may also be seen as an indicator of where efforts should be concentrated. For example, Wang, H. et al. (Chapter 13) and Lyons et al. (Chapter 7) point to the heavy concentration of emissions in a small number of sectors which implies that in some cases we should zone in on particular sectors where changes are likely to have the most impact. At the same time we need to be cautious about how we measure and evaluate change in particular places. If, for example, greenhouse gas emission reductions are achieved by simply relocating 'emitting' industries (Wang, H. et al., Chapter 13), we have not solved the problem. This does, however, raise the question of how problems are defined in different contexts, whose interests are served by a given project, and not least what the environmental benefits may be.

Another issue highlighted by a number of authors focuses on the mix of firms in a particular country, for example in India, Colombia and Africa (Ashton and Shenoy, Chapter 2; Van Hoof, Chapter 12; Olayide, Chapter 3). Multinational and large indigenous companies (e.g., Tata in India) can have international quality environmental standards, but penetrating the very large number of small companies that are heavily constrained in terms of finance, knowledge and awareness is a major issue. It should be pointed out, however, that this is not unique to the developing country context. Smaller companies in the Commonwealth of Pennsylvania had lower rates of reuse practice also (Lyons et al., Chapter 7). Focusing on technological solutions for the largest emitters may obscure more holistic attempts to establish a truly sustainable society that moves toward a society that gives co-priority to environmental sustainability and development and a wider redefinition of 'engineering common sense' across all forms of business (Hayter, 2008).

The motivations behind IE-related policies are variable, with implications for the forms taken by IE practice. Boons et al. (Chapter 5) identify a distinction between European countries prioritising resource conservation (e.g., Portugal) and those supporting IE as part of broader sustainability initiatives (e.g., the Netherlands), sometimes closely tied to regional development (e.g., France). Globally, a similar distinction can be drawn with

Japan, for example, prioritising resource use efficiency, and the US practice, favouring economic development, but without a supportive policy framework. There is a stark contrast, though, typified by China and the US (Liu et al., Chapter 10, this volume, and Lowitt, Chapter 4). Both nations' EIPs are attempting a co-operative approach to environmental management. Whereas, China is using EIPs to curb environmental damage in the context of rapid industrialisation, local economic development bodies in the US are assuming certain environmental principles and attempting to use EIPs to generate economic growth. A much better understanding is needed of how those motivations feed into policies, and how companies and other stakeholders, each with their own priorities, engage and respond. For example, bodies such as NISP in the UK or the Pennsylvania DEP in the US have data available to reconstruct residue flows. Given that databases follow the policy, it is very difficult to know the extent to which such flows may be present elsewhere and thereby how effective the policies actually are.

A major feature of many of the chapters in this book is the importance of institutional practices in getting IE/IS off the ground, as conceptualised and analysed by Spekkink (Chapter 9, this volume). A particular issue that emerges from the chapters herein is the constraints imposed by a scalar institutional disconnect. Van Hoof (Chapter 12) found in Colombia that regional authorities did not follow through on national policies in Colombia, while in China Liu et al. (Chapter 10) argued that regional authorities are constrained by national policies. Probably the most germane differences apply to broadly defined developed and developing countries, certainly in terms of the capacity of poorer countries to fund IE/IS practices where governance structures and business practices are more poorly established or less amenable to the types of transactions necessary for IE/IS practices to emerge. Not only did the multi-scalar institutional setting in China provide a poor framework for the UK's approach to IS facilitation, but the lack of guidance to and stringent enforcement of regulations were also constraining factors (Wang, Q. et al., Chapter 6).

Although the attempt to closely copy an overseas programme discussed by Wang, Q. et al. (Chapter 6) is unusual, the idea of building institutional capacity locally by importing expertise is far from unique. This is also a feature of some of the African examples presented by Olayide (Chapter 3), e.g., the involvement of a UN body and a North American university. Noticeably, however, those institutions appear to be working in concert with local organisations and initiatives. Both the Africa and India cases indicate that for developing countries there is a potential for developing IE activity, which in some cases has a foundation in practice pre-dating industrialisation. Thus, whilst attention should be paid to the environmental performance of emerging large-scale industrial plants, the environmental impact and opportunities embedded in more traditional economic operations should not be overlooked. Developing countries may nurture quite distinctive forms of IE, whilst still participating in the global exchange of academic insight and practice.

Notably, stable institutional practices do not emerge overnight, and whilst relatively stable over the short to medium term they do face periodic crises that may cause current institutional practices to evolve into new forms (Gibbs 2006; Hayter, 2008). However, change is a constant feature of policy, which alongside fluctuating economic performance suggests that a capacity for change and responsiveness to circumstances is a prime requirement for IE practices to become embedded anywhere, let alone everywhere.

Whilst there is a widespread presence of IE globally, the depth and breadth of practices remains questionable. A much longer book could be written, one suspects, on case studies of non-IE practices. However, as is often the case with new technological trajectories they may begin with incremental innovations that accumulate over time to create highly significant changes, if the associated demographic, social, financial, industrial and demand conditions are appropriate (Hayter, 2008; Perez, 2010; Dicken, 2011). Thus, as Chertow (2007) argues, there is a role for an IS (or indeed IE) researcher to highlight such practices as in an attempt to institutionalise and embed such practices into the everyday business model. Critical to that endeavour, however, is understanding the institutional context of IE (including IS) and the form of embeddedness under which that context emerges (Boons and Howard-Grenville, 2009). More work needs to focus on the extent to which different regions or countries can learn from each other's experiences if the context is similar. So whilst it is unlikely that many developing countries could replicate the capital intensive and large-scale programmes being carried out in China, there may be considerable value, for example, to exploring successful examples of agricultural or resource extractive practices across developing countries.

Given the enormous variation which still exists between different places, both despite and because of the globalised world economy and the potential of information technology, geographic context remains an important element in human activity. IE, as other areas of economic and/or sustainability endeavour, is deeply rooted in the places in which it is either happening or envisioned. There is potential for IE-related steps to make a significant contribution to development by providing both a cleaner environment and cost savings (Smith et al., 2010), providing that the challenges to implementation can be overcome and that lessons drawn from elsewhere are informed by awareness of differences of context in terms of the industrial composition, policy, social practices and economy.

IE research has an essential role to play in understanding and explaining instances of IE, and in providing a critical analysis of a socio-geographic, as well as technical, phenomenon. This is no academic dalliance. Whilst there are distinctions between analytical and normative research, not to mention direct involvement with practice, the contribution from all, decidedly including the benefit of critical insight, is needed to help lay the foundations for the suitable deployment of IE strategies that could suitably contribute to development that is sustainable.

REFERENCES

Ashton, W. and M. Shenoy (2015), 'Industrial ecology in India: converging traditional practice and modern environmental protection', in P. Deutz, D. Lyons and J. Bi (eds), *International Perspectives on Industrial Ecology*, Cheltenham, UK and Northampton, MA, USA: Edward Elgar, pp. 12–29.

Boons, F.A.A. and J. Howard-Grenville (eds) (2009), *The Social Embeddedness of Industrial Ecology*, Cheltenham, UK and Northampton, MA, USA: Edward Elgar.

Boons, F., W. Spekkink, R. Isenmann, L. Baas, M. Eklund et al. (2015), 'Comparing industrial symbiosis in Europe: towards a conceptual framework and research methodology', in P. Deutz, D. Lyons and J. Bi (eds), *International Perspectives on Industrial Ecology*, Cheltenham, UK and Northampton, MA, USA: Edward Elgar, pp. 69–88.

Branson, R. and P. McManus (2015), 'Bilateral symbiosis in Australia and the issue of geographic proximity', in P. Deutz, D. Lyons and J. Bi (eds), *International Perspectives in Industrial Ecology*, Cheltenham, UK and Northampton, MA, USA: Edward Elgar, pp. 126–141.

Chertow, M.R. (2007), '"Uncovering" industrial symbiosis', *Journal of Industrial Ecology*, **11** (1), 11–30.

Dicken, P. (2011), *Global Shift: Mapping the Changing Contours of the World Economy*, New York: Guilford Press.

Gibbs, D. (2006), 'Prospects for an environmental economic geography: linking ecological modernization and regulationist approaches', *Economic Geography*, **82** (2), 193–215.

Hayter, R. (2008), 'Environmental economic geography', *Geography Compass*, **2** (3), 831–850.

Jensen, P.D., L. Basson, E.E. Hellawell, M.R. Bailey and M. Leach (2011), 'Quantifying "geographic proximity": experiences from the United Kingdom's National Industrial Symbiosis Programme', *Resources, Conservation and Recycling*, **55**, 703–712.

Liu, L., B. Zhang and J. Bi (2015), 'Institutional context of eco-industrial parks development in China: environmental governance in industrial parks and zones', in P. Deutz, D. Lyons and J. Bi (eds), *International Perspectives on Industrial Ecology*, Cheltenham, UK and Northampton MA, USA: Edward Elgar, pp. 157–174.

Lowitt, P. (2015), 'Eco-industrial development in the United States: analysing progress from 2010–2015', in P. Deutz, D. Lyons and J. Bi (eds), *International Perspectives on Industrial Ecology*, Cheltenham, UK and Northampton, MA, USA: Edward Elgar, pp. 46–68.

Lyons D., M. Rice and L. Hu (2015), 'Industrial waste management improvement: a case study of Pennsylvania', in P. Deutz, D. Lyons and J. Bi (eds), *International Perspectives on Industrial Ecology*, Cheltenham, UK and Northampton, MA, USA: Edward Elgar, pp. 108–125.

Olayide, O.A. (2015), 'Industrial ecology, industrial symbiosis and eco-industrial parks in Africa: issues for sustainable development', in P. Deutz, D. Lyons and J. Bi (eds), *International Perspectives on Industrial Ecology*, Cheltenham, UK and Northampton, MA, USA: Edward Elgar, pp. 30–45.

Patchell, J. (2015), 'The intersection of industrial symbiosis and product-based industrial ecologies: considerations from the Japanese home appliance industry', in P. Deutz, D. Lyons and J. Bi (eds), *International Perspectives on Industrial Ecology*, Cheltenham, UK and Northampton, MA, USA: Edward Elgar, pp. 175–190.

Perez, C. (2010), 'Technological revolutions and techno-economic paradigms', *Cambridge Journal of Economics*, **34** (1), 185–202.

Smith, M.H., K. Hargroves and C. Desha (2010), *Cents and Sustainability*, London: Earthscan.

Spekkink, W. (2015), 'Varieties of industrial symbiosis', in P. Deutz, D. Lyons and J. Bi (eds), *International Perspectives on Industrial Ecology*, Cheltenham, UK and Northampton, MA, USA: Edward Elgar, pp. 142–156.

Van Hoof, B. (2015), 'Institutional capacity for sustainable industrial systems in Caldas, Colombia', in P. Deutz, D. Lyons and J. Bi (eds), *International Perspectives on Industrial Ecology*, Cheltenham, UK and Northampton, MA, USA: Edward Elgar, pp. 191–208.

Wang, H., Y. Lei and J. Bi (2015), 'Greenhouse gases reduction strategies for eco-industrial parks in China', in P. Deutz, D. Lyons and J. Bi (eds), *International Perspectives on Industrial Ecology*, Cheltenham, UK and Northampton, MA, USA: Edward Elgar, pp. 209–227.

Wang, Q., P. Deutz and D. Gibbs (2015), 'UK-China collaboration for industrial symbiosis: a multi-level approach to policy transfer analysis', in P. Deutz, D. Lyons and J. Bi (eds), *International Perspectives on Industrial Ecology*, Cheltenham, UK and Northampton, MA, USA: Edward Elgar, pp. 89–107.

Index